Transgressions

critical Australian Indigenous histories

Transgressions

critical Australian
Indigenous histories

Ingereth Macfarlane
and Mark Hannah
(editors)

ANU
THE AUSTRALIAN NATIONAL UNIVERSITY

E PRESS

ANU
E PRESS

Published by ANU E Press and Aboriginal History Incorporated
Aboriginal History Monograph 16

National Library of Australia
Cataloguing-in-Publication entry

Title:	Transgressions [electronic resource] : critical Australian Indigenous histories / editors, Ingereth Macfarlane ; Mark Hannah.
Publisher:	Acton, A.C.T. : ANU E Press, 2007.
ISBN:	9781921313448 (pbk.)
	9781921313431 (online)
Series:	Aboriginal history monograph
Notes:	Bibliography.
Subjects:	Indigenous peoples–Australia–History.
	Aboriginal Australians, Treatment of–History. Colonies in literature.
	Australia–Colonization–History. Australia–Historiography.
Other Authors:	Macfarlane, Ingereth.
	Hannah, Mark.
Dewey Number:	994

Contacting Aboriginal History
All correspondence should be addressed to Aboriginal History,
Box 2837 GPO Canberra, 2601, Australia.
Sales and orders for journals and monographs, and journal subscriptions:
T Boekel, email: sales@aboriginalhistory.org, tel or fax: +61 2 6230 7054
www.aboriginalhistory.org

ANU E Press
All correspondence should be addressed to:
ANU E Press, The Australian National University, Canberra ACT 0200, Australia
Email: anuepress@anu.edu.au, http://epress.anu.edu.au

Aboriginal History Inc. is a part of the Australian Centre for Indigenous History, Research School of Social Sciences, The Australian National University and gratefully acknowledges the support of the History Program, RSSS and the National Centre for Indigenous Studies, The Australian National University.

Cover design by ANU E Press
Cover photo: Clint Spencer. iStockphoto, File Number: 4387298

Table of Contents

List of Illustrations

Contributors

Thalia Anthony wrote this paper in the transitional period between completing her PhD thesis in history and recommencing her law degree, both at The Australian National University. She is currently a lecturer in the Faculty of Law, University of Sydney. Thalia is passionate about interdisciplinary Indigenous studies and embraces this volume's expression of critical Indigenous histories.

Jillian Barnes has a business background in arts marketing and industrial management consulting. She has recently worked on a documentary film in Central Australia with members of the Arrernte community choir at Hermannsburg. This article was written during her doctoral research in History at the University of Sydney. Her thesis, 'Tourism's possession of the Centre': Seeing and performing kinship and belonging at Uluru, 1929-1958', will be submitted in 2007. She has edited *Historia*, and tutored in a new History subject at the University of Sydney titled 'Race relations and Australian frontiers'. She was awarded the Australasian Pioneers Club Prize for her Honours thesis in Australian history in 2000.

Devin Bowles' paper is based on his work for a Master of Arts in anthropology at The Australian National University, 2003. He is now studying for an Honours degree in psychology at The Australian National University.

Angelique Edmonds completed her PhD at the Centre for Cross Cultural Research, The Australian National University in 2007. She trained as an architect at the University of NSW and Kingston University in London and completed a Master of Philosphy at Cambridge University. Her PhD research focused upon Aboriginal relationships to place and expressions of Aboriginal agency in determining the structure of their living environments. At the time of research and writing of this paper, Angelique was living in the Roper River Region of South East Arnhem Land, contracted by the Northern Territory government to facilitate a community planning project for future housing in Ngukurr.

Dennis Foley is a Fulbright Scholar, a Visiting Fellow at The Australian National University and a lecturer at the Australian Graduate School of Entrepreneurship, University of Swinburne, forging a new field in Indigenous entrepreneurship. He has completed postdoctoral studies at The Australian National University in the Centre for Aboriginal Economic Policy Research, the National Centre for Indigenous Studies, and the College of Business and Economics. His publications cross several disciplines, from Indigenous literature and history, to business management-entrepreneurship and education. Dennis's principle areas of research are Indigenous entrepreneurship and Indigenous epistemology. His PhD recently won the 2006 Best Doctoral Thesis Award, Gold Medal, World Business Institute. Although an academic in the western definition, Dennis was born in his matrilineal place and is of salt-water law. His blood connection to this land is with the Gammeray, the Gatlay and the Gaimai. This also includes the sub-groups of the Cannaigal and the Boregal. His father is a descendant of the Capertee/Turon River people of the Wiradjuri, north of Bathurst. Dennis identifies as a descendent of the Gai-mariagal people.

Mark Hannah studied history and archaeology at the University of New England. He completed his PhD at The Australian National University in 2005. His research concentrated on the Queensland settler state's attempt to regulate Indigenous marriage practices in the policy epoch commonly referred to as the era of 'protection' (the late nineteenth to early twentieth centuries), when customary marriage practices were largely displaced by a new settler orientated marriage regime. He is presently preparing to undertake further research in the Department of Anthropology at the London School of Economics.

Shino Konishi is a lecturer in Indigenous Australian studies and history at the Koori Centre, University of Sydney. Her research interests concern histories of race, the body, and gender with a particular focus on the eighteenth century exploration of Australia and cross-cultural encounters between Aboriginal peoples and Europeans. Shino identifies with the Yawaru people of Broome, Western Australia.

Kathy Lothian is a PhD student in the School of Historical Studies at Monash University, writing a biography of philosopher Professor Peter Singer. She has interests in indigenous histories, immigration, ethnicity and life writing. At the time of writing the paper in this volume, she had recently completed a Master of Arts thesis on Black Power in Australia.

Ingereth Macfarlane has been the Managing Editor of *Aboriginal History* journal since 2001. She is currently completing research for a PhD in the Australian Center for Indigenous History, The Australian National University, looking at the long-term history of the interactions of people and places in the western Simpson Desert, northern South Australia.

Jessie Mitchell completed her history doctorate at The Australian National University in 2005, examining life on the first Indigenous missions and protectorate stations in south-eastern Australia, for which she was awarded the Australian Historical Association Serle Prize in 2006. This paper was written during the second year of her thesis. Jessie currently heads ACT Shelter, a low-income housing advocacy body.

Jane Mulcock completed a PhD in anthropology at the University of Western Australia in 2002. Her research focussed on experiences of belonging, spirituality and indigeneity amongst Anglo-Celtic settler-descendants in Australia. These themes have carried through into her recent postdoctoral research at the University of Western Australia on beliefs, values and practices associated with native and introduced plant and animal species. Her current research interests focus on human-animal interactions and management of urban wildlife. She has published a number of journal papers been involved as an editor and co-author of *The salinity crisis* (2001, UWA Press) and *Anthropologists in the field* (2005, University of Colombia Press).

Naomi Parry completed her PhD in 2007 in History at the University of New South Wales, called '"Such a longing": black and white children in welfare in New South Wales and Tasmania, 1880-1940'. Her work on Musquito began when, as a Tasmanian with an interest in Indigenous issues, she was asked to write an entry for the Australian Dictionary of Biography (published in the 2006 Supplement), and discovered that there was much more to the story, and the historiography, of this man. Her second Australian Dictionary of Biography 'missing person' was Maria Lock, foremother of the contemporary Darug community, who lived a very different colonial Indigenous life.

Jinki Trevillian is an historian and writer who completed her PhD at The Australian National University in 2003. The research for her doctoral thesis, 'Talking with the Old People: histories of Cape York Peninsula, 1930s-1950s', took Jinki from the government archives of southern cities to far North Queensland. Her aim was to learn about history as told by the people who lived it. Jinki is committed to historical research and writing that builds bridges of understanding between individuals, institutions and the broader community.

Preface

This volume brings together an innovative set of readings of complex interactions between Australian Aboriginal people and colonisers. It has its origins in 2003 when Mark Hannah, then a doctoral student in the Centre for Cross Cultural Research at The Australian National University, invited a group of early career scholars to meet in Canberra. They brought their diverse social science and humanities backgrounds to the uncovering of creative Indigenous responses to the colonial encounter in Australia, and fresh ways of writing about these. Their studies were focused in diverse parts of Australia and on different time periods, but shared a common interest in developing critical re-assessments of Australian colonial and anti-colonial histories. Their meeting encouraged face-to-face exchanges that could short-circuit the isolation often experienced by cross-disciplinary, original scholars. It also emphasised writerly aspects of creative thinking, promoting the portrayal of character, alternative prose styles and inventive narrative forms. The authors' responses to these invitations have flavoured the commissioned papers presented here. The critical and creative drives which inform them shines out in their writing. They are exciting and sometimes surprising in the angles they take, and the cross-overs of genre or subject that they offer.

The underlying theme that has informed the collection, and given the book its title, is that of 'transgression'. This owes its force and tone to Michel Foucault's account of the necessary dynamic that exists between transgression and limit. He points out that transgressions and limits exist and can be identified only because of each other. We know what constitutes the limit, not by tracing or re-stating the boundaries, but by crossing over them. Transgression 'forces the limit to face the fact of its imminent disappearance, to find itself in what it excludes'.[1]

> Perhaps [transgression] is like a flash of lightning in the night which, from the beginning of time, gives a dense and black intensity to the night it denies, which lights up the night from the inside, from top to bottom, and yet owes to the dark the stark clarity of its manifestation, its harrowing and poised singularity; the flash loses itself in this space it marks with its sovereignty and becomes silent now that it has given a name to obscurity.[2]

Elizabeth Povinelli (2006) frames these concerns in terms of the interplay between individual freedom and social constraint:

> Insistently driving into the thicket of social life's material and discursive conditions, [Foucault] sought not a new collective bargaining agreement to extend rights to new communities and identities, but to interrogate the limits of each and every such bargain. How do we make things that

are in reality, though not a part of knowledge, *actual*? … Why am I governed *like this* rather than like that, here and now?[3]

By exploring the mechanisms by which limits are set and maintained, unexamined cultural assumptions and dominant ideas are illuminated. We see the expectations and the structures that inform and support them revealed, often as they unravel. Such illuminations and revelations are at the core of these papers: in the relationship of a contemporary historian to an eighteenth century French ethnographic observer (Konishi); in the longings expressed in people's explorations of variant indigeneities (Mulcock); in the politics of the establishment of the Tent Embassy (Lothian); in Indigenous leadership in various forms (Parry, Foley); in the creation of iconic representations of Aboriginal identity (Barnes); in rethinking legal aspects of land tenure and the working relationships of the northern pastoral industry (Anthony); in tracing the patterns of missionary attitudes to Aboriginal male sexuality (Mitchell); in the emotional freight of religious conversion (Bowles); in an emphasis on romance as a dynamic of identity (Trevillian); and in Indigenous ceremonial life played out within the structures of a built environment (Edmunds).

Mark Hannah is thanked for his initiatives in bringing together the authors, shaping the form of the volume and organising the refereeing process. We are grateful to the referees for their valuable comments. Finalisation of the editing and production of the monograph was carried out by Ingereth Macfarlane for the Board of Aboriginal History. The authors are warmly thanked for their patience and willingness to see the project through to completion, loyal to the idea of a collection of writers with shared interests. Geoff Hunt and Bernadette Hince provided skilful copy-editing. The ANU E Press have been indispensable in the publication of the volume.

Ingereth Macfarlane
Canberra, September 2007

References

Foucault, M 1977, 'A Preface to Transgression' in *Language, Counter-memory, Practice*, Cornell University Press, Ithaca.

Povinelli, EA 2006, *The Empire of Love: toward a theory of intimacy, genealogy and carnality*, Duke University Press, London.

ENDNOTES

[1] Foucault 1977: 28.

[2] Foucault 1977: 35.

[3] Povinelli 2006: 158.

François Péron and the Tasmanians: an unrequited romance

Shino Konishi

François Péron was my first. A slight man with a sickly aspect, blind in one eye and possessing a long patrician nose that gave him an imperious air,[1] he had a tendency to be self-indulgent, was intensely political in his relationships, and was not averse to machination against anyone he developed a dislike for. He could easily tell the odd lie or bend the truth if he saw any benefit to himself in it. He certainly could not be accused of mincing his words. His dedication to self-justification and self-aggrandising was exasperating to say the least.

I first encountered Péron when I was an undergraduate history student. I found him repellent; almost everything he said was disagreeable. Initially I was only interested in refuting him, dissecting his words and proving that he was an ignorant egomaniac. It was what he said about indigenous people and how he perceived women that offended me. He could be callously clinical in his descriptions. He never refrained from running his cold eye over the body of a black man or woman, focussing on any physical quality he saw as lacking, aberrant, or simply unattractive. At times, he even seemed ridiculous. He lacked self-awareness and humility, so never missed an opportunity to present himself as a hero, a role that rested precariously on his slender frame.

Encountering others who felt the same way I did, it seemed that his way with words and his negative appraisals provoked strong reactions.[2] He is indeed a treasure trove of objectionable quotations. Yet, over the years I have begun to look beyond the snatches of description that spark such ire, humoured his ludicrous self-aggrandising, and slowly began to change my opinion of Monsieur Péron. When once I just dismissed him, now I try to engage with him. Without realising it I have developed a relationship with him, and like all romances it is turbulent. At times he appals me and I detest him. Then at other times, I affectionately imagine I see through his pompous façade, and see how he truly is. I guess I have cast myself in the role of tragic heroine, and want to redeem my man.

François Péron significantly changed my life. He was the first to make me want to become an historian. He was my first primary source — his writings, the first object of my study. While I have since developed relationships with others, he is still my first, and as such the most significant. I have journeyed to the other side of the world to see his handwritten letters and journals, to study the marginalia he wrote on drawings and texts, to touch the same paper on which he spent the last years of his short life writing, to feel whether he left any hidden remnant of himself imprinted on the surface. I also wanted to walk through the town from which he departed on his epic voyage; the town whose people he imagined had affectionately wished 'Ah, may you ... return once more to your country, and the gratitude of your fellow citizens!'[3] as he set sail for my side of the world. I have done all this in order to understand him better; to grasp what it was exactly that made him say those terrible things.

In 1800, at the tender age of 25, Péron was the last to join the expedition to the Great South Land. This was a scientific expedition devised by the veteran seadog, Post-Captain Nicolas Baudin, a voyage to the Southern Ocean and *Terra Australis*, to discover the natural history of this still incompletely charted territory. This expedition would eventually be co-opted by the newly formed *Société des Observateur de l'Homme* and intrigue none other than the future emperor Napoleon Bonaparte. The expedition was to transcend Baudin's humble amateur naturalist fantasies. However, I am jumping ahead, for how are you to know the significance of these things? I must return to Péron's life prior to the expedition so we can discern how he became that self-confessed 'irresponsible, scatter-brained, argumentative, indiscreet', opinionated, and alienating man, 'incapable of ever giving way for any reason of expediency'.[4]

François was not born into a wealthy family, and his father died at an early age. So he was guided on the usual trajectory of an intellectually curious, eighteenth-century French man from the lower orders: he was encouraged to join the seminary. In the course of one of Napoleon's numerous campaigns he was forced to enlist, and became a prisoner of war at the age of 19. After his release he moved to Paris, and under the patronage of Master Petitjean, he enrolled in a medical degree, becoming a student of the esteemed men of science, and members of the *Société*, Antoine-Laurent de Jussieu and Georges Cuvier.[5] Upon hearing of the expedition to *Terra Australis*, Péron abandoned his studies and immediately entreated his mentors to recommend him to the expedition. He was promptly assigned the post of zoologist. More importantly, he was also to serve as the expedition's anthropologist, a science still in its infancy. An artefact of its recent inception was the disparity between the two anthropological treatises that served as Péron's guidelines. Georges Cuvier's was inspired by the nascent nineteenth-century science of comparative anatomy, while Joseph-Marie DeGérando's *Instructions* were more commensurate with the eighteenth-century philosophical approach of Jean-Jacques Rousseau.[6] Péron's own ethnography precariously straddles both approaches, revealing his inexperience and naïvety.

F.ᵗ PÉRON.

Il s'est desseche comme un arbre charge des plus beaux fruits qui succombe a l'excès de sa fécondité

(Voyez l'Eloge de la vie de l'auteur)

Figure 1.1: Fois. [i.e. Francois] Peron, nd, engraving by Lambert designed by Lesueur, Charles Alexandre, 1778-1846, Allport Library and Museum of Fine Arts, Tasmania

I had not anticipated arriving at Rousseau so early in this story. In order to best describe his significance, I need to jump ahead from Péron joining Baudin's expedition, skipping over the departure of the *Geographe* and the *Naturaliste* from Le Havre on the 19 October 1800 amid the fanfare and delight of the local citizens.[7] I also need to skip past the ships' stop at the Île de France (Mauritius) where they lost a significant proportion of their crew, disaffected by the slow trip and scant provisions for which Post-Captain Baudin was apportioned most

3

of the blame.[8] I want to pass over the brief visits the *Geographe* and the *Naturaliste* made to Western Australia including their first encounters with Aboriginal people, and even skip their longer sojourns in Tasmania and Port Jackson.[9] In fact I want to skip over all of the events on the journey that changed him. Instead, I want to introduce you to Péron about halfway through the expedition, just after his departure from Port Jackson on 18 November 1802, when as we will see he had already become a disappointed man.[10]

It is at this stage of the journey that Péron chose to conclude the first volume of his journal. Although he and Louis de Freycinet are the joint authors of the four volume journal of the expedition, *Voyage of Discovery to the Southern Hemisphere*, Péron wrote volume one by himself. At this stage of the voyage the ships were about to return to France, by way of the southern coast of Western Australia. The last chapter describes the results of his dubious experiment intended to compare the physical strength of indigenous men with that of European men, using a newly invented mechanical contraption known as Regnier's dynamometer.[11]

It is within this apparently objective and empirical context that Péron launches into a typically derogatory and bitter description of the Tasmanian people. He begins his attack with a minutely detailed disquisition on their bodies,[12] easing into his subject matter by stating that the Tasmanians' height is similar to that of Europeans. The head attracts Péron's attention because he thinks it 'uncommonly large', and oddly proportioned, being much longer than it is wide. His eye sweeping down the length of the body, François turns to the torso, and appears to take a more positive tack. The Tasmanian men's shoulders are broad, their loins 'well formed', and their buttocks 'sizeable',[13] though due to his economic phrasing it is difficult to say whether he appreciates their form or not.

However, as his eye descends to the legs Péron's aim becomes clear. He has elaborated on the muscular stockiness of their torso only to heighten the feebleness of the Tasmanians' extremities. His eye can discern 'scarcely any muscle'. Even Péron's syntax highlights their scrawniness, for he ends the sentence by describing the way their abdomens project over their spindly legs like an inflated 'balloon'. This vignette on the Tasmanians' bodies is classic ethnography à la Péron, a dish that has often been tasted.[14]

But it is not just their bodies that come under attack — he also dismisses Tasmanian society, polity, abode, arts and diet. Péron's entire description is damning. It inexorably and predictably leads to his pronouncement that 'the inhabitant of these regions unites all the characters of man in an unsocial state, and is, in every sense of the word, the *child of nature*'.[15] This is a familiar sentiment to any student of Aboriginal history. And it is here, with his self-indulgent use of italics, that the reason for Péron's ire reveals itself. He is striking out against those 'vain sophists' who 'attribute to savages all the sources of happiness and every principle of virtue'.[16]

Now Rousseau can enter the story. As a student François had been influenced by that eminent philosopher. He was seduced by the fantasy of the Noble Savage, a child of nature, not only more virtuous than civilised man, but physically superior in both form and function. So at first glance Péron's vitriolic attack on the body of the Tasmanians appears to be fuelled by the bitter disappointment of a former acolyte; by the realisation that his deeply held faith was a mere phantasm.

My first sympathetic understanding for François came from believing that his disillusionment with 'J.J'[17] (as he intimately referred to Rousseau) was heartfelt and emotional, perhaps nourished by the passion of losing his father. His filial tragedy led me to suspect that he could not take the disappointment of a fallen paternal figure such as Rousseau lightly. I believed that the tragic romance was between Rousseau the mentor and Péron the succeeding disciple. Naturally, I concluded that the Tasmanians were merely innocent unfortunates caught in the crossfire, purely a means to Péron's end of proving that Rousseau was a charlatan *philosophe*. The idea that the Tasmanians themselves played almost no role in shaping these derogatory European attitudes was compelling, and seemed to be a view commonly held by other writers.[18]

However, re-reading Péron again and again, I have come to question this belief, for Péron was not always damning in his appraisals of the Tasmanians. It seems that his vitriolic fire was not sparked by Rousseau alone, but also fanned by the Tasmanians: not by their debasement and corporeal deviancy as Péron implies, but rather by their cool indifference to him, their reluctance to play the foil to his heroic self-imaginings. So I have come to the conclusion that François' unrequited romance was not with Rousseau at all, but instead with the Tasmanians.

I will now return to François, as he was on 13 January 1802: a prodigy in the science of natural history, idealistic, expectant, and full of vim and vigour. His enthusiasm should no doubt partly be attributed to the relief of finally catching sight of Tasmania after an arduous 61-day journey from Timor marked by dysentery, death and despair. It was on this fateful day that he first encountered the Tasmanians.

François beheld an Arcadian vision when he saw the Tasmanian coast. Despite the brisk temperatures he stood on the deck of the *Geographe* transfixed by the sight of the 'lofty mountains', the inland plains which rose 'in amphitheatres' over the whole island and the 'immense forests'.[19] He listened to the calls of the seabirds that circled the ships and the dolphins' splashes as they danced in the *Geographe's* wake. All the sights and sounds contributed to François' solemn feeling that he had 'touched the extreme boundary of the southern world'.[20]

His admiration of the landscape grew as the ships sailed into the d'Entrecasteaux Channel in search of fresh water. The lush green of the vegetation and prodigious mountains, combined with the beautiful plumes of the local parrots and majestic swans led François to declare that it was the 'most picturesque and pleasant' place they had seen during their long voyage.[21] It was in this halcyon environment that Péron first glimpsed the Tasmanians.

As the ships approached the shore two men fleetingly appeared on the beach, disappearing as the ships neared. Then, shortly after the French disembarked, another two men appeared. The braver of the two immediately bounded down the rise to greet them. This young man captivated Péron with his athleticism for he 'seemed rather to spring from the top of the rock than to descend from it'.[22] His physicality made him appear 'strong' and the only defect he appeared to have was an apparent looseness to his joints. François scanned the Tasmanian's face, and upon seeing that his eyes were 'lively and expressive', concluded that his 'physiognomy had nothing fierce or austere' about it.[23]

This figure bewitched François. He was his Noble Savage, a man of impressive physical strength and dexterity with an open and guileless demeanour. Péron's compatriot Freycinet immediately embraced the man and François followed suit. It was in this fleeting caress that Péron got his first inkling that his appreciation was not reciprocated. The aloof Tasmanian seemed to receive the French embrace with an 'air of indifference'. But in the fever of excitement from finally beholding this fabled noble savage, Péron overlooked this minor rebuff. Instead, he interpreted this distance as a sign that physical displays of affection had little meaning to the man, a theory he would later apply to all Tasmanians.[24] But for the time being, Péron was enchanted by the man's insatiable curiosity.

Immediately after their embrace, or possibly even during, the Tasmanian ran his hands over the Frenchmen's clothes, marvelling at their white skin and their layers of attire. Opening their jackets and lifting their shirts, perhaps even rolling up their sleeves and tugging at their waistbands, he inspected their skin, punctuating his fervid manoeuvring with 'loud exclamations of surprise' and stamping a rapid little tattoo with his feet.[25] The French boat then caught his eye, and he rushed over to inspect it with the same zeal. Ignoring the men still seated aboard he jumped in and immediately began running his hands along the boards, the mast and so forth.

He was distracted momentarily by a bottle of arrack given to him by one of the bemused sailors. Holding the bottle in the sun he slowly turned it, catching the rays of light that glinted off its surface, but then promptly threw it overboard, returning his attentions to the boat.[26] The flurry of activity as one of the 'vexed' sailors splashed into the water to rescue the valuable liquor did not distract the Tasmanian who by then was endeavouring to push the boat off and master the art of sailing for himself. François was charmed by the man's display of energetic inquisitiveness, and impressed by his deductive reasoning, for he would later write with patronising warmth that they were 'the most striking demonstrations of attention and reflection which we had ever seen among savage nations'.[27]

While this scene was being played out in the water, Péron and Freycinet wandered further ashore to meet the second Tasmanian in a somewhat less frantic exchange. This man's salt-and-pepper hair and beard suggested that he was more than 50 years old. While obviously anxious and frightened by the strangers' sudden appearance, he still managed to give an impression of 'kindness and candour'.[28] After the obligatory scrutinising of their white skin and dishevelling of their clothes, he beckoned two women to join them on the beach.

Taking a moment to deliberate, the women approached, though this time the elder of the two took the lead. Her complete nakedness revealed that the skin of her belly was a topography of 'furrows' and ridges, a telltale sign for Péron that she had mothered many children.[29] The younger woman nursed a baby girl, giving Péron an excuse to linger over his description of the shape and fullness of her bosom. But when he lifted his gaze to her face he was taken aback by her expression as she openly returned his stare. Unlike the 'kind and friendly' countenance of the older couple, this young woman had 'fire' burning in her eyes.[30] Yet, as her eyes flitted back to her baby they changed, becoming warm with affection as she fondled and cared for it in a display of 'maternal love' that François could only assume was a peculiarity of women the world over. Again, Péron overlooked her momentary flintiness in his enchantment of their presence.

After this meeting Péron's compatriots wished to move on to begin their scientific transactions, but François opted to stay with the two women and the Tasmanian patriarch in an endeavour to 'collect some words of their idiom'.[31] Meanwhile the young man continued his active engagement with the sailors, gathering wood and lighting a fire upon realising the Frenchmen's desire to warm themselves. As both parties converged at the fire François had another opportunity to delight in the innocence of these *children of nature*.

Suddenly the young woman let out a scream, which 'alarmed' everybody. Upon realising the cause of her distress the French were filled with mirth, laughing heartily at her childlike mistake. Having mistaken a sailor's gloves for a hand, she feared that this alien man could simply detach it 'at pleasure'.[32] It is this first stage of the romance, during the attraction that François feels at first sight of the Tasmanians, that the ill-fated bottle of arrack again re-enters the story.

During this initial flirtation, Péron's boorish seduction routine of condescendingly laughing at the Tasmanian woman soon causes the romance to stall. Under the cover of this distraction, the elderly patriarch takes the opportunity to take the same bottle of arrack that had been given his son and carry it off towards his camp.[33] The loss of such a valuable resource, comprising 'a great part' of their 'stock', necessitates the sailors' vigorous repossession of the bottle, but the erratic behaviour of the Frenchmen concerning this *gift* incites much discontent in the old man, and ignoring the French gestures of appeasement and requests to stay, the Tasmanian family immediately take their leave, and temporarily exit the story.

Despite this hiccup in the budding relationship, François was still confident in his ability to worm his way into the noble savages' affections, for *tomorrow is another day*, so he replaces his anthropologist hat with his zoologist one for a spot of shell collecting.

Now I would like to open on a new scene. Later that afternoon a party of Frenchmen, hoping to alleviate their disappointment at not finding fresh water with a collecting success, ventured further along the shore and discovered a Tasmanian hut and canoes.[34] After inspecting them and evaluating their apparent lack of sophistication and workmanship, they again met the Tasmanian family whose number had since swelled to nine.

The family rushed towards their visitors with cries of delight and joy, the earlier altercation forgotten.[35] They took the sailors back to their hut where the hospitable family prepared a simple meal of broiled shellfish, which the Frenchmen found to be 'succulent and well-flavoured'. In reciprocation for their fine meal the guests decided to regale the Tasmanians with a spirited rendition of *La Marseillaise*,[36] though Péron insisted that its true anthropological purpose was to 'see what effect our singing would have on our audience'.[37] The Tasmanians did not appear surprised by the sudden rendition, though responded to the music with 'diverse contortions' and 'odd gestures'; the French could barely contain their laughter. But the Tasmanians' immediate 'exclamations of admiration' at the conclusion of the stirring anthem led Péron to infer that their strange reactions were positive. Encouraged by this reaction Péron decided to entertain them with another song.[38]

Almost imagining the lights dimming and a change in tempo, François advanced his romantic dalliance one step, from attraction to seduction. The French began by crooning some of their 'tender airs'. Even though the Tasmanians appeared to 'comprehend the sense of these' romantic ballads, they seemed strangely unaffected.[39] After what I can only imagine was an uncomfortable period of silence, a new character entered, the Tasmanian belle Ouré-Ouré, who broke the awkward atmosphere as she introduced the next scene.

Ouré-Ouré was about 16 or 17 years of age, and thought to be the younger sister of either the energetic young man or his flinty wife. François freely admitted that she attracted their keenest attention. Her complete nudity and 'delicate' form could not be ignored, but François, in a moment of chivalry, refrained from clinically describing her body, and only conceded that she seemed beguilingly unaware that there could be anything indecent or immodest about her 'absolute nudity'.[40] He perceived her glances toward them to be 'affectionate and expressive', though acknowledged that Freycinet had drawn more of her attention. François and the Tasmanians were now advancing to the next stage of the romance, the mutual flirtation.

For François, Ouré-Ouré was a natural coquette: delivering affectionate glances and winning smiles, and possessing a fine figure. Yet, when she took a more active role in the flirtation Péron's reaction became ambivalent, perhaps belying either the limited experiences that almost saw him join the seminary, or his unmediated preference for white skin.[41] In short, her coy preening was simultaneously enticing and disturbing. 'Taking some burnt charcoal in her hands, she crushed it so as to reduce it to a fine powder' then daubed it all over her face, expressing a confident and satisfied attitude towards her beauty regimen.[42] The Frenchmen were flattered by her attentions and amused to discover that 'fondness for adornment … prevails in the hearts' of all women, but Péron was also distressed by how 'frightfully black' it made her.[43] Yet in a romantic gesture François accepted this new look of Ouré-Ouré's and later seized the opportunity to try to usurp Freycinet in her affections. Noticing that she owned a bag made of rushes he thought to himself 'as this girl had also shewn me some marks of regard' I will venture 'to ask her for this little trifle'.[44] At his behest she immediately gave him the bag, and moreover accompanied it with 'an obliging smile' and 'some tender expressions' that he lamented not being able to understand. In response to this flirtation François inundated her with presents, including a handkerchief, a hatchet and a hammer, despite having been ordered by his captain to be sparing with his gifts.[45]

François was enamoured not only with the Tasmanians' hospitality and camaraderie, or Ouré-Ouré's affections, but also with the playful mischievousness of the children, and the ease with which he felt he had conversed with the Tasmanians despite their not being able to understand each other. Upon bidding their adieus the French were accompanied back to their boat by the Tasmanians who met the other French sailors, most of whom also noticed Ouré-Ouré's considerable attractions and festooned her with even more gifts. The Tasmanians' seeming commitment to the budding relationship was evident in their reluctance to allow the Frenchmen to leave.[46]

This day would be François' most romantic with the Tasmanians, full of laughter and affection. He was impressed not only by how the family had embraced their visitors but also the warmth they had shown one another. Later he would reflect that on that day he 'saw realized with inexpressible pleasure, those charming descriptions of the happiness and simplicity of a state of nature, of which I had so often read, and enjoyed in idea'.[47] Yet only two days later, on 15 January, Péron would begin to rethink this evaluation.

On that fateful day Péron was completely oblivious to how events would play out. In fact he was not even thinking of the Tasmanians, but instead was busy charting the marshy Port of Swans in a small boat, marvelling at the local countryside and wildlife. The party of naturalists discovered a river, which they named after the celebrated hydrographer Fleurieu, and Péron decided that a European colony should be established there, as the river would supply the settlement with water all year round.[48]

Meanwhile, hostilities between the French and indigenes flared over on Bruny Island. That day a small party of the French had ventured out on a fishing expedition. Shortly after landing they encountered a group of Tasmanians. Péron later learned that a burly midshipman by the name of Jean Maurouard, anticipating the study Péron would later conduct with his dynamometer, had also decided to test the strength of the infamously physically adept noble savages.[49]

Upon meeting the Tasmanians the French again presented them with gifts, and to all intents and purposes the 'natives' seemed friendly, inducing Maurouard to feel at liberty to try something new. Selecting the Tasmanian who 'appeared to be the most robust', he indicated his desire to engage in a little roughhousing. Planting his feet firmly in the sand, the Frenchman grabbed the Tasmanian's wrist and gestured that both should 'pull as hard as possible'.[50] Assuming that his gestures were fully comprehended the midshipman engaged in numerous feats of strength, repeatedly toppling or throwing his opponent into the sand. Mighty Maurouard won out every single time, but as the game was played amid much laughter and frivolity he did not anticipate the Tasmanian reaction.

Tiring of wrestling and collecting fish, the Frenchmen decided to withdraw to the ship, so again said their goodbyes and presented more gifts. His back turned to the Tasmanians as he pushed the boat out into the water. Maurouard was struck in the shoulder with a spear.[51] The point grazed the midshipman's shoulder blade and lodged in the flesh between his neck and shoulder. The Frenchmen immediately sprang into action. Sub-lieutenant St. Cricq drew his pistol, and with the unstoppable Maurouard charged back up the rise to find the attacker. Baudin reports in his journal that they then noticed seven or eight armed men, who did not react upon spying the pursuing Frenchmen. The Frenchmen, seemingly struck by their peculiarly uninterested demeanour, decided that it was most prudent to return to the ship, and retreated back down the rise without any further incident.[52] But Péron reports the story slightly differently.

When Péron heard news of this attack a few days later on his return from the Port of Swans he was filled with horror. How could those noble savages whose company he had so thoroughly enjoyed only days earlier have behaved so barbarically? But then perhaps he recalled those brief incidents during his first day when their response had been cool or indifferent, not to mention their attempt to steal the arrack. Perhaps those minor rebuffs by the Tasmanian men preyed on him. He certainly remembered the hostile attacks that they had suffered on the west coast of New Holland. Possibly the Tasmanian men were not as different from their mainland neighbours as he first thought. Péron judged this attack to be a 'perfidious and cowardly' display of brutality.[53] He immediately assumed that it was a vindictive response to their resounding defeat at the hands of Maurouard.

It never occurred to him that the Tasmanians might have been demonstrating their own indigenous game of skill, the art of spear dodging, or that the Tasmanians might have tired of their presence and wanted the interlopers to leave. In fact Péron cannot even entertain the notion that the Tasmanians have any motivation other than an inherent 'destructive instinct',[54] because to him they are little more than a cipher for his fanciful projections. His penchant for melodrama, which becomes more and more pronounced over the course of his journey, reveals itself in his retailing of this incident. According to his narrative the French immediately gave pursuit, and he claims they would have 'punished them as they deserved' had the cowards not already 'escaped among the rocks, or hid themselves among the brambles'.[55] This would not be the only time that Péron allowed his fantasies to obscure the truth.

After a reprieve of only a few days, the French had another encounter with the Tasmanian men that played out in a similar fashion, again resulting in 'violent aggression'.[56] For a second time Péron was absent so missed out on the action, but at his request the botanist Leschenault wrote him a report, so he had all of the important details. That is to say, the report described the violent events, mentioning neither how the Tasmanians were encountered nor what their attitude had been, because after the spearing of Maurouard the French could only see the Tasmanian men's actions as inexplicably and instinctively violent.

This day began with a party of Frenchmen, led by Jean Félix Emmanuel Hamelin, captain of the *Naturaliste*, and including the artist Nicolas-Martin Petit, setting out in order to make some progress on their ethnographic research. After meeting a group of Tasmanians Petit drew some portraits of the men as they sat in repose smiling and talking. Despite their relaxed demeanour Petit was soon to realise that they were not merely passive anthropological subjects, for once Petit had finished the portraits, one of his subjects suddenly grabbed hold of the drawing. In the ensuing struggle of wills Petit steadfastly held on to his work, forcing the Tasmanian to relinquish his hold and up the ante by seizing and brandishing 'a log of wood' at Petit. Thanks to the spearing of Maurouard the French were on guard against potential attacks, so the rest of the party immediately rallied to the artist's side. The increased support induced the man to surrender his claim to his portrait, though not his indignation. Despite French attempts to placate the Tasmanians with another round of gifts, they were sent running back to their ships with a volley of rocks.[57]

The botanist Jean-Baptiste Louis Claude Leschenault reported this second attack to Péron, who included it in the official journal of the voyage. Leschenault's report contained the critique of Jean-Jacques Rousseau which would come significantly to influence Péron: 'I am astonished, … to hear sensible people aver, that men in a state of nature are not wicked.'[58] He goes on to say it is preposterous to believe that the natives never played the role of aggressor. Two attacks were evidently enough for Leschenault to reject the claim that the Tasmanians were noble savages. François on the other hand, with lingering memories of Ouré-Ouré, still had a soft spot for the women.

On the last day of the month, after almost two weeks with little contact, Péron came across a group of Tasmanians. Following Leschenault's advice to the letter he turned back 'without hesitating a moment'.[59] Beating a hasty retreat along the shoreline he happened to meet sub-lieutenant François Antoine Boniface Heirisson. Bolstered by this extra support, he decided to return to where he had seen the 'natives'. Realising that they had no chance of catching the Tasmanians if they chose to avoid them, Péron and Heirisson signalled their good intentions by calling out, holding up their presents so they could be seen, and 'waving their handkerchiefs'.[60] The group eventually submitted to these entreaties and stopped, allowing Péron and Heirisson to catch up. It was as he approached that François realised that 'they were women, and that there was not a single male among the party'.[61] This realisation instantly lifted his spirits. Unfortunately these women were not to live up to Péron's fantasies, for they were hardly shy and malleable coquettes.

From the outset the women were in control. It was the women who allowed the Frenchmen to draw near, the women who instructed them to sit, and the women who made them disarm.[62] The Frenchmen not only had to submit to the women's instructions but also had to tolerate their interrogations and mockery. Péron thought that they seemed 'often to criticise our appearance', and laughed 'heartily at our expense'.[63] When the surgeon Jérôme Bellefin attempted to repeat their earlier success with the Tasmanians by singing to them, the women again seemed to appreciate it, but one, who they later learned was called Arra-Maida,[64] mimicked his 'action and the tone of his voice', and then began to sing and dance herself.[65] Her singing had such an unfamiliar melody that Péron thought it difficult to 'give any idea of music' and her dancing plainly shocked Péron: her contortions and 'attitude' bordered on 'indecent', forcing him to primly note that these savage people were still absolute 'strangers to all the delicacy of sentiment and conduct' that was a natural 'consequence of complete civilization'.[66]

Péron's earlier ambivalence regarding Ouré-Ouré and her seduction routine was only exacerbated when he was confronted by these brazen paramours. Having been tantalised by Ouré-Ouré and entranced by her demure flirtations which allowed him to play the role of chivalrous seducer, he was clearly taken aback at being forced into the role of blushing coquette himself. However, his surprise at this inversion of roles paled in comparison to the women's attempt to transform the Frenchmen's appearance. Once Arra-Maida had finished her performance she approached Péron. From her rush bag, similar to Ouré-Ouré's, she took some charcoal and began crushing it between her hands just as Ouré-Ouré had done, but instead of powdering her own face she begun applying it to Péron's. After finishing his face Arra-Maida then blackened Heirisson's. Even though both men 'submitted to this obliging piece of caprice', and Péron even recognised that the Tasmanians might have the same disdain for white skin that Europeans had for black, this meeting with the women cooled Péron's ardour for the Tasmanians.[67]

In contrast to his chivalrously discreet account of the delectable Ouré-Ouré, Péron openly stared at these women, and then described their bodies in clinical and derogatory detail, picking out any flaw, no matter how minor. His description is loaded with negative adjectives, and a sense of their utter degradation is suggested by his syntax, which scans their bodies from top to bottom, cataloguing an exhaustive account of imperfections.[68] He concluded his general assessment of the women by stating that 'in a word, all the particulars of their natural constitution were in the highest degree disgusting'.[69] Péron acknowledged that the young girls possessed an 'agreeable form and pleasant features' but unfortunately their 'nipples were rather too large and long'.[70] It seems that for Péron signs of the women's transgressive behaviour and nature were now physically manifested in their bodies.

Even though Péron's opinion of the Tasmanian men and women had become jaded, he was not the one to end the romance. Despite his ambivalence regarding the attractiveness of the women Péron stayed with them as long as he could, playing the dupe to their 'many tricks' and 'drolleries' and enjoying a 'merry' time. As he followed them home from their fishing expedition musing on the unjust burdens imposed on savage women, he was suddenly roused from his reflections by one woman's 'loud cry of terror'. The women had just caught sight of the manned French boats.[71] The realisation that there were more intruders waiting just off the shore ignited their fears, and all but one of the women fled towards the forest. The indomitably courageous Arra-Maida hectored her fleeing sisters and eventually convinced them to escort the party back to their boat. As they neared the shore Péron realised that the 'husbands' of these women had also converged where the boats were moored, but instead of being fearful they appeared to be filled with 'malevolence' and suppressed anger, which Péron assumed to be consequent to their 'inability to contend' with the superior Europeans.[72] Yet the Tasmanians seemed to have decided that the best way to contend with the French trespassers was to spurn their advances by evading them and giving the Frenchmen an apparently unambiguous sign of their disdain.

On 3 February, only a few weeks after their first meeting, the French returned to Bruny Island.[73] On seeing two women walking down the mountain to the sea, two of the French who had yet to encounter the Tasmanian women immediately ran towards them hoping for a closer look. When the women realised they were being pursued they sprinted off, disappearing before the men were able to catch them. Disappointed, the entire French party continued along the coast, and eventually spied a huge bonfire that appeared to have been burning since the night before. As they approached the pyre they realised that it was surrounded by 'almost all the presents' that the French had given to the Tasmanians. Like any jilted lover Péron was in denial. Instead of recognising that the Tasmanians were breaking up with him, he imagined that this bonfire and deliberate return of their gifts was just a manifestation of their 'puerile curiosity'. He deluded himself by thinking that 'these uninformed men threw away what no longer pleased or amused them',[74] and refused to recognise that it was actually he and his compatriots who no longer pleased the Tasmanians.

Had this romance been a fiction rather than being based on historical events the story would have ended here, perhaps with Péron mourning the end of the affair, or moving on to look for another race of impossible noble savages. But the harsh and prosaic reality of the situation was that Péron and the French lingered, unwanted, in Tasmania for a few more weeks, having other meetings with the Tasmanians and making further attempts to study these children of nature. The French continued to try to draw their portraits, document their vocabularies, discern whether or not they indulged in 'kisses and tender caresses', and test their physical strength with their dynamometer.[75] Their attentions were frequently rebuffed, and encounters usually ended in violent or aggressive altercations, with the French having to resort to drawing their weapons.

One particularly exciting encounter for Péron involved a dispute over his jacket. Having been offered many gifts, one of the Maria Island Tasmanians decided he wanted Péron's jacket and repeatedly asked for it. After being denied one too many times he grabbed his spear and threatened the Frenchman with it. Péron later wrote that he 'seemed to say, "Give it to me, or I will kill you"'.[76] This scene, in which Péron portrays himself as the quintessential cool, calm, and collected hero, continues with Péron laughing at the man and pretending it was all a joke. Suddenly, Péron grabbed hold of the spear end, and pushed it away from his face. Coolly, the hero then simply pointed at his handsome sidekick, First Class Seaman B.J. Rouget, who had his musket aimed at the aggressor, and 'added one single word of his own language (*mata*), death'.[77] The man immediately surrendered his claim to the jacket.

As I read over this scene again, I have to wonder if it really did play out in this way. Was Péron so calm in the face of death? Did the Tasmanians really have such a 'treacherous disposition'?[78] Or was it yet another example of Péron's overactive imagination and self-aggrandising fantasies? Having read Péron numerous times I wonder if this scene isn't a bitter and desperate attempt to save face after being rebuffed and jilted by the Tasmanian noble savages.

So why did I develop some sympathy for François, this vindictive, 'irresponsible, scatter-brained, argumentative', and 'indiscreet' man? It was not because he lost his father at an early age, and not even because he was a prisoner of war held at three different compounds while still a teenager. My change of heart was because after years of reading him again and again, I recognised that he had been searching and longing for something that did not exist. He had adopted such a passionate faith in a singular idea that it bordered on religious zeal. He was desperate to find the perfect noble savage, a *tabula rasa* on which to project his fantasies of an ideal human society. When he finally found it on the temperate shores of Tasmania, he did not anticipate that things would play out the way they did. He never expected that his offerings and paternalistic guidance would be rejected, that the noble savages would refuse to do his bidding and be model subjects for his study, and that they would fail to behave as Rousseau had led him to believe. So he reacted with the vindictiveness of a rejected lover.

So you may ask again, why do I sympathise with Péron? The answer is simply because his quest mirrored my own. As an indigenous historian I have combed these first contact narratives for any accounts and revelations about pre-contact Aboriginal people in order to greater understand the heartbreaking experiences and momentous changes that colonisation wrought for indigenous Australians. Despite seeing myself as standing at the opposite end of a temporal and colonial abyss from François Péron and his eighteenth-century European counterparts, I now realise that we are in some instances uncomfortably aligned. For I, like François, have idealistic fantasies about Aboriginal society and have attempted to impose this romanticised vision on the historical record. In doing so I have come to realise that I have inadvertently glossed over the complexities and idiosyncrasies of pre-contact Aboriginal society, and that I have ignored the playful and amicable relations that were formed in those first moments of contact. I have been blind to the power that the indigenous people had in those early colonial encounters. Like Péron I made the mistake of misinterpreting and misjudging the agency of eighteenth-century Aboriginal people. I sympathise with François because unlike him I eventually recognised this, and now I can fall in love with the Tasmanians and other indigenous historical figures all over again.

References

Baudin, Nicolas 1974, *The Journal of Post Captain Nicolas Baudin Commander-in-Chief of the Corvettes Géographe and Naturaliste, assigned by Order of the Government to a Voyage of Discovery*, Christine Cornell (trans.), Libraries Board of South Australia, Adelaide.

Cuvier, Georges 1978, 'Note Instructive Sur Les Recherches A Faire Relativement Aux Différences Anatomiques Des Diverses Races D'Hommes' in Jean Copand and Jean Jamin (eds), *Aux Origins de L'Anthropologie Française: Les Mémoires de la Société des Observateurs de l'Homme en l'an VIII*, Le Sycomore, Paris: 171-176.

Degérando, Joseph-Marie 1969, *The Observation of Savage Peoples*, FCT Moore (trans.), University of California Press, Berkeley and Los Angeles.

Hughes, Miranda 1988, 'Tall Tales or True Stories? Baudin, Peron, and the Tasmanians, 1802', in Roy Macleod and Philip F Rehbock (eds), *Nature in its Greatest Extent: Western Science in the Pacific*, University of Hawaii Press, Honolulu: 65-86.

Jones, Rhys 1988, 'Images of Natural Man', in J Bonnemains, E Forsyth and B Smith (eds), *Baudin in Australian Waters: The Artwork of the French Voyage of discovery to the Southern Lands 1800-1804*, Oxford University Press, Melbourne: 35-64.

Laissus, Yves 1988, 'François Péron: A Biographical Note', in J Bonnemains, E Forsyth and B Smith (eds), *Baudin in Australian Waters: The Artwork of the French Voyage of discovery to the Southern Lands 1800-1804*, Oxford University Press, Melbourne: 31-34.

Lesueur, Charles-Alexandre, *François Péron*, William Henry Smith Memorial Library, Indiana Historical Society, Indianapolis.

O'Brien, Patty 1999, 'Divine Browns and the Mighty Whiteman: Exotic Primitivism and the Baudin Voyage to Tasmania in 1802', *Journal of Australian Studies* 63: 13-21.

Péron, François 1809, *A Voyage of Discovery to the Southern Hemisphere, performed by Order of the Emperor Napoleon, During the Years 1801, 1802, 1803, and 1804*, Richard Phillips, London.

Péron, François, n.d., 'Conférence addressee à 'Messieurs les professeurs', décrivant les aborigines et leur moeurs près de Port Jackson', *Dossier 9: Expédition aux Terres Australes. Notes de Voyage, côtes Est et Sud de la Nouvelle Hollande (auteurs divers)*, No. 09032, Transcription de J Bonnemains, Collection Lesueur, Muséum d'histoire naturelle du Havre.

Plomley, NJB 1983, *The Baudin Expedition and the Tasmanian Aborigines 1802*, Blubber Head Press, Hobart.

Sankey, Margaret 2004, 'The Aborigines of Port Jackson, as seen by the Baudin Expedition', *Australian Journal of French Studies* 41(2): 117-125.

ENDNOTES

[1] Charles-Alexandre Lesueur, François Péron.

[2] Hughes 1988; O'Brien 1999.

[3] Péron 1809: 16.

[4] Deleuze, *Voyage*, 2, t. 1, 1824: 47, cited in Laissus 1988: 31.

[5] Laissus 1988: 31-32.

[6] Cuvier 1978; DeGérando 1969; Hughes 1988: 67-72.

[7] Péron 1809: 16.

[8] Péron 1809: 42-53.

[9] Péron 1809: 71-4.

[10] Péron 1809: 311-2.

[11] Péron 1809: 222, 311-312; Sankey 2004: 118-119.

[12] Péron 1809: 313.

[13] Péron 1809: 313.

[14] Plomley 1983: 161; Jones 1988: 46; Hughes 1988: 75.

[15] Péron 1809: 313.

[16] Péron 1809: 312.

[17] Péron n.d.: Feuille A, verso, 'Conférence addressee à 'Messieurs les professeurs', décrivant les aborigines et leur moeurs près de Port Jackson', *Dossier 9: Expédition aux Terres Australes. Notes de Voyage, côtes Est et Sud de la Nouvelle Hollande (auteurs divers)*, No. 09032, Transcription de J Bonnemains, Collection Lesueur, Muséum d'histoire naturelle du Havre.

[18] O'Brien 1999: 21.

[19] Péron 1809: 171.

[20] Péron 1809: 171.

[21] Péron 1809: 172.

[22] Péron 1809: 173.

[23] Péron 1809: 173.

[24] Péron 1809: 173.

[25] Péron 1809: 173-4.

[26] Péron 1809: 173-4.

[27] Péron 1809: 174.

[28] Péron 1809: 174.

[29] Péron 1809: 175.

[30] Péron 1809: 175.

[31] Péron 1809: 175.

[32] Péron 1809: 176.

[33] Péron 1809: 176.

[34] Péron 1809: 177.

[35] Péron 1809: 177.

[36] Jones 1988: 45.

[37] Péron 1809: 177.

[38] Péron 1809: 177.
[39] Péron 1809: 178.
[40] Péron 1809: 178.
[41] Péron 1809: 196-7; Hughes 1988: 81.
[42] Péron 1809: 178.
[43] Péron 1809: 178.
[44] Péron 1809: 179.
[45] Baudin 1974: 302.
[46] Péron 1809: 180.
[47] Péron 1809: 181.
[48] Péron 1809: 183-4.
[49] Péron 1809: 184.
[50] Baudin 1974: 305.
[51] Baudin 1974: 305.
[52] Baudin 1974: 305.
[53] Péron 1809: 185.
[54] Péron 1809: 187.
[55] Péron 1809: 185.
[56] Péron 1809: 186.
[57] Péron 1809: 186.
[58] Péron 1809: 186.
[59] Péron 1809: 195.
[60] Péron 1809: 196.
[61] Péron 1809: 196.
[62] Péron 1809: 196.
[63] Péron 1809: 196.
[64] Péron 1809: 200.
[65] Péron 1809: 197.
[66] Péron 1809: 198.
[67] Péron 1809: 198.
[68] Péron 1809: 196-7.
[69] Péron 1809: 197.
[70] Péron 1809: 197.
[71] Péron 1809: 199.
[72] Péron 1809: 199.
[73] Péron 1809: 200.
[74] Péron 1809: 200.
[75] Péron 1809: 217-9, 222.
[76] Péron 1809: 220.
[77] Péron 1809: 220.
[78] Péron 1809: 221.

Moving Blackwards: Black Power and the Aboriginal Embassy

Kathy Lothian

It is February 1972, and Canberra's Parliament House lawns are a busy, thriving protest site. Only metres from the front steps of the building a green-striped beach umbrella marks the spot where, on Australia Day, several Aboriginal activists set up camp. Now the umbrella has been joined by several tents. Cardboard placards display roughly-drawn slogans proclaiming the activists' anger and intentions: 'DESTROY ARNHEM LAND WE DESTROY AUSTRALIA'. 'WHY PAY TO USE OUR OWN LAND'. 'WHICH DO WE CHOOSE. LAND RIGHTS OR BLOODSHED!' [1] *Above them all, flapping from the umbrella's canopy, the sign that binds them: 'Aboriginal Embassy'. To stand on the road, with the big White building behind, and the small Black encampment in front, is to stand in a tense middle ground between two worlds of mutual incomprehension. While the machinery of the nation churns behind, the lawns in front play host to young Aboriginal people stretched out in the summer's morning. There might be tea drinking, guitar playing, planning, debating. Later, there might be exchanges with passers-by, leaflets being handed out, or photographers angling for the best frame. For a time, the Embassy has become Canberra's most curious landmark, its goings-on featured in newspapers around the country. In the press photos, several young men steadily return the camera's gaze. They stand before their creation, their clenched black fists defiantly raised.* [2]

Black Power

In the late 1960s, in that liminal space between the end of federal government policies of assimilation and the beginning of self-determination, stood one group of Aboriginal activists who were certain that they would overcome. Along with older and more conservative campaigners, they rejected assimilation and the White dominance of Aboriginal affairs. But it was the depth of their anger, their impatience and their disenchantment that marked their politics as new. This group was dismissive of a worldview that counselled eventual change. They were tired of the letter writing and petitioning, the focus on equality and multiracial togetherness of the dominant Aboriginal organisations. While they were intensely proud of their Aboriginality, in a way that was much more vocal than their elders had been, their reading of Black American activists had also been enlightening. They not only recognised the parallels of poverty, racism and political powerlessness between themselves and other oppressed minorities, but were also coming to learn that legislative change, no matter how grand or

19

symbolic, was no guarantee that their problems would be addressed. It was time for new tactics to be considered.[3]

These were the activists of the Aboriginal Embassy, that enduring symbol of Aboriginal demands for land rights. But the Embassy is much more than a story about land. It is also a story about these activists, their preoccupations and their alignment with Black Power. Black Power was an attitude that manifested itself in numerous ways through the late 1960s and early 1970s. It was embraced by both pragmatic Indigenous activists committed to reconciliatory approaches and, although they were in a minority, those inclined towards a revolutionary and violent solution. At its heart, however, Black Power represented an overt rejection of the lack of power in Aboriginal lives. For some activists, this meant a drastic reshuffling of Aboriginal organisations where Whites held important decision-making roles. Others saw the adoption of Black Power ideas as a way of focusing on a positive reclamation of Aboriginal identity. For others, the fight against racism and poverty was paramount.[4]

The first unmistakable Black Power upheaval was felt in August 1969, when activists in the Victorian Aborigines Advancement League invited Caribbean Black Power leader Roosevelt Brown to visit. Shortly afterwards, and claiming to be 'enlightened' by him, they issued a statement that described the proper role of Whites within the organisation as 'standing back' while Aboriginal decision-makers did their job.[5] Over the next couple of years the shockwaves rippled, as the idea took hold among other organisations — the Foundation for Aboriginal Affairs in Sydney, and the national umbrella organisation, the Federal Council for the Advancement of Aborigines and Torres Strait Islanders (FCAATSI). Here, a bitter clash at the 1970 annual conference resulted in the formation of a new organisation. In the National Tribal Council, it was declared that Aborigines would decide their own priorities, free from paternalistic White 'do-gooderism'.[6]

An even more militant organisation was formed at the end of 1971, when Denis Walker, the son of long-time Aboriginal campaigner Kath Walker, announced the formation of the Black Panther Party of Australia. Once described by the *Australian* as a 'calm young man',[7] he was now known for his abrasive and provocative militancy. 'Everything was taken off you with a gun', he declared. 'The only way you are going to get it back is with a gun'.[8] Along with his 'field marshals' — young Aboriginal men including Paul Coe, Gary Foley, Gary Williams and Billy Craigie, as well as Jim Doherty and Sam Watson — Walker had declared his commitment to the American Party's revolutionary ideology of armed self defence of the Black community and the 'eventual overthrow of the system'.[9] Just as the American Panthers had done, the Australian Panthers demanded a United Nations–supervised plebiscite to be held among Aborigines in order to determine 'the will of black people as to their national destiny'.[10]

The American Panthers were, Walker argued, teaching Blacks to 'stand up and assert their rights — and they're getting them'.[11]

The end of 1971 and beginning of 1972 saw a flurry of militant activity by Black Power activists. In Brisbane, a demonstration over racism resulted in complete chaos. Queensland activist Pastor Brady and other Aborigines threw punches at the police. Walker climbed onto the roof of a car to address the demonstrators, holding his arms in a giant V. Stones were thrown, a policeman kicked as he lay on the ground.[12] By the end of the day, nine Aborigines had been arrested, including Walker. Outside the courthouse following their hearing, they gave a collective Black Power salute and later, in an interview, Walker explained the mood. It was, he said, the beginning of a 'big breakout'; the first time that Blacks had said 'we're going to do it our way and to hell with the authorities'.[13]

Late in the year, the Captain Cook memorial in Hyde Park, Sydney, was covered with land rights slogans. Several days later, a tower at La Perouse was graffitied with clenched fist symbols of Black Power, along with 'Black is beautiful', 'Black is proud', and 'Pigs are suckers'.[14] In Victoria, the walls of the Advancement League headquarters were decorated with clenched black fists and Black Power slogans directed against 'honkies' and the slow transition to Black control within the organisation.[15] Early in January 1972, Michael Anderson achieved momentary celebrity by reminding Australians of Evonne Goolagong's trip to South Africa in 1970. Anderson was a Black Power activist originally from Walgett, a town in country New South Wales that had been targeted by the Freedom Rides in 1965. He attended the Australian Open tennis tournament wearing a 'Black Power is Black On' badge, asked Goolagong to become a spokesperson for Black Power and to decline the MBE she received in the New Year's honours list.[16]

Despite this show of militancy, Black Power activists actually held much in common with their predecessors. Although Black Power activists were generally more outspokenly and confidently Aboriginal than older Indigenous campaigners, many of the differences between the new guard and the old were attitudinal and stylistic. Just as previous campaigners had done, Black Power activists campaigned for equal rights and protested loudly about the status of Aboriginal citizenship. In addition, as Heather Goodall and others have shown, the fight to regain land among militant campaigners of the 1960s and 1970s was also an important goal with a long precedent.[17]

By the late 1960s, however, campaigns for land were increasingly being fought not only on moral grounds, but also on the basis that Aborigines had particular rights that stemmed from their status as Indigenous people. Two of the most significant campaigns of this decade were those fought by the Gurindji and the Yolngu. Supported by Aborigines both moderate and radical, these land claims became powerful national symbols of the fight for land rights. Together, they contributed to a growing expectation that the importance of land to Aboriginal people would find an appropriate governmental response.[18]

The policy announcement, when it eventually came, was a harsh blow. On 25 January 1972, Prime Minister McMahon's statement boasted of the achievements in Aboriginal Affairs, and proclaimed empathy with the 'Aboriginal [desire] to have their affinity with the land with which they have been associated recognised by law'. Nonetheless, and despite the recommendations of the Office of Aboriginal Affairs, McMahon's statement effectively denied Aboriginal land rights. Instead, his vision was for a system of 'special purpose' leases, conditional upon Aboriginal peoples' 'intention and ability to make reasonable economic and social use of the land'.[19] The response from Black Power activists was instantaneous.

The tents

The Embassy's focus on land is underlined from the very beginning. The very first announcements by Michael Anderson, who is fast surpassing his initial claim to fame as an intimidator of Evonne Goolagong, are that 'the land was taken from us by force — we shouldn't have to lease it', and that the group would remain on the lawns until 'the Government reconsiders its statement'.[20] In early February, the Embassy announces its official 'land rights policy'. It is a five point program demanding ownership of all reserves in Australia, preservation of sacred lands, Aboriginal ownership of the Northern Territory as well as areas of 'certain cities', and six billion dollars as compensation for all other land.[21]

Throughout February, orange, green and white tents sprout overnight on the Parliament House lawns, and the number of protesters begins to swell. Over the next few months, John Newfong can often be seen around the encampment. Newfong is an Indigenous activist and journalist from Stradbroke Island, and has become an official Embassy spokesman. One can imagine him standing his ground on the lawns, in earnest discussion with reporters. Perhaps he gestures to the spot above the entrance to the main tent, to explain the significance of the two flags that now fly alongside the 'Embassy' placard. One, he might say, is an African international unity flag in black, green and red stripes, adopted by activists to represent the people, the land and the blood shed by Aborigines who have died in defence of their country. The other, a black and brown flag to signify the people and the land, is overlaid with a white spear and four crescent shapes surrounding it, signifying four men seated around a campfire.[22]

This is clearly no ordinary protest and Peter Howson, the Minister for the Environment, Aborigines and the Arts, is disturbed. The declaration of an Embassy, he worries, implied the existence of a sovereign state or separate nation. This, he insists, 'cut[s] across the Government's expressed objection to separate development'.[23] From his viewpoint as a political conservative, Howson is right to worry. The

Embassy does not merely hint at the existence of a separate nation. It is a self-evident statement.

Black pride

While the Embassy did represent one of the earliest explicit declarations of Aboriginal sovereignty, Aborigines had long been aware of their separateness from the life of the nation. In fact, the rejection of 'whiteness' as 'rightness' was the foundational politics for many Black Power activists. For these campaigners, the essence of Black Power lay in its refusal to internalise a sense of inferiority. To be a Black Power activist was to have a positive sense of one's identity. It was to build a new set of truths. As Victorian activist Bruce McGuinness put it, a 'Blackward step' would be 'a forward step'.[24]

Some Black Power activists drew upon Black American activism to promote an overtly 'Black' image. The 'Afro' was a popular hairstyle for those who were 'black and beautiful'. Walker dressed in the black leather jacket and dark sunglasses of the Black Panthers, while Redfern activist Bob Bellear chose the Panthers' black beret.[25] Clenched black fists began to appear everywhere: at demonstrations, on badges, in leaflets and newsletters. Aspects of Black American language found their way into activist dialogue. 'Honky' or 'the Man' was the terminology used to describe the white oppressor, 'Uncle Tom' the label given to those seen to be in collusion with him. In 1972, McGuinness announced that the old book of rules had been torn up. The new book's title was 'Black is beautiful, right on brothers and sisters, and screw you whitey'.[26]

Activists also found reading material that resonated with their own life experiences and desires. McGuinness recommended Frantz Fanon's *The Wretched of the Earth* and Stokely Carmichael and Charles Hamilton's best-selling *Black Power* as useful guides for Aboriginal Black Power activists. The latter book, which promoted the need for Black people to eschew coalitions with Whites and to 'redefine themselves', McGuinness wrote, 'should be a prized possession of every Aborigine'.[27] Bobby Seale, Eldridge Cleaver, George Jackson and Angela Davis were also useful background reading.[28] It was Malcolm X's autobiography and speeches though, that most captured the imaginations of some of the younger Aborigines, with his uncompromisingly militant rejection of White culture, his pride in being Black, his belief in Black nationhood, and his call for self-defence 'by any means necessary'.[29]

Adopting these visual and rhetorical symbols of Black America did not deter Black Power activists from calling for pride in Aboriginality. Bob Maza, for instance, was an Indigenous activist from Queensland, who had been living in Melbourne during the late 1960s and had moved to Sydney in the early 1970s. From 1968 he began an urgent campaign to 'create an awareness of the Koorie as a race', pointing to the honour, integrity and self-discipline of the 'old

Aborigines'.[30] In June 1969 he suggested that Malcolm X's teaching and example could do much to enhance this self-discovery. 'I only hope that when I die I can say I'm black and it's beautiful to be black. It is this sense of pride which we are trying to give back to the aborigine [sic] today', he claimed.[31] Malcolm X taught him, he argued, that it was possible to 'walk tall and with pride', and that only a positive self-image could effectively challenge the internalised impact of White supremacy.[32] Law student and Redfern activist Paul Coe agreed, believing that that Black Power was all about actively working against assimilationist paradigms through the 're-instating of black culture wherever … possible'.[33]

It was this position on Black Power that Maza carried with him when he attended a Black Power conference in America in September 1970. After attending workshops with other Black Power delegates and meeting Black American groups around the country afterwards, he was 'burning with passion' to implement some of the ideas he had gleaned. He was particularly impressed by Amiri Baraka's National Black Theatre in Harlem. They were 'so powerful', and 'so strong'. Maza loved the way they were using theatre as a teaching medium and so, with a little theatre experience of his own behind him, helped to establish a National Black Theatre (NBT) in Redfern, in 1972.[34]

This multifaceted theatre and community place was a space that could be used as a childcare facility during the day, where Black Panthers were known to participate in poetry readings for local children, and where community meetings were held. Carole Johnson, a dancer with a Black American company, had remained in Australia after her tour finished and it was here that she trained the dance division of the theatre. An art workshop produced sculptures, carvings and ceramics, as well as posters for demonstrations. Drama and writing workshops taught basic skills, and 'Ebony Profile' was established as a Black casting agency for advertising, television and film.[35]

Black theatre was a consciously political undertaking from the beginning. The performers and writers involved aimed to put forward what they saw as a specifically Aboriginal view of social reality and to challenge White audiences. NBT was consequently often described as 'protest theatre', but its function was much broader. It was actively intent on exploring those factors that constituted Aboriginality. The theatre's creative works were to be used as tools for recovering a different historical tradition and for putting forward Aboriginal narratives of dispossession. They would counter White-controlled images of Aboriginality and promote Black pride. This version of Aboriginality would not only declare its separateness from white Australia but also would celebrate it and teach it to others. For many, Aboriginal theatre was no less powerful than the Aboriginal Embassy or the Black Panther Party in achieving political goals or promoting Black Power.[36] The theatre of NBT lay in the idea that there was no significant slippage between the parts the actors were playing and the reality of their lives once they had left the stage. Life on reserves and missions, in fringe towns and inner urban communities, seasonal work, racial violence, the continuing impact of colonialism and the intersections between past and present provided the creative impetus for Aboriginal theatre. So too did the political activities of the theatre's actors, many of whom, as playwright Gerry Bostock observed, were involved in multiple spheres of activism. Those involved in Black theatre were just as likely to be found working with Aboriginal community organisations or at the Aboriginal Embassy — because, Bostock argued, they knew that 'to do the job that has to be done involves struggle on many fronts, and you can't devote yourself to one area'.[37]

The tents

As the months drag on into autumn and then into winter, the Embassy protesters lose none of their conviction, nor their anger. Although they leave — for jobs, families, other cities — there is reunion around the tents on the weekends, and talk of land rights in the air. And when the protestors come together to discuss their goals, there is talk of other things too. They know that the tents are a devastating visual reminder of the aftermath of dispossession, and they know that 'land rights' and 'civil rights' are intimately connected. If you were to pass by the Embassy during these months, a staffer might hand you a flyer listing a broad range of concerns. You might learn of an 'Aboriginal Embassy Manifesto', which begins by asking whether Aborigines have 'received a fair deal' in return for losing their land. It points to inequalities in education, wages and the law, as well as extremely high mortality statistics. Or, you might chance across an information sheet titled 'Why an Embassy?' It begins with a denunciation of the government's policy on land, but moves swiftly to paint a picture of Aboriginal living conditions — high unemployment and infant mortality, malnutrition, gonorrhoea, scurvy, tuberculosis, gastroenteritis and trachoma. [38]

To attempt to deal with these problems, many of the Embassy campaigners are actively involved in 'community survival programs' in inner-city Sydney. As much as their commitment to land rights, it is their daily confrontation with poverty and racial oppression that binds them. One of these activists is Gary Foley. From Nambucca Heads in northern New South Wales, he has been a significant figure in the Black Power movement in Sydney for several years. He also loves a good argument. When an elderly White woman approaches him one day as he is lying on the Embassy lawns, full of moralistic advice for the demonstrators, it is all the encouragement he needs. 'Listen! Lemme tell you something!' He jabs his finger at her. 'We've done alright in the past two years in Sydney without people like you. And we're going to do alright for a long time to come. We're going to get our bloody land, even if we have to fucking well take it!' [39]

Black independence

For young Redfern activists, racism was a constant presence. It permeated every facet of their lives but found its clearest expression in their frequent encounters with the police — which arose, they were certain, from an official campaign of intimidation, harassment, and high-level surveillance.[40] Police behaviour at the Empress Hotel (the 'Big E'), or the Clifton Hotel in Regent Street was a typical example. 'It was like a taxi rank', Foley claimed. 'They'd come in and beat the shit out of everyone inside, arbitrarily arrest anyone who objected, and when the wagons were full they'd drive off and lock people up on trumped-up charges'.[41] Simply to be on the streets of Redfern late at night was enough to contravene the 'unofficial curfew'. If you were on the streets after 10 pm, recalled activist Chicka Dixon, 'brother, you're taking a chance'.[42]

It was Foley, his cousin Gary Williams and Paul Coe who eventually took decisive action. Coe, Foley claimed, 'started trying to convince me and Williams that we could do something about [police harassment]'. He began encouraging them to read political literature, but was becoming particularly enthusiastic about his discovery of a campaign called the 'Pig Patrol' that the Black Panthers had begun in America. He handed the information to Foley. 'This is a great idea. Read this'.[43]

These activists realised that, while they could not trail police around the streets with loaded weapons as the Black Panthers were doing, the techniques were nonetheless easily adapted for Redfern. They could at least carry notebooks and pencils. Thus armed, some activists entered the 'Big E' one Saturday evening in 1969. 'As the pigs began to do their nightly act we started writing down everything that they were doing', Foley recalls. 'We wrote down their numbers, their van numbers, who they were arresting'.[44] After several months, a group of activists including Williams, Foley, Paul and his sister Isobel Coe, Tony Coorey, Les Collins, Lyn Thompson, Shirley Smith (Mum Shirl) and James Wedge had amassed a vast amount of incriminating evidence.[45]

What followed was a series of meetings between these activists and Hal Wootten, Dean of Law at the University of New South Wales. They were, he noted, an 'impressive group', intensely proud of their Aboriginality, and determined to solve the social problems that beset their community.[46] The first Aboriginal Legal Service of New South Wales was consequently launched only a short time later. While activists relied heavily on the assistance of sympathetic White lawyers, this was the first organisation in the state to be conceived, established and controlled by Aborigines since the Aborigines Progressive Association in 1937.

Institutional racism was crippling Aboriginal life in Redfern in other areas as well, and young Black Power activists continued to seek a solution. Coe continued to read about the Black Panther community survival projects in the United States — free clothing, political education classes, free food programs, and a news service, as well as a 'Free Breakfast Program' for children, and a 'People's Free Medical Research Health Clinic'. Party Chairman Bobby Seale had promoted the programs as means of 'organising the people', and letting them know 'that in this time, in our time, we must seize our right to live, and we must seize our right to survive'.[47] When Gordon Briscoe, an inaugural council member of the Legal Service, visited a Redfern house in June 1971 on business related to the service, he was outraged. Inside, the Aboriginal client was so ill that he was unable to speak, his impoverished family unable to afford medical attention.[48]

The determination to 'seize the time' that Aboriginal activists had shown in their establishment of the Legal Service was redeployed. Within only a few weeks, the Aboriginal Medical Service had opened for business a few doors down from the Legal Service in Regent Street, Redfern. Here volunteers provided basic health care and developed programs to counteract the increasing numbers of patients coming to the service with health problems caused by malnutrition.[49] Free fruit and vegetables were delivered to Aboriginal families, and the Breakfast for Children Program provided Aboriginal schoolchildren with breakfast on school mornings where otherwise they might have eaten nothing.[50]

Although Foley and other Black Power activists readily acknowledged the way in which these programs were inspired by the American Black Panther Party,[51] the programs were, nonetheless, a response to the unique conditions of the Aboriginal community. Transformed to meet the needs of inner-city Aborigines, activists also understood them as being embedded within the fight for land rights. For Briscoe, the services represented 'the contemporary extension of the historical resistance to white superiority.' They were statements of independence and self-assertion, aimed at getting White society to recognise that 'this is our land and we mean to get it back'.[52] For Coe the Legal Service had a definite role outside the provision of legal assistance. It was, he argued in 1975, an interim step leading towards a Black nation. 'I believe, and always have believed', he maintained, 'that the Aboriginal people have never ever relinquished their sovereignty or their rights ... that we have always been and still are, a nation within a nation — that we are a sovereign people.'[53]

The tents

In July, in the midst of the crisp Canberra winter, the Embassy stands firm. Now it has gained a new emblem. While the black and brown flag with its traditional insignia still flies, politicians who cast their gaze over the lawns from their office windows cannot fail to be struck by the new addition. A new flag, arresting in its design and colours of black, red and yellow, boldly underscores the Embassy's assertion of Aboriginal nationhood. [54]

From the beginning, the McMahon Liberal government has been affronted by the existence of the tents. Former Prime Minister John Gorton had raised the possibility of their removal at the very first sitting of parliament that year. But now, Ralph Hunt, Minister for the Interior, is finally able to approve the new ordinance to make it illegal to camp on Parliament's doorstep. [55] *Now it is possible to act. Six days after Aborigines around the country march in a national demonstration for land rights, the police move. It is only the first of two bloody and brutal encounters with the protestors. On both occasions, they march in military style from Parliament; their dark uniforms a stark contrast with the Whiteness of the building. On both occasions, the violence is frightening. Despite the insistence of the protestors that 'We Shall Not Be Moved!', several activists find themselves ferrying the injured to hospital. When it is all over, the remaining Aborigines cluster in little groups, looking dazed.* [56]

Few want to abandon their Embassy. A meeting after the second violent removal of the tents reveals not only the protestor's resolve, but also the depths of their anger. Chicka Dixon reminds everybody of the need for 'sustained action'. Foley wants to show the government that they mean business — with a few Molotov cocktails. Walker suggests that, if the tents are removed for a third time, some sort of 'destruction' be inflicted on White society. [57] *But many protestors also fear that a further confrontation with police will result in deaths.* [58] *In the afternoon of 30 July, after re-establishing the Embassy and spending the day on the lawns with hundreds of White supporters, the Embassy staff allow police a passage through the crowd, and the tents are peacefully removed.* [59]

***

Although the defiant image of the Aboriginal Embassy continues to stand as one of the most significant moments in twentieth century Aboriginal political history, the connection with Black Power activism has often been overlooked. Certainly, not all Embassy supporters aligned themselves with Black Power. The Embassy, in its encapsulation of the claim to land rights, had the wide support and participation of Aborigines from the entire political spectrum. Yet in July 1972, when the McMahon Liberal government attempted the Embassy's removal, there they were, dozens of activists with clenched black fists thrust in the air. Amid the chants of 'LAND RIGHTS — NOW!', Walker strode the lawns in his Black Panther jacket, waving the Aboriginal flag. John Newfong, Paul Coe, Michael Anderson, Cheryl Buchanan, Gary Foley, Billy Craigie, Ambrose Golden-Brown, Tony Coorey and Roberta Sykes, many of them Redfern activists from the Medical and Legal services, all defended the tents. Bob Maza, along with Anderson, brought the National Black Theatre to the lawns, where it performed 'the whole history of Aboriginal/European conflict' in its 'Embassy dance'.[60] Despite their defeat by police, the feeling that they had won a moral victory was running high. Surely their claims could no longer be ignored?[61]

In the 35 years since the first erection of the Embassy, its significance as a marker of the demand for Aboriginal land rights has taken on legendary qualities, and those demands have remained as urgent as ever before. Erected again and again since 1972, the Embassy now maintains a constant — if uneasy — presence among the tourist surrounds of Old Parliament House. In this time the encampment has been variously described as an 'eyesore' and a place of pilgrimage. It has inspired artwork and has been the target of several firebomb attacks.[62]

Although the Embassy's symbolic importance to Indigenous people was recognised in 1995 when it was listed on the Register of the National Estate,[63] White Australia has either continued to avert its gaze from this organic and ramshackle reminder of the Indigenous presence in Australia, or has continued to seek its physical removal. In the most recent governmental attempt to erase the Embassy, Minister for Territories, Jim Lloyd, has argued that the site would be better served by an authorised and structured exhibition. Here, camping would be disallowed and carefully controlled displays would provide an educative function for tourists.[64] Perhaps more symbolically, in the Bicentenary year of White occupation of Australia, the seat of Australian government simply moved away. It now lies further up the hill, where the main view from the front steps is not a shabby Aboriginal encampment but a sweeping expanse of manicured lawn down to the old White building and onwards to the war memorial.

References

Primary documents

'Aboriginal Embassy', n.d., Flyer authorised by Sammy Watson Jr., Aboriginal Embassy, Canberra, Mitchell Library Ephemera Collection.

'Aboriginal Embassy, Canberra' (text of an information sheet handed out by the Aboriginal Embassy), reprinted in *Newsletter on Aboriginal Affairs,* No. 1, April 1972.

'Aboriginal Embassy Manifesto', reproduced in Scarfe, Allan and Scarfe, Wendy 1974, *The Black Australians: Aboriginals — the past and the future,* Melbourne: 54.

Anderson, Michael n.d., 'Why an Embassy?', unpublished typescript, Australian Institute of Aboriginal and Torres Strait Islander Studies, PMS 5101.

Black Panther Party of Australia, 'Platform and program. What we want. What we believe' January 1972, FJ Riley and Ephemera Collection, State Library of Victoria.

Commonwealth Government 1972, 'Australian Aborigines: Commonwealth Policy and Achievements', Statement by the Prime Minister, The Rt Hon. William McMahon, C.H., M.P.', 26 January.

Eggleston, Elizabeth, Personal Papers, Monash University Archives, MON 79.

Eggleston, Elizabeth, Research Files, Monash University Archives, MON 81.

National Tribal Council September 1970, 'Policy Manifesto', Australian Institute for Aboriginal and Torres Strait Islander Studies, P14565.

National Tribal Council January 1971, Constitution, Australian Institute for Aboriginal and Torres Strait Islander Studies, P14566.

Newspapers and media sources

AAL Newsletter

Aboriginal Quarterly

The Age

The Australian, Weekend Australian

'Black Power: Queensland riot' November 1971, *This Day Tonight*, Australian Broadcasting Commission, Brisbane

Broadside

Canberra News

The Courier Mail

Herald (Melbourne)

Identity

Koorier

Ningla A' Na, documentary film, 72 minutes, dir. Allesandro Cavadini, Australia 1972

New Dawn

Smoke Signals

Sunday Australian

Sydney Morning Herald

Tribune

Secondary sources

'Black Panther Party of Australia — Brisbane Chapter, Manifesto Number One', and 'Black Panther Party of Australia — Brisbane Chapter, Manifesto Number Two', in Richards, Michael J 1972, 'The writers and the Aboriginals, being an analysis of the treatment of the Aboriginal race in the writing of Australian history', BA thesis, University of Queensland: Appendix.

Bostock, Gerry 1985, 'Black Theatre', in Jack Davis and Bob Hodge (eds), *Aboriginal writing today: papers from the 1st national conference of Aboriginal writers held in Perth, Western Australia, in 1983*, Canberra: 63-73.

Bostock, Lester 1973, 'Black Theatre in New South Wales', *New Dawn*, September: 14.

Breitman, George (ed.) 1966, *Malcolm X Speaks: selected speeches and statements*, London.

Briscoe, Gordon 1978, 'Aboriginal health and land rights', *New Doctor* (Journal of the Doctors' Reform Society), April: 13-15.

Dow, Coral 2000, 'Aboriginal Tent Embassy: icon or eyesore?', Social Policy Group, Parliament of Australia, 4 April 2000, accessed 19 July 2006, <http://www.aph.gov.au/LIBRARY/Pubs/chron/1999-2000/2000chr03.htm>

Eggleston, Elizabeth 1970, 'Aborigines and the administration of justice: a critical analysis of the application of criminal law to Aborigines', PhD thesis, Monash University.

Foley, Gary 1975, 'The history of the Aboriginal Medical Service: a study in bureaucratic obstruction', *Black News Service*, no. 5, August: 4.

—— 1988a, 'One Black life', *Rolling Stone Yearbook*: 107-111.

—— 1988b, 'Talking history', *Land Rights News*, vol. 2, no. 8: 30-31.

Gilbert, Kevin 1994, *Because a White man'll never do it* (2nd edn), Sydney.

Goodall, Heather 1996, *Invasion to Embassy: land in Aboriginal politics in New South Wales, 1770-1972*, Sydney.

Kemp, Kevon 1972, 'Theatre the Black Muslim way, for the good of Aborigines — and whites', *The National Times*, 13-18 November: 20.

Lothian, Kathleen 2002, '"A Blackward step is a forward step": Australian Aborigines and Black Power, 1969-1972', MA thesis, Monash University.

Mayers, Naomi and Paul Coe 1976, 'Aboriginal Medical Service submission to the Senate Standing Commission on Social Environment', 17 April 1973, Senate Standing Committee on Social Environment: Report on the Environmental Conditions of Aborigines and Torres Strait Islanders and the Preservation of Their Sacred Sites'.

Newfong John 1972, 'The Aboriginal Embassy: its purpose and aims', *Identity*, July: 4-6.

Robinson, Scott 1993, 'Aboriginal Embassy, 1972', MA Thesis, Australian National University.

—— 1994, 'The Aboriginal Embassy: an account of the protests of 1972', *Aboriginal History* 18(1): 49-63.

Seale, Bobby 1970, *Seize the time: the story of the Black Panther Party* (Rep.), London.

Statement from the Aboriginal Tent Embassy re the third firebomb attack, *ABC Indigenous news*, 17 August 2004, accessed 19 July 2006, <http://www.abc.net.au/message/news/stories/s1179624.htm>

Taffe, Sue 2005, *Black and white together. FCAATSI: the Federal Council for the Advancement of Aborigines and Torres Strait Islanders 1958-1973*, St Lucia.

Tatz, Colin, and McConnochie, Keith (eds) 1975, *Black viewpoints: the Aboriginal experience*, Sydney.

Liz Tompson (ed.) 1990, *Aboriginal voices: contemporary Aboriginal artists, writers and performers*, Sydney.

Wootten, Prof. JH 1973, 'The New South Wales Aboriginal Legal Service', in Lorna Lippmann (ed.), *Aborigines in the 70s: Seminars 1972-1973*, Centre for Research into Aboriginal Affairs, Monash University, Melbourne: 157-177.

—— 1993, 'Aborigines and police', *The University of New South Wales Law Journal* 16(1): 265-301.

ENDNOTES

[1] *Sydney Morning Herald*, 28 January 1972; *The Tribune*, 1-7 February 1972.

[2] See, for instance, *The Tribune*, 27 March – 3 April 1972.

[3] These issues are explored in more depth in Lothian 2002: 35-46 passim.

[4] Lothian 2002: 35-46 passim.

[5] *Smoke Signals*, September 1969: 3; *AAL Newsletter*, October 1969: 2-3.

[6] See Taffe 2005: 257-266; National Tribal Council, Policy Manifesto, September 1970, National Tribal Council, Constitution, January 1971.

[7] *Australian*, 20 May 1971.

[8] *Tribune*, 8 December 1971.

[9] *Sunday Australian*, 5 December 1971; *Australian*, 19 January 1972; 'Black Panther Party of Australia — Brisbane Chapter, Manifestos Number One and Two' in Richards 1972: Appendix.

[10] Black Panther Party of Australia, *Platform and Program. What We Want. What We Believe*, January 1972, FJ Riley and Ephemera Collection, State Library of Victoria.

[11] *The Herald* (Melbourne), 12 January 1972.

[12] *Courier-Mail*, 24 November 1971; *Australian*, 24 November 1971; 'Black Power: Queensland Riot' November 1971, *This Day Tonight*, Australian Broadcasting Commission, Brisbane.

[13] *Sydney Morning Herald*, 25 November 1971.

[14] *Sydney Morning Herald*, 3 December 1971.

[15] *Sydney Morning Herald*, 16 December 1971.

[16] *Australian*, 6 January 1972.

[17] See Goodall 1996 generally.

[18] See, for example, Taffe 2005: 164-216 passim.

[19] Commonwealth Government 1972, 'Australian Aborigines: Commonwealth Policy and Achievements'.

[20] *Canberra News*, 27 January 1972; Goodall 1996: 339.

[21] *Newsletter On Aboriginal Affairs*, No. 1, April 1972: 5.

[22] 'Aboriginal Embassy, Canberra' (text of an information sheet handed out by the Aboriginal Embassy), reprinted in *Newsletter on Aboriginal Affairs*, No. 1, April 1972. These flags can both be clearly seen in a photograph accompanying Newfong 1972: 4-6.

[23] *Canberra News*, 31 January 1972.

[24] *Identity*, November 1972: 4.

[25] See footage of these activists in *Ningla A' Na*.

[26] *Identity*, November 1972: 4. More generally, see Lothian 2002, chapter 4.

[27] *AAL Newsletter*, October 1969: 6; *The Koorier*, vol. 1, no. 7: 12. Lothian 2002: 133-134.

[28] Lothian 2002: 133-134.

[29] In Breitman 1966: 96.

[30] *The Koorier*, vol. 1, no. 5, 27 January 1969: 1; *Smoke Signals*, April-June 1969: 3.

[31] *Broadside*, 12 June 1969: 4.

[32] Bob Maza, cited in Tompson (ed.) 1990: 162-163.

[33] Paul Coe, cited in Colin Tatz and Keith McConnochie (eds) 1975: 105; but see also footage in *Ningla A' Na*.

[34] *Weekend Australian (Review)*, 2-3 January 1999: 15.

[35] Kemp 1972: 20; Bostock 1973: 14; 'Basically Black', *New Dawn*, December 1972: 2.

[36] Gilbert 1994: 121.

[37] Bostock 1985: 69.

[38] 'Aboriginal Embassy Manifesto', reproduced in Scarfe and Scarfe 1974: 54; Anderson, Michael n.d., 'Why an Embassy?'; see also 'Aboriginal Embassy', n.d., Flyer authorised by Sammy Watson Jr.

[39] See footage in *Ningla A' Na*.

[40] See Eggleston 1970: 17-81 passim.

[41] Foley 1988a: 109; see also Foley 1988b: 30.

[42] Tatz and McConnochie (eds) 1975: 36; see also Wootten 1993: 268.

[43] Foley 1988a: 108.

[44] Foley 1988a: 109.

[45] Foley 1988a: 109; Robinson 1993: 33.

[46] Wootten 1973: 159.

[47] Seale 1970: 473.

[48] Briscoe, Gordon 1972, 'Towards a health programme for Aborigines', paper presented to the Aboriginal Health Service seminar, Monash University, 14-17 May 1972, in Elizabeth Eggleston Research Files, Item 195.

[49] Foley 1975: 4; Mayers and Coe 1976, 'Aboriginal Medical Service submission to the Senate Standing Commission on Social Environment'.

[50] *New Dawn*, May 1972: 3; *Aboriginal Quarterly*, vol. 2, no. 3, March 1980: 11.

[51] Foley 1988b: 30.

[52] Briscoe 1978: 14.

[53] Paul Coe, cited in transcript of *Lateline*, 22 May 1975, in Elizabeth Eggleston Personal Papers, Item 178.

[54] Robinson 1993: 131 f/n 120.

[55] Robinson 1993: 116, 140.

[56] See footage in *Ningla A'Na*.

[57] See footage in *Ningla A'Na*.

[58] Robinson 1993: 164-165; Robinson 1994: 58-60.

[59] Robinson 1993: 168-171; *Ningla A' Na*.

[60] *Ningla A' Na*; Bostock 1973: 14.

[61] *Ningla A' Na*.

[62] Dow 2000; Statement from the Aboriginal Tent Embassy re the third firebomb attack 2004.

[63] Dow 2000.

[64] *The Age*, 10 December 2005.

Criminal justice and transgression on northern Australian cattle stations

Thalia Anthony

The remote interior of northern Australia represented a site of transgression for both pastoral colonisers and Aborigines alike. From the northern frontier period in the late nineteenth century until the 1966 Equal Pay decision, a unique relationship existed on cattle stations in which pastoralists and their Aboriginal workers deviated from government control. Despite Aboriginal protection legislation that prevailed elsewhere in northern Australia, pastoralists created their own jurisdiction over Aboriginal people. This jurisdiction bypassed the assimilationist tendencies of government policy, by allowing Aboriginal people to practice customs and ceremonies, and retain connections to country.[1] At the same time, it maximised the capacity for pastoralists to exploit Aboriginal labour. Therefore, both pastoralists and Aboriginal people benefited from transgressing official 'Aboriginal Acts'.

However, this source of transgression was at the mercy of the pastoralist. Accordingly, it came to a sudden halt in the late 1960s with the introduction of labour-saving machines and the 1966 Equal Pay decision. These developments rendered Aboriginal workers redundant. They were transferred from the cattle station to the government sphere of welfare and criminal justice.[2] They were subsequently denied connections to country, and their historic labour contribution went largely unrecognised.

This paper suggests that the pastoralists' jurisdiction represented a repository of feudal power. The term 'feudal' is used to refer to an interdependent labour relationship between the landed and the landless, but one that is ultimately controlled by the landholder. The landless are answerable to the proprietor, rather than the state. The state is mostly complicit in this decentralised power exercised by those who produce an economic surplus from their land.[3] In northern Australia, the state recognised the economic value of the cattle industry, and its complicity manifested through regulations as well as negligent oversight of pastoralists' power over Aboriginal workers. The consequences were twofold. On the one hand it resulted in impoverished conditions for Aboriginal workers and their dependants. On the other hand it enabled Aboriginal workers to transgress the intransigent nature of protection policies. While the interdependent relationship with pastoralists also involved assimilation, its effect was retrained due to the rights afforded to Aboriginal people on stations.

Transgression from state powers operated on cattle stations across northern Queensland, Northern Territory and Western Australia. These stations north of 'Capricorn' employed Aboriginal people on an unprecedented scale in Australia. Despite the fact that each station was autonomous and geographically isolated, there was a distinct pattern of feudal relationships. This was because the mutual dependence between pastoralists and Aboriginal workers provided a stable means of labour exploitation. This is discerned from oral histories of Aboriginal people, pastoralists and protectors; government reports, and official correspondence. When pastoralists' dependence ceased in the late 1960s, so did its jurisdiction for transgression. As Peter Yu describes, Aboriginal people were forced into 'severely overcrowded native welfare reserves' or 'hastily gazetted refugee camps'.[4] This paper considers the growth of the pastoralists' jurisdiction (including the underpinning colonial land system) and the capacity for Aboriginal transgression within this jurisdiction, and concludes with the consequences of the demise of Aboriginal employment on cattle stations and possibilities for the future.

Feudal transgression: a more elucidatory means of classifying cattle stations

Traditionally, relationships on northern cattle stations have been classified in terms of 'free or forced' employment. Both sides of the debate ground their arguments in notions of power. The proponents of the 'forced labour' argument suggest that cattle station managers exercised power brutally over Aboriginal workers.[5] In turn, the workers were powerless to resist. In the 1980s Raymond Evans drew attention to 'striking parallels across time and space between the condition of the slave and the unfree Aboriginal worker'.[6] Both were denied economic rights of pay and freedom of movement in the labour market.

By contrast, from the late 1980s cultural historians such as Ann McGrath and Henry Reynolds emphasised the Aborigines' 'creative adaptation' to stations that afforded them agency.[7] This 'accommodationist' school highlights the cultural leverage granted to Aboriginal workers to stay on their land and maintain kinship ties. McGrath summarises this cultural revisionist position as follows: 'Aboriginal station dwellers co-operated with the white people, but they were never truly colonised'.[8]

The traditional focus on the degree of power exercised between cattle station managers and their workers does not appreciate the context of the cattle station as a land jurisdiction. Possession of land gave pastoralists rights over Aboriginal workers. At the same time, Aboriginal workers who conformed acquired rights over the station land. By making the feudal notion of land jurisdiction a central issue, it explains how Aboriginal workers benefited from the relations — by retaining ties to their land but *at the same time* being exploited — by pastoralists making residence contingent on Aborigines' labour contribution. Therefore, labour was neither free nor forced, but dependent on the land jurisdiction of the pastoralist.

Intersection between feudal land laws and power

In northern Australia, pastoralists' jurisdiction over Aboriginal people reflects the corresponding feudal rights to land and power. The feudal legal system is based on multiple layers of land possession beneath the ultimate title of the Crown. Each landholder is entitled to exercise power over their land and dispossessed workers. Consequently, feudal law does not centre power in one authority. When Australia was colonised, Britain introduced feudal land tenure throughout Australia. However, it was only in the pastoral north that feudal relations accompanied these laws. This is because landholders had an interest in exercising their right to power over 'landless' Aboriginal workers. This section will consider the role of Australian feudal land laws in dispossessing Aboriginal people, and dividing power between the state on behalf of the Crown and the pastoralist.

The feudal property principle, known as the 'Doctrine of Tenures and Estates', served colonial objectives of land expropriation and control. The Doctrine of Tenures provides for a 'single devolving chain of title' by ensuring that 'no land in which the Crown has granted an interest is ever without a legal owner'.[9] The Doctrine of Estates articulates the interests of those who hold land from the Crown to grant their estate to a lessee.[10] The Doctrine of Estates and Tenures, therefore, allows coexisting interests in one piece of land at the same time. In northern Australia feudal laws materialised due to pastoralists' need for Aboriginal labour. Not only did they have to answer to the 'Crown' by fulfilling lease requirements on their land,[11] but they also had to accommodate Aboriginal land interests in order to guarantee their labour. Throughout the rest of Australia, feudal tenure tended towards a nominal form of Crown control.

Feudal law was a powerful vehicle for Australian land conquest, as it justified Crown control and legitimised Aboriginal dispossession. Feudal tenure, as the source of Australian property statute and case law, meant the Crown could parcel out huge tracts of land to productive and loyal tenants while retaining ownership. This stratified system of land law was routinely implemented in other English, French and Spanish settlements, via a land lease system, to allow the Crown ultimate control.[12]

The High Court in *Mabo v Queensland* [13] confirmed the feudal origins of Australia's land law. The majority claimed that the Crown acquired ultimate title, known as 'radical title', of all Australian land upon colonisation. Each substantive judgment made some reference to this feudal essence of land law as expressed in the Doctrine of Tenures and Estates. Despite recognising native title, these judgments upheld the feudal basis of Australian land law. In his majority judgment, Justice Brennan reiterated that the tenurial principle that 'all lands are holden mediately or immediately of the Crown, flows from the adoption of the feudal system'.[14] He posited that because colonial lands were the patrimony of the coloniser nation, the origins of Australia's land tenure were found in the traditional belief that after the Norman Conquest in 1066, 'the King either owned beneficially and granted, or otherwise became Paramount Lord of, all land in the Kingdom'.[15]

The *Australia Courts Act* 1828 (Imp.) was the statutory instrument for the formal implementation of feudal laws. It traced all Australian land possession to Crown grants.[16] Common law precedent affirmed feudal tenure in *Attorney-General v Brown*. This 1847 NSW Supreme Court decision overruled a challenge to the Crown's sovereign title over tenures. Chief Justice Stephen explicitly stated that since settlement the 'waste lands' of the colony were in the 'Sovereign's possession; and that, as his or her property, they have been and may now be effectually granted to subjects of the Crown'.[17] He referred to the British constitutional principle that the sovereign is the legal *'universal occupant'*.[18]

To sustain the imposition of feudal tenure laws in Australian common law, the corresponding fiction of *terra nullius* — land belonging to no one — was invoked to show there was no pre-existing property title to universal Crown title. International law upheld that states could acquire foreign land legally, and apply their laws automatically, where land was *terra nullius*.[19] This doctrine was manufactured to include territories inhabited by 'backward peoples', due to the purported benefits of Christianity and European civilisation, and Vattel and Blackstone's eighteenth-century notion that land uncultivated could be claimed by occupation, as it would lead to land 'improvement'.[20] Their position drew on the modern justification of private property rights advanced by seventeenth century philosopher John Locke. This holds that common lands brought into production would 'first begin a title of property'.[21] This was confirmed in the Privy Council's judgment *Re Southern Rhodesia*.[22] In *Attorney-General v Brown*, Chief Justice Stephen rejected that there were Aboriginal proprietors at the time of settlement, as all of the country was considered 'waste land'.[23] The assertion of feudal land tenure in Australia, therefore, was predicated on the Crown's abnegation of existing Aboriginal land arrangements.

The interests of the landholder and the state are held together by a common endeavour to enforce the position of the 'landless'. Proprietors enforce this directly, and brutally, with the backing of the state. In this respect their direct dispensation of power reflects their direct interest in the land. By contrast, the Crown's interest in land is nominal and their exercise of power is remote. Therefore the dissemination of Crown title means the Crown's powers are reduced to a 'seigneurial means of expression',[24] and become the 'weakest link' in the feudal chain.[25] In northern Australia, the Crown as supreme landlord had ultimate title to land but actual possession was in the hands of the pastoralists.[26] The pastoralists used their possession initially to dispossess Aboriginal people of their land, to quell their resistance and then to exploit and control Aboriginal workers. For this reason, Queensland colonial commentator Walter Tyrwhitt stated, pastoralists were the 'natural aristocracy' in the social hierarchy due to their land claims.[27]

Pastoralists' governance on the frontier

On northern frontiers, Australian colonisers assumed local powers over Aboriginal people. These colonisers were almost invariably pastoralists. The *Adelaide Advertiser* reported in 1904 regarding Western Australia, 'As the settlement extends farther out the country formerly occupied exclusively by the natives passes into the hands of the pastoralists.'[28] The pastoralists used their powers to take Aboriginal land and exploit their labour. Pastoralists' direct control over Aboriginal people was a counterpoint to the weak centralised authority that rested in the hands of the colonial government in the nineteenth century and the Aboriginal Chief Protector in the twentieth century.

Historians such as Rosalind Kidd and Bain Attwood employ Foucauldian notions of fragmented power to explain the power distribution on the northern frontier.[29] They infer that there is no order between the decentralised powers of pastoralists and the centralised power of the state. This approach overlooks the unity of the pastoralists' and the state interests to retain land and sovereignty against Aboriginal people. This represents a feudal dissemination of power, in which the government is complicit to the landholders' jurisdiction. This is because the landholder can most effectively exploit land and labour.

Therefore, while pastoralists transgressed government controls of Aboriginal lives outside of stations, governments tended to sanction their powers. Pastoralists had a mandate to manage Aboriginal people working on their stations due to the profits they reaped.[30] In Queensland, land was leased on the condition that Aboriginal inhabitants would be removed by the pastoralist.[31] In the Northern Territory, Regulation 14 under the *Aboriginals Ordinance* 1918 gave the pastoralist the power to maintain the worker, their relatives and dependants.[32] These examples demonstrate that pastoralists' rights to land conferred entitlements to rule.

The proclamations of pastoralists and administrators reveal the concurrent view that pastoralists were the legitimate dispensers of Aboriginal justice. Pastoralists in the Northern Territory claimed that they were 'far removed from the restraints of formal law' and therefore 'every man was his own policeman'.[33] In 1904 the Northern Territory Government Resident, Charles Dashwood, claimed the lack of police in pastoral areas obliged pastoralists to contend with native depredations.[34] In 1890 the South Australian Minister responsible for the Northern Territory, JL Parsons, declared, 'Leave the native question alone and the natives will be obliterated.'[35]

Pioneering pastoralists inculcated in Aboriginal minds the notion that they possessed an indeterminate amount of force. Northern Queensland commentator Sir Raphael Cilento stated, 'In the absence of law, the squatters took their own vengeance, and it was devastating.'[36] In the first decade of Northern Territory settlement, Lindsay Crawford, the first manager of the Victoria River Downs station, asserted, 'we have held no communication with the natives at all, except with the rifle'.[37] Prominent missionary and Protector of Aborigines in the East Kimberley, Reverend JB Gribble, in 1884 noted the disproportionate punishment exacted by Queensland settlers who 'go out in parties fully armed' in reaction to Aborigines spearing their cattle.[38] These punitive raids, despite being public knowledge, went unchecked by governments. By exercising their own force, pastoralists installed their dominant reign mercilessly. This went on to be a powerful instrument for the discipline of Aboriginal labour even after such force had subsided.

Normalised pastoralists' jurisdiction

The need for Aboriginal labour in the northern colonies by the late nineteenth century meant that pastoralists continued to control Aboriginal lives, but in a more refined manner. On cattle stations pastoralists assumed the role of welfare provider.[39] This offset the powers of the bureaucratic 'protectorship' that controlled virtually every aspect of Aboriginal lives on the 'outside'.[40] Rosalind Kidd points to the role of pastoralists as ration distributors, which gave them 'horrifying' power to punish Aboriginal people by withholding rations.[41] Nonetheless, Aboriginal people on stations were able to transgress government controls, and to a degree, negotiate their relationship with their pastoral managers. This was a result of the new employment relationship that had elements of mutual dependence, obligations and loyalties, despite the dominant position of the pastoral lord.

The shift in control strategies from violence to labour discipline was consolidated in the 1930s when Aboriginal people were being born on stations and had become accustomed to their labour relationship with pastoralists.[42] Consequently, there was a reduction in Aboriginal people's physical resistance to pastoralists' occupation. In addition, pastoralists realised by the 1930s that 'white' labour was not going to fill the labour needs of the industry.[43] The Territory's Chief Protector of Aboriginals, Baldwin Spencer, noted that pastoralists had become 'dependent' on Aboriginal workers.[44] Aboriginal labour was not only abundant, with thousands of Aboriginal people on stations, but also highly skilled. Their familiarity with the environment made them competent stockworkers, and their hunting abilities translated into mustering abilities. They were a stable labour force as they lived on station property (which was usually their traditional country), as well as a cheap labour source because pastoralists did not generally pay them wages.[45] Aborigines were therefore revalued in terms of their 'usefulness' to 'whites'.[46]

The shift represented, in Foucauldian terms, the 'normalisation' of power.[47] Normalised discipline is just as powerful as violent punishment as a means of social control.[48] It 'hierarchizes' power, rather than displays it 'in its murderous splendor'.[49] Modernist political philosophers, such as Max Weber,[50] conflate normalisation (or 'civilisation') with the development of the modern bureaucratic state, and indeed this would apply to the bureaucracy formed to police the Aboriginal protection legislation. However, in the pastoral north, normalised power remained localised.

Contemporary writings reveal that pastoralists conceived themselves as the new paternalists.[51] In *We of the Never-Never* (1907), one of the best-known and earliest literary representations of Northern Territory labour on Elsey Station, Jeannie Gunn, wife of pastoralist Aeneas Gunn, projected the new compassion. Contrasting colonisers' relentless approach to cattle spearing on the frontier,[52] she advocated 'the judicious giving of an old bullock at not too rare intervals' in order to keep the Aborigines 'fairly well in hand'. Her response of 'granting fair liberty of travel, and a fair percentage of calves or their equivalent in fair payment' reflects changing mentalities from frontier violence to paternalism.[53] Furthermore, Albert Wright perceived violence towards his Aboriginal stockmen and their dependants as an undeserved wrong on 'his *own* people'.[54] These portrayals represent the changing attitudes towards Aboriginal people as their labour contribution increased.

Northern pastoral lords over their feudal estate and workers

The growing paternalism went hand in hand in hand with pastoralists' increased confidence over their land tenure. Pastoralists saw themselves as entitled to the land they had conquered. Pastoralist Billy Cox who 'ruled' the 'vast' Louisa Downs Station in the Kimberley for 50 years, and passed it on to his son and grandson, was attached to the idea that the 'station was theirs by right'.[55] Many pastoralists conceived themselves as lords who bestowed rights over their land and dependent workers. These pastoralists likened themselves to 'cattle barons' and 'cattle kings', even if their castles were made out of grass.[56] According to pastoralist Albert Wright, it was necessary for Aborigines under the new property regime to conform to station life. The 'inevitability' of losing their land meant Aborigines had to transform 'their very selves'; the choices were 'to die, or to serve'.[57] Over Aboriginal land and labour, the pastoralists were self-professed feudal lords.

Pastoralists' conceptions of their supremacy in the property hierarchy spread to the parliamentary realm. They resembled 'aristocratic squatters' who exercised political sway over the microcosm of their lease and the macrocosm of colonial legislature.[58] As self-entitled 'natural rulers',[59] they pointed to their respectability, affluence and civilisation. Their proprietary status meant large numbers of people depended on them, which qualified them for parliament.[60] North Queensland pastoralist and explorer Oscar de Satge, who served three terms in the Legislative Assembly between 1869 and 1888,[61] wrote that the successful manager of a large station might aspire to fill any position from magistrate to Premier.[62]

However, it was on the landholder's property that lordship powers would materialise most effectively. These powers were exercised over 'their' Aboriginal workers in a multiplicity of guises.[63] On smaller stations, particularly those run by the owner, Aboriginal workers tended to be closely controlled by the manager, who would reward their duty with liberal treatment and incentives. There, Aboriginal workers were more inclined to develop strong allegiances to pastoralists and their wives.[64] On the bigger stations, such as Victoria River Downs, managers tended to exercise more discretion with their workers and treat them as dispensable.[65] When it was owned by the British company Vestey's, the Aboriginal Protector and writer Xavier Herbert observed forceful treatment and abusive language.[66] These managers were much more focused on meeting budget outcomes set by distant owners.[67]

Nonetheless, on both small and large stations, pastoralists and their wives exercised a lordship over Aboriginal workers. They demanded loyalty and discipline, which they often commanded by virtue of their control over rations and residence on the pastoral lease. From her experience of early Northern Territory stations, Mrs Dominic D Daly emphasised the need 'to keep the aboriginal in his proper place'.[68] Michael Durack claimed that station managers and head stockmen tried to be 'kind and just' to the best of their ability. But any more than that could not be expected in their circumstances, which necessitated productive and disciplined labour.[69]

The paternal quality of pastoralists' lordship is indicated by their wide use of possessive pronouns. They referred to their Aboriginal workers as 'our Aborigines'.[70] Imbued with a clear sense of hierarchy, many pastoralists and their wives literally saw their role as one of master over servant. They conceived it as their duty to civilise Aborigines to European standards. Their proprietary position, physically and morally, endowed them with a right and obligation to impose discipline on Aboriginal workers. They exerted their supreme position directly on Aboriginal workers with whom they lived and worked, including domestic servants on the homestead, station hands and stockworkers on droving camps.

The terminology of lord,[71] master[72] and servant[73] seeps into contemporary pastoralists' descriptions of relations between station managers and workers. It is particularly deeply infused into accounts regarding Aboriginal workers in the homestead.[74] Female domestic servants even had to address the children of their employers with the title of 'Master or Miss'.[75] By classifying their Aborigines along these feudal lines, pastoralists could justify their 'firm but fair' treatment and significant labour controls over inferior workers. The Federal Minister for Home Affairs (1928-29), CLA Abbott, claimed that the 'faithfulness of blacks' in the Territory is contingent on a good and kindly 'boss' and 'missus'.[76]

However, the lordly supremacy station masters and mistresses assumed not only endowed them with rights, but also obligations. The responsibilities attendant to their 'patrimonial jurisdiction'[77] included the maintenance of Aboriginal workers and their dependants, amounting to whole communities of Aboriginal people on stations. Pastoralists provided them with rations, including food, clothes and tobacco, land to live on, and shelter in some instances.[78] Pastoralists took on the government's official role to 'protect' and provide for Aborigines.[79] Pastoralists' feudal rights over Aboriginal people, therefore, were inseparable to their obligations.

Lordly responsibilities for the welfare and upkeep of workers depended on Aborigines' conformity to the station domain. This would entrench Aboriginal loyalty and dependence on the cattle station. 'Adequate tucker', according to Mary Durack, was assured to Aborigines as long as they 'played the white man's game'.[80] With her sister, Elizabeth, Mary Durack wrote of their Aboriginal workers: 'They work for us because we give them 'tucker' and whatever else they need. We give them what they want because we need them to work for us — just a matter of convenience from both points of view.'[81] Michael Durack is even more forthcoming in pointing out the lordly obligations imposed on him as part of his dependence on Aboriginal station labour:

> Many seem to imagine that the white man has the big end of the stick in this bargain, but I don't think this is the case. There are those of us who consider we would fare better with four or five skilled stockmen in place of a dozen not wholly reliable black abos whose lubra and picanninies must be clothed and fed as well. 'Then why not?' you ask. It is a big step. The blacks have been at the station for a long, long time. We are, in a negative way, attached to them and they to us.[82]

In northern Australia, the pastoralists rather than the government were the self-proclaimed benefactors of Aboriginal people. Federal Minister for Territories Paul Hasluck wrote that managers of Kimberley stations in the 1930s served as feudal 'overlords' by providing their 'serfs' with 'stability and contentment'.[83]

Nonetheless, 'white man's burden' on cattle stations furthered the economic interests of the industry. It enabled the pastoralist to express their lordly will over land *and* labour for a profitable outcome.

The strength of pastoralists' jurisdiction in the face of government legislation

Pastoralists' personal power endured in the twentieth century despite — and sometimes because of — burgeoning bureaucracies. The introduction of Aboriginal 'protective' legislation gave wide-sweeping powers to the Chief Protector of Aboriginals and the 'protectorship' under him. Their role was to regulate the lives of Aborigines, by restricting their movements, place of residence, family life, and expenditure of Aborigines' money.[84] These 'Aboriginal Acts' were common across northern Australia: *Aboriginal Protection Act and Restriction of the Sale of Opium Act* (Queensland 1897), *Aborigines Act* (Western Australia 1905), and *Aboriginals Act* (Northern Territory 1910).

The Aboriginal Acts applied onerously to Aboriginal people in missions, on government settlements and in town employment. The Northern Territory Chief Protector of Aborigines, Dr CE Cook observed, 'The Aborigines employed on cattle stations were no problem. The problems were on the missions.'[85] He attributed this to the 'relationship between the management and the Aboriginals [on cattle stations] which worked in the interests of both of them'. By contrast, Aborigines on missions were far removed from home territories,[86] and missionaries sought to replace Aboriginal interests in their land and culture with an interest in Christian 'civilisation' and morality.[87]

However, the Protector often acquiesced to the power of the pastoralist over Aboriginal workers, either pursuant to the Act or with disregard to the Act. Pastoralism was how the legislation's objective of uplifting and protecting Aborigines would be met, according to Baldwin Spencer, the Territory's Chief Protector in 1913.[88] R Marsh of the Federal Department of Territories, wrote in 1954, '[T]he pastoralists in maintaining aboriginal dependents are doing the job which would otherwise fall to the Government.'[89] Despite this rhetoric, the form in which pastoralists managed Aboriginal people did not always comply with the assimilation agenda of governments.

A key feature of the Aboriginal Acts was the introduction of employment permits for Aboriginal workers.[90] These gave station managers the power to employ as many Aboriginal workers as they chose. Managers could buy these permits for a small price so long as they were deemed of 'good repute', in the 'protector's opinion'.[91] Ruby de Satge, who worked on a Queensland station, described the 1897 legislation in the following terms, '[T]he Act means that if you are sitting down minding your own business, a station manager can come up to you and say, 'I want a couple of blackfellows' … Just like picking up a cat or a dog.'[92]

The minimal government regulations concerning permit conditions, and the lack of government monitoring of station conditions,[93] meant the permits effectively gave employers a green light to exercise unlimited control over Aboriginal workers. Aboriginal workers were denied access to the bargaining process, freedom of movement or the right to refuse to work.[94] Stockworker John Watson at Fitzroy Downs stated that the protectors gave managers permits to 'work them [Aborigines] as they saw fit' and 'take charge of their welfare'.[95] Armed with permits, pastoralists were granted 'the status of "protector"', according to Eric Lawford who worked at Christmas Creek. He said:

It gave them [pastoralists] the same authority as the policemen, who were also protectors. If there was any trouble with the blackfellas then the police used to be called in to sort it out. But, because he was the permit holder and as such a protector, the station manager could do pretty much as he liked.[96]

In the exceptional case where district protectors refused to grant permits due to poor living conditions, such as Ted Evans' rejections of applications by Vestey's managers at Victoria River Downs, pastoralists used their political clout to override the protectors' decisions. Evans reflected, 'that's the kind of power and lobbying you're up against when you try to do something'.[97] Humanitarians at the 1933 Aboriginal Welfare Conference referred to the protectionist legislation, as protecting the pastoralist rather than Aboriginal worker.[98]

The alignment of pastoral and state interests is epitomised by the fact that a number of pastoralists served as official protectors. The Western Australian Minister responsible for Aboriginal Affairs (1914-19), Rufus H Underwood, commented that appointing pastoralists to positions of protectors was akin to 'leaving a hawk to protect a chicken'.[99] More commonly, however, police took up the role.[100] Their struggle to juggle it with other duties, and their close relations with pastoralists, meant police unofficially devolved their duties. They are reported to have carried out their responsibilities in relation to the Territory's *Aboriginals Ordinance* in a detached manner, making their inspection of employment conditions 'nominal and superficial'.[101]

Non-payment of wages as a source of pastoralists' authority

The non-payment of wages was endemic on northern Australian cattle stations well into the twentieth century. This phenomenon emerged as part of a broad system of pastoral lords' rights and obligations. Low labour costs not only assisted in maximising pastoralists' surplus, but also made possible a large-scale and dependent workforce. Inducements other than wages, such as rights of Aboriginal communities to live on their country, more effectively enforced ties of the Aboriginal worker to the pastoralists' jurisdiction.

In addition, pastoralists perceived it as their right to extract labour from Aboriginal workers without pay. Aborigines, as they saw, had an obligation to work for the pastoralist. According to Aboriginal spokesperson, Noel Pearson, Aboriginal work 'for slave labour rates of pay, or no pay at all', was perceived by pastoralists as 'an *exaction of responsibility* from Aboriginal people'.[102] Like feudal lords, pastoralists' surplus extraction from workers was a matter of 'dues' rather than commodity relations. The feudal lord's use of its superior land claim was the means of labour exploitation, as the landless could only stay on the lord's land in exchange for their labour.[103]

Some workers were aware that they were short-changed, particularly in later station years, but did not have the power to stand up to management and demand wages. John Watson articulates the situation of non-waged dependence accordingly, 'The Aboriginal people knew they were being exploited but they didn't have any choice.'[104] Stockworker Barney Barnes emphatically compared the lack of money on stations in the 1940s to being kept in a prison.[105] Moreover, Northern Territory Administrator, AR Driver, was forthright in conveying that non-payment of wages fostered 'a system of *serfdom*' in which employers 'were able to maintain strict control of a subject people'.[106]

Where legislation provided for Aboriginal wages, there were government regulations that allowed pastoralists to bypass this requirement, aside from the frequent illegal employment of Aboriginal workers without employment permits. Notably, wages did not have to be paid where the pastoralist provided for Aboriginal workers' dependants on stations. Under Regulation 14 of *The Aboriginals Ordinance* 1918-43, the Chief Protector had the power to exempt an employer from the 'payment of wages' to an Aboriginal person maintaining 'relatives and dependants'.[107] However, in reality, the relatives and dependants were themselves workers, contributing to the upkeep of the homestead and station property.[108] A stockworker at Fitzroy Downs, Jock Shandley, claimed that the managers 'really made [the dependants] work for their tucker, for their bread and beef'.[109] In addition, dependants were relegated to 'black camps', where accommodation usually comprised 'scrap' material, if anything at all,[110] and their food rations were of the lowest standard in the station hierarchy.[111]

After World War II, the Federal government increasingly 'maintained' Aboriginal children as part of its assimilation policy.[112] Consequently, pastoralists no longer had financial responsibility for Aboriginal children (or the elderly[113]), and were therefore required to pay wages to Aboriginal workers. However, they continued to bypass this requirement through the 'booking down system'. This involved crediting Aboriginal wages on the station store books and then charging excessive prices at the store. Through this common mechanism, pastoralists avoided cash payment of wages.[114]

This maintenance of worker communities typifies the feudal process of exploitation. It is not simply that Aboriginal workers were not paid, but they were rendered dependent on pastoralists for rations and access to land in lieu of wages.[115] However, the relationship of dependence between pastoralists and Aboriginal workers provided Aboriginal people with an opportunity to command rights that they would have otherwise been denied under the protection of the government, particularly rights to their land and customs. Aboriginal workers, by asserting their connections to country, transgressed many controls imposed on Aboriginal people on the 'outside'.

Aboriginal transgression

The unique relationship that developed on northern Australian cattle stations by the 1930s provided rights and obligations to Aboriginal workers. The pastoralists' jurisdiction not only allowed pastoralists to transcend state power, but also the Aboriginal worker escaped the full impact of state 'protection'. By living on stations, which were on or near their 'homelands',[116] Aboriginal workers and their dependants could transgress policies of protection and assimilation, which often involved removal from traditional country. As part of the working arrangement, whole Aboriginal communities lived on the property. This enabled them to retain aspects of their customary systems.[117] Pastoralists came to accept that Aboriginal workers would continue their cultural practices, and often encouraged them as a means of maintaining their labour force.[118] This working relationship based on rights and obligations on both sides, can be framed as feudal because at its heart was a common interest in land, albeit for very different reasons.

Aboriginal memories convey that within station life there was an endeavour to 'keep alive' their land connections.[119] Riley Young of Yarralin pointed out that labour conditions enabled the otherwise frightened and dispossessed Aborigines to 'look after the land' and 'keep the place'.[120] Aboriginal workers' ongoing ties to their land were more than a matter of residence. They actively pursued customary and ceremonial rites that furthered their land interests and moral economy. The general rule was that masters did not interfere directly with 'tribal matters', such as religious rituals, so long as they did not jeopardise the station's economic venture.[121]

The unyielding determination of Aboriginal workers to retain their land connection was one factor that prevented them from becoming an enslaved labour force. Manning Clark claimed that cultural intransigence precluded Aborigines from being reduced to slavery in the north, although he also recognised that in the south-eastern colonies, particularly Tasmania, it had devastating consequences for Aboriginal communities.[122] The northern experience confirms by corollary the cardinal maxim that 'neighbours made difficult slaves'.[123] The well-known slave theorist Orlando Patterson proposed that the fundamental element of slavery — 'natal alienation' — was almost impossible to achieve with natives in a conquered land.[124] The master, not the slave, was the intruder in an established native community.[125]

An integral aspect of the relationship between pastoralists and stockworkers was the allowance for *dependants* to reside on the station. This meant that Aboriginal communities could nurture kinship ties and share their resources in accordance with traditional social relations. Communities could also maintain their languages, express their Aboriginal identity and practice cultural rites.[126] These ongoing ties allowed Aboriginal workers to transgress broader government attempts to assimilate Aboriginal people. Aboriginal people on the pastoralists' jurisdiction faired well compared to their counterparts on the 'outside'. The benefits for those on the 'inside' became patently clear after Aboriginal communities were removed from stations *en masse* after the 1966 Equal Wage decision. After their removal, Aboriginal people had restricted access to their land and customary practices.

In addition, the Aboriginal 'moral community' that was fostered on stations was a counterpoint to the morality of the pastoralists. It allowed workers to resist the domination of the pastoralists' way of life. Their ongoing kinship ties and customs were powerful factors in providing workers with autonomy from their masters. It also set Aboriginal station workers apart from slave conditions, which rupture family and community ties.[127] The slave master seeks to impose a slave morality that is foreign to the slave, whereas on cattle stations it suited pastoralists to have relatives and dependants live on station land.[128] This is because it offset wages, created a stable workforce and provided an additional pool of labour. Ties of kinship gave Aboriginal good reason to remain on stations and made it difficult for Aborigines to leave on a permanent basis. On the Victoria River Downs Station in the Northern Territory, 75% of Aborigines were dependants of stockworkers.[129]

However, the real opportunity to practice customary rites was in the wet season when Aboriginal people on stations were allowed to go 'walkabout'. Adult initiation and other important ceremonies were conducted in this season. Aboriginal workers asserted this right even when pastoralists, such as May MacKenzie, regarded it as 'awkward and annoying'. MacKenzie was frustrated 'that the tribe could never be persuaded to stay over the traditional time of walkabout, but went as inevitably as the season came, taking the boys just as they would have been most useful'.[130] However, generally pastoralists granted leave for 'walkabout' as a component of the station relationship of rights and obligations. They would sometimes provide rations for Aboriginal people to take with them. But walkabout also occurred in a period when pastoralists were happy to dispense with the labour force. It was allowed only during the months of the non-mustering wet season (November-March), known as the 'slack season', when managers were happy to forego responsibility for their upkeep.[131] Jimmy Bird remembered that Aboriginal workers 'had to wait until manager said we could go'.[132]

Nevertheless, Aboriginal workers fondly recall their annual 'walkabout' in the wet season. Lochy Green's recollection of the Partukurru, or initiation time, at Myroodah Station illustrates the Aboriginal experience. He described the pastoralists' concurrence with the traditional Aboriginal law business, which is indicated by their provision of rations during this period:

> That law business used to be held during the wet season, which was a holiday time on the stations. The managers used to let the Aboriginal people alone during that time, as long as they came back to the station when it was time to start work again … The law men used to call people from all the other stations to come down for a big meeting — took rations with them.[133]

Many Aboriginal workers were active in shaping their relationships with pastoralists and the manner in which they performed their work. Norbert Elias points out that 'civilizing' processes, including work, involve interactions between individuals that weave patterns of 'interdependence'.[134] This is apparent on northern cattle stations, where both the pastoralists and the Aboriginal workers' livelihood hinged on their coexistence. On the homestead, bonds of friendship would occasionally grow between Aboriginal servants and their 'missus'.[135] When mustering, pastoralists would recognise the skills of Aboriginal workers and assign them supervisory roles.[136] Stockworkers assumed independent responsibility over their tasks, and expressed a pride in their work.[137]

Conclusion: limits of Aboriginal transgression and ways forward

The capacity for Aboriginal workers to transgress government protection and assimilation policies, was ultimately at the will of the pastoralists' jurisdiction. As long as pastoralists were dependent on Aboriginal labour, Aboriginal rights would be accommodated. However, once their labour value diminished, so did their rights. Therefore, the suggestion by cultural historians that Aboriginal rights on cattle stations indicate 'agency' must be considered within the context of the pastoralist's jurisdiction. Because the pastoralists had land and capital, they were able to dispense with the relationship of mutual dependence as it suited them. This rendered Aboriginal workers' land connections vulnerable to pastoralists' authority and legal rights to land.

This is starkly apparent in light of the mass retrenchments in the 1970s, and the removal of Aboriginal communities from station properties across northern

Australia. This was precipitated by the Equal Wage decision of 1966 and the pursuant Pastoral Award 1968, which pastoralists claimed made Aboriginal labour unaffordable. However, it was not the only factor. The introduction of motorcycles and helicopters to mustering practices had already begun to undermine the role of Aboriginal stockworkers on horseback.[138] Peter Yu described the Aboriginal expulsion from stations as breaking 'the back of the feudal relationship between station managers and Aboriginal families ... precipitat[ing] a refugee crisis of enormous proportions'.[139] Lawford explained that the expulsion did 'a lot of damage up here; it really disrupted our communities'.[140] Their rights to their land were restricted as the feudal land tenure system prevailed.[141]

For Aboriginal people to transgress ongoing government attempts to assimilate Aboriginal communities, they need to establish their own jurisdiction on their land. This could require resources to run their own cattle stations and other sustainable industries.[142] Former stockworker John Watson laments the destructive practices of aerial mustering to the land, which would be better protected by Aboriginal people.[143] He states, 'The Aboriginal people have an intimate understanding of the natural environment, but we haven't been given the opportunity to apply that knowledge in modern jobs'.[144] The development of sustainable industries in northern Australia could revitalise the historic labour contribution of Aboriginal cattle workers. This form of economic self-determination would offer more than a fragile right to their culture and land. Rather, if appropriately supported by governments, it could create a long-term platform for Aboriginal rights and reconciliation.

References

Primary sources

Albrecht, FW 1957, 'Work Among Aborigines Living at Cattle Stations', *Finke River Mission News Letter*, Unpublished, Alice Springs, May, Mortlock Library (SA), PRG 868.

Allen, JW 1943, 'Aborigine Station Employees – Northern Territory: memorandum for the Minister for the Interior, Canberra from the Secretary, Northern Territory Pastoral Lessees' Association', 27 November 1943, National Archives of Australia (NAA) (Canberra), A452/54; 1955/506.

Driver, AR 1949, 'Correspondence to the Secretary, Department of the Interior', 6 July, NAA (Darwin), CA1070, F1, 43/24.

Giese, HC 1981, *Interview with Dr C. E. (Mick) Cook*, Darwin, 2 March 1981, Northern Territory Archives Service, NTRS 226 (Oral history transcript) TS179, 60.

Gillespie, LL 1962, *Child Endowment for Aboriginal Children on Cattle Stations in the Northern Territory*, Memorandum to the Director, Department of Social Services, Adelaide, 31 October 1962, NAA (Canberra): A885, B456 Part 2.

Goodes, HJ 1960, *Child Endowment for Aboriginal Children on Cattle Stations in the Northern Territory*, Memorandum to the Minister, 17 March, 1960, NAA (Canberra): A885, B456, Part 2.

Hall, Victor Charles 1966, *Outback Policeman's Diary*, Unpublished, Mortlock Library (SA), D5184 (Lit Ms).

Lambert, CR 1953, 'Employment and Payment of Aborigines in the Northern Territory: correspondence from the Secretary for Department of External Territories to the Administrator of the Northern Territory', 29 January, National Archives (Darwin), CRS F1 Item: 1953/307.

Marsh, R 1954, 'Maintenance of Aboriginal Dependants on Pastoral Leases: Memorandum from the Assistant Secretary, Department of Territories, No. 51/1634', February 1954, NAA (Canberra), A452/54; 1955/303.

McCaffery, RK 1953, 'Maintenance Payment to Dependants of Aboriginal Employees on Pastoral Properties: Circular Memorandum no.72 from Acting Director of Native Affairs to District Superintendent, Darwin, Acting Superintendent, Alice Springs, and patrol officers', 4 September, NAA (Darwin), CRS F1: 1953/307.

McGrath, Ann 1978, *Interview with Noel and Dorothy Hall*, Darwin, 28 August, Northern Territory Archives Service, NTRS 226 (Oral history transcript) TS230 (Box 14).

Stephenson, Mary C 1982, *Interview with E. C. (Ted) Evans*, Darwin, April-June, Northern Territory Archives Service, NTRS 266 (Oral history transcript) TS46 (Box3).

Thonemann, HE (Northern Territory Pastoral Lessees' Association) 1933, in *Report of Debates: Conference of Representatives of Missions, Societies, and Associations Interested in the Welfare of Aboriginals to Consider the Report*, Transcribed by the Commonwealth Attorney-General's Department, Melbourne, 12 April 1933, NAA (Canberra), CRS A1 33/8782.

Wilson, Winifred 1952, *Dietary Survey of Aboriginals in the Northern Territory*, Commonwealth Department of Health, Alice Springs, Noel Butlin Archives (Canberra), 42/14.

Secondary Sources

Abbott, CLA 1950, *Australia's Frontier Province*, Angus & Robertson, Sydney.

Commonwealth of Australia 1911, 'An Ordinance Relating to Aboriginals (1911)', Notified in Gazette, 8th January 1912, 61-66.

Commonwealth of Australia 1918, 'An Ordinance Relating to Aboriginals (1918)', Home and Territories Department.

Alavi, Hamza 1975, 'India and the Colonial Mode of Production', *Economic and Political Weekly* X (August): 1235-62.

Altman, Jon and Whitehead, PJ 2003, 'Caring for country and sustainable Indigenous development: Opportunities, constraints and innovation', CAEPR Working Paper No. 20/2003.

Amin, Samir 1976, *Unequal Development: an essay on the social formations of peripheral capitalism*, translated by Brian Pearce, Monthly Review Press, New York.

Anderson, Perry 1978, *Passages from Antiquity to Feudalism*, Verso, London.

Anon 1935, 'Report on W.A. Aborigines: Protector agrees with most of findings', *The Advertiser*, Adelaide, 16 March: 8.

Attorney-General v Brown (1847) 1 Legge 312.

Attwood, Bain 1992, 'Introduction', in Bain Attwood and John Arnold (eds), *Power, Knowledge and Aborigines*, Journal of Australian Studies Special edn, La Trobe University Press, Melbourne: i-xiv.

Barnes, Barney 1988, 'You can go back to your place if you want to', in Paul Marshall (ed.), *Raparapa Kularr Martuwarra ... All right, now we go 'side the river, along that sundown way: stories from Fitzroy River drovers*, Magabala Books, Broome: 255-283.

Bell, Dianne 1988, 'Choose Your Mission Wisely: Christian colonials and Aboriginal marital arrangements on the northern frontier', in Tony Swain and Deborah Bird Rose (eds), *Aboriginal Australians and Christian Missions: ethnographic and historical studies*, Australian Association for the Study of Religions, Adelaide.

Bennett, MM 1928, *Christison of Lammermoor*, 2nd edn, Alston Rivers, London.

Berndt, Catherine and Berndt, Ronald M 1983, *The Aboriginal Australians: the first pioneers*, Pitman, Melbourne.

Berndt, Ronald M and Berndt, Catherine 1987, *End of an Era: Aboriginal labour in the Northern Territory*, Australian Institute of Aboriginal Studies, Canberra.

Bhuta, Nehal 1998, 'Mabo, Wik and the Art of Paradigm Management', *Melbourne University Law Review* 22 (1): 24-41

Bird, Jimmy 1988, 'They can't break us down', in Paul Marshall (ed.), *Raparapa Kularr Martuwarra ... All right, now we go 'side the river, along that sundown way: stories from Fitzroy River drovers*, Magabala Books, Broome: 89-105.

Birtles, Francis E 1909, *Lonely Lands: through the heart of Australia*, NSW Bookstall Co., Sydney.

Biskup, Peter 1973, *Not Slaves, Not Citizens: the Aboriginal problem in Western Australia, 1898-1954*, University of Queensland Press, St Lucia.

Bisson, TM 1994, 'The "feudal revolution"', *Past and Present* 142 (Feb): 1-18.

Blackstone, William 1830, *Commentaries on the Laws of England*, Bk II, London.

Broadhurst, R 1987, 'Imprisonment of the Aborigine in Western Australia, 1957–85', in K Hazlehurst (ed.), *Ivory scales – Black Australians and the law*, University of NSW Press, Kensington.

Buchanan, Gordon 1933, *Packhorse and Waterhole: with the first overlanders to the Kimberleys*, Angus & Robertson, Sydney.

Bush, Michael L 1996, *Serfdom and Slavery: studies in legal bondage*, Longman, London.

Cilento, Raphael 1959, *Triumph in the Tropics: an historical sketch of Queensland*, With Clem Lack, Smith & Paterson, Brisbane.

Clark, CMH 1962, *A History of Australia*, vol. I, Melbourne University Press, Melbourne.

Collier, James 1911, *The Pastoral Age in Australasia*, Whitcombe & Tombs, London.

Daly, Mrs Dominic D 1887, *Digging, Squatting and Pioneering Life in the Northern Territory of South Australia*, Sampson Low, Marston, Searle & Rivington, London.

de Satge, Oscar 1901, *Pages from the journal of a Queensland squatter*, Hurst and Blackett, London.

Donovan, PF 1981, *A Land Full of Possibilities: a history of South Australia's Northern Territory*, University of Queensland Press, St Lucia.

Durack, Mary 1965, *The Courteous Savage: Yagan of Swan River*, Thomas Nelson, Melbourne.

Durack, Mary 2000a, *Sons in the Saddle*, Omnibus edn, Kings in grass castles; Sons in the saddle, Random House, Sydney.

Durack, Mary 2000b, *Kings in Grass Castles*, Omnibus ed., Kings in grass castles; Sons in the saddle, Random House, Sydney.

Durack, Mary and Durack, Elizabeth 1935, *All-About: the story of a Black community on Argyle Station, Kimberley*, The Bulletin, Sydney.

Edgeworth, Brendan 1994, 'Tenure, Allodialism and Indigenous Rights at Common Law: English, United States and Australian land law compared after *Mabo v Queensland*', *Anglo-American Law Review* 23(4): 397-434.

Elias, Norbert 1982, *The Civilizing Process: state formation and civilization*, Jephcott, Edmund ed., vol. II, Basil Blackwell, Oxford.

Evans, Raymond 1984, 'Kings' in Brass Crescents: defining Aboriginal labour patterns in colonial Queensland', in Kay Saunders (ed.), *Indentured Labour in the British Empire, 1834-1920*, Croom Helm, London: 183-212.

Foucault, Michel 1978, *The History of Sexuality*, translated by Robert Hurley, vol. 1: An Introduction, Random House, New York.

Green, Lochy 1988, 'All right, I'm looking for a job, I'll join you', in Paul Marshall (ed.), *Raparapa Kularr Martuwarra ... All right, now we go 'side the river, along that sundown way: stories from Fitzroy River drovers*, Magabala Books, Broome: 184-194.

Gribble, Rev. J. B. 1884, *'Black But Comely.' Or, Glimpses of Aboriginal Life in Australia*, Morgan and Scott, London.

Gunn, Mrs Aeneas (Jeannie) 1990, *We of the Never-Never*, Arrow Australia, Sydney.

Haebich, Anna 1992, *For Their Own Good: Aborigines and Government in the Southwest of Western Australia 1900-1940,* University of Western Australia Press Nedlands.

Hasluck, Paul 1988, *Shades of Darkness: Aboriginal Affairs 1925-1965*, Melbourne University Press, Melbourne.

Herbert, Xavier 1975, *Poor fellow my country*, Collins, Sydney.

Hess, Michael 1994, 'Black and Red: the Pilbara pastoral workers' strike, 1946', *Aboriginal History* 18(1): 65-83.

Hogg, Russell 2001, 'Penality and modes of regulating indigenous people in Australia', *Punishment and Society* 3(3): 355-379.

Huggins, Jackie 1987/88, '"Firing on in the Mind": Aboriginal Women Domestic Servants in the Inter-War Years', *Hecate: The Counter-Bicentenary Issue* 13 (2): 5-23.

Huggins, Jackie 1995, 'White Aprons, Black Hands: Aboriginal Women Domestic Servants in Queensland', *Labour History: Special Issue — Aboriginal workers* 69 (Nov): 188-195.

Hunt, Alan and Wickham, Gary 1994, *Foucault and Law: towards a sociology of law as governance*, Pluto Press, London.

Kidd, Rosalind 1997, *The Way We Civilise: Aboriginal Affairs — the untold story*, University of Queensland, St Lucia.

Kidd, Rosalind 2004, *Stolen Wages — A National Issue*, Address to the Garma Festival, 9 August 2004, <http://www.griffith.edu.au/centre/cpci/pdf/ros_kidd_garma.pdf>

Krader, Lawrence 1975, *The Asiatic Mode of Production: sources, development and critique in the writings of Karl Marx*, Van Gorcum & Comp. B.V., Assen.

Lawford, Eric 1988, 'Crowbar saved my life', in Paul Marshall (ed.), *Raparapa Kularr Martuwarra … All right, now we go 'side the river, along that sundown way: stories from Fitzroy River drovers*, Magabala Books, Broome: 1-31.

Lewis, Darrell 1997, *A Shared History: Aborigines and White Australians in the Victoria River District, Northern Territory*, Create-a-Card, Darwin.

Locke, John 1924, *Two Treatises on Government*, Book II, Everyman's Library, London.

Lukin Watson, Pamela 1998, *Frontier Lands & Pioneer Legends: how pastoralists gained Karuwali land*, Allen & Unwin, Sydney.

Mabo v Queensland [No. 2] (1992) 175 CLR 1.

McGrath, Ann 1987, *'Born in the Cattle': Aborigines in cattle country*, Allen & Unwin, Sydney.

McGrath, Ann 1997, 'The history of pastoral co-existence', *Native Title Report - July 1996 to June 1997*, Report of the Aboriginal and Torres Strait Islander Social Justice Commissioner to the Attorney-General as required by section 209 of the Native Title Act 1993, <http://austlii.law.uts.edu.au/au/other/IndigLRes/1997/4/2.html>, 13.

McMahon, Monica 1977, 'Colonial Domination: Aborigines in the Northern Territory 1911-1934. Background to attitudes and policies', Honours thesis, The Australian National University.

Melbourne Correspondent 1904, 'Black Slavery: a strong indictment', *The Advertiser*, Adelaide, 19 April: 5.

Merlan, Francesca 1978, '"Making People Quiet" in the Pastoral North: reminiscences of Elsey Station', *Aboriginal History* 2(1): 71-102.

Mukhia, Harbans 1981, 'Was there Feudalism in Indian History?' *The Journal of Peasant Studies* 8: 273-310.

New South Wales v The Commonwealth ('*the Seas and Submerged Lands Case*') (1975) 135 CLR.

Newton-King, Susan 1999, *Masters and Servants on the Cape Eastern Frontier*, Cambridge University Press, Cambridge.

North, Douglass C and Thomas, Robert Paul 1973, *The Rise of the Western World: a new economic history*, Cambridge University Press, Cambridge.

Patterson, Orlando 1982, *Slavery and Social Death: a comparative study*, Harvard University Press, Cambridge.

Pearson, Noel 1999, *Our Right to Take Responsibility*, Discussion Paper, Cape York Land Council, Cape York, June.

Post Office v Estuary Radio Ltd. (1968) 2 QB 740.

Re Southern Rhodesia [1919] AC 211.

Reid, Gordon 1990, *A Picnic with the Natives: Aboriginal-European relations in the Northern Territory to 1910*, Melbourne University Press, Melbourne.

Reynolds, Henry 1981, *The Other Side of the Frontier: an interpretation of the Aboriginal response to the invasion and settlement of Australia*, History Department James Cook University, Townsville.

Rose, Deborah Bird 1991, *Hidden Histories: Black stories from Victoria River Downs, Humbert River and Wave Hill stations*, Aboriginal Studies Press, Canberra.

Rowse, Tim 1987, '"Were You Ever Savages?" Aboriginal insiders and pastoralists' patronage', *Oceania* 58(2): 81-99.

Saunders, Kay 1982, *Workers in Bondage: the origins and bases of unfree labour in Queensland 1824-1916*, University of Queensland Press, St Lucia.

Schubert, Leslie A 1992, *Kimberley Dreaming: the century of Freddie Cox*, Words Work Express, Mundurah.

Scully, Pamela 1977, *Liberating the Family? Gender and British slave emancipation in the rural Western Cape, South Africa, 1823-1853*, Heinemann, Portsmouth.

Sen, Bhowani 1962, *Evolution of Agrarian Relations in India, including a study of the nature and consequence of post-Independence agrarian legislation*, People's Publishing House, New Delhi.

Shandley, Jock 1988, 'In those days you couldn't cry', in Paul Marshall (ed.), *Raparapa Kularr Martuwarra ... All right, now we go 'side the river, along that sundown way: stories from Fitzroy River drovers*, Magabala Books, Broome: 32-88.

Shaw, Bruce (ed.) 1992, *When the Dust come in Between: Aboriginal viewpoints in the East Kimberley prior to 1982 as told to Bruce Shaw*, Aboriginal Studies Press, Canberra.

Shepherd, FP 1935, *General Report on the Investigation of Pastoral Leases in the Northern Territory 1933-1935*, Presented to the Federal Department of the Interior, Canberra, 1935, National Archives (Darwin), NN F987, 2 (Schedule F: Conditions of Leases).

Sing, Peter and Ogden Pearl 1992, *From Humpy to Homestead: the biography of Sabu*, P. Ogden, Darwin.

Spencer, Baldwin 1913, 'Preliminary Report on the Aboriginals of the Northern Territory', The Northern Territory of Australia Report of the Administrator for the Year 1912, Commonwealth of Australia, *Parliamentary Papers*, No 45 of 1913 at 42-3.

Stevens, Frank S 1968, *Equal Wages for Aborigines: the background to industrial discrimination in the Northern Territory of Australia*, Aura Press, Sydney.

Thorpe, Bill 1992, 'Aboriginal Employment and Unemployment: colonised labour', in Claire Williams with Bill Thorpe (eds), *Beyond Industrial Sociology: the work of men and women*, Allen & Unwin, Sydney: 88-107.

Turley, David 2000, *Slavery*, Edited by Fasolt, Constantin, New Perspectives on the Past, Blackwell Publishers, Oxford.

Tyrwhitt, Walter Spencer Stanhope 1888, *The New Chum in the Queensland Bush*, New ed., W.H. Allen, London.

Vattel 1797, *The Law of Nations*, Bk I, London.

Walker, Jan 1988, *Jondaryan Station: the relationship between pastoral capital and pastoral labour, 1840-1890*, University of Queensland Press, St Lucia.

Watson, John 1988, 'We know this country', in Paul Marshall (ed.), *Raparapa Kularr Martuwarra ... All right, now we go 'side the river, along that sundown way: stories from Fitzroy River drovers*, Magabala Books, Broome: 207-254.

Weber, Max 1967, 'The Meaning of Discipline', in HH Gerth and C Wright Mills (eds), *From Max Weber: essays in sociology*, 6th ed., Routledge & Kegan Paul, London, 1967: 253-264.

Wharton, Herbert (ed.) 1994, *Cattle Camp: Murrie drovers and their stories*, University of Queensland Press, Brisbane.

The Wik Peoples v Queensland (1996) 187 CLR 1.

Wood, Ellen Meiksins 1991, *The Pristine Culture of Capitalism: a historical essay on old regimes and modern states*, Verso, London.

Wright, Judith 1960, *The Generations of Men*, Oxford University Press, London.

Yu, Peter 1994, 'Aboriginal Peoples, Federalism and Self-Determination', *Social Alternatives* 13 (1): 19-24

ENDNOTES

1 Schubert 1992: 77.

2 Hogg 2001: 355; Broadhurst 1987.

3 Anderson 1978: 147.

4 Yu 1994: 19.

5 Saunders 1982: 76.

6 Evans 1984: 203.

7 Reynolds 1981: 135.

8 McGrath 1987: 175.

9 *The Wik Peoples v Queensland* (1996) 187 CLR 1: 90 (Brennan CJ).

10 *Wik*: 128 (Toohey J).

11 Such as fencing, irrigating and stocking: Shepherd 1935.

12 Sen 1962: 46.

13 *Mabo v Queensland* [No. 2] (1992) 175 CLR 1.

14 *Mabo*: [25].

15 *Mabo*: [49].

16 Bhuta 1998: 25.

17 *Attorney-General v Brown* (1847) 1 Legge 312: 316.

18 Emphasis inclusive *Attorney-General v Brown*: 317-8.

19 *Post Office v Estuary Radio Ltd.* (1968) 2 QB 740 (Diplock LJ); *New South Wales v The Commonwealth* ('the Seas and Submerged Lands Case') (1975) 135 CLR: 388 (Gibbs J).

20 Blackstone 1830: 106-8; Vattel 1797: 100-101.

21 Locke 1924: 141.

22 *Re Southern Rhodesia* [1919] AC 211: 233-4 (Lord Sumner).

23 *Attorney-General v Brown*: 318-9.

24 Bisson 1994: 8.

25 Edgeworth 1994: 429-31.

26 Wood 1991: 50.

27 Tyrwhitt 1888: 78.

28 Melbourne Correspondent 1904: 5.

29 Kidd 1997: ix-xxi, 1-17; Attwood 1992: iii-iv.

30 Biskup 1973: 16.

31 Lukin Watson 1998: 14.

32 Thorpe 1992: 91.

33 Buchanan 1933: 117.

34 Gunn 1990: 141.

35 Donovan 1981: 184 .

36 Cilento 1959: 185.

37 Lewis 1997: 3.

38 Gribble 1884: 30-1.

39 Berndt and Berndt 1983: 98.

40 See Commonwealth of Australia 1918, *Aboriginal Ordinance* 1918 s5(1)(b).

41 Kidd 2004.

42 McGrath 1987.

43 Thonemann 1933: 20-1.

44 Spencer 1913: 43.

45 Spencer 1913: 40.

46 Hess 1994: 68-9.

47 Foucault 1978: 144.

48 Hunt and Wickham 1994: 49.

49 Foucault 1978: 144.

50 Weber 1967: 239.

51 Durack 1965: 22-3.

52 Merlan 1978: 87.

53 Gunn 1990: 187.

54 Emphasis added. Wright 1960: 156.

55 Schubert 1992: 150.

56 Durack 2000b: iii; Schubert 1992: 40.

57 Wright 1960: 155.

58 Saunders 1982: 41-2.

59 Collier 1911: 316.

60 Walker 1988: 74-5.

61 Lukin Watson 1998: 23.

62 de Satge 1901: 98.

63 Alavi 1975: 1243; Mukhia 1981: 276.

64 McGrath 1987: 64.

65 Riley Young interview in Rose 1991: 151.

66 Herbert 1975.

67 Mary C Stephenson 1982, *Interview with E. C. (Ted) Evans*, Darwin, April-June 1982, Northern Territory Archives Service, NTRS 266 (Oral history transcript) TS46 (Box3): 39 (Tape 2,Side A).

68 Daly 1887: 75.

69 Hasluck 1988: 59.

70 Durack and Durack 1935: 25; Huggins 1987/88: 9; Bennett 1928: 227.

71 For example Birtles 1909: 203.

72 For example Durack 2000a: 49.

73 For example Hall 1966: 179.

74 Huggins 1987/88: 11.

75 Huggins 1995: 195.

76 Abbott 1950: 150.

77 Karl Marx cited in Krader 1975: 202.

78 McGrath 1997: 13.

79 See Commonwealth of Australia 1918 *Aboriginal Ordinance* 1918 s5(1)(b).

80 Durack 2000a: 49.

81 Durack and Durack 1935: 25.

82 Letter to the *Western Australian* (1935) reproduced in Hasluck 1988: 59.

83 Hasluck 1988: 54.

84 Huggins 1995: 188.

85 HC Giese 1981, *Interview with Dr C. E. (Mick) Cook*, Darwin, 2 March 1981, Northern Territory Archives Service, NTRS 226 (Oral history transcript) TS179, 60.

86 Merlan 1978: 74.

87 Bell 1988: 341.

88 Cited in Reid 1990: 195.

[89] R Marsh 1954, 'Maintenance of Aboriginal Dependants on Pastoral Leases: Memorandum from the Assistant Secretary, Welfare Division, Federal Department of Territories, No. 51/1634', February, National Archives (Canberra), A452/54; 1955/303: 1.

[90] See Commonwealth of Australia 1911, *Aboriginals Ordinance* 1911 (NT) s8(1); *Aboriginals Ordinance* 1918 (NT) s22(1).

[91] Walter Kingsmill, Western Australian Legislative Council, *Report of the Select Committee appointed to report upon The Aborigines Bill* (1904): 4.

[92] Huggins 1987/88: 7.

[93] Even in the high tide of 'official' protection in the 1930s there were only 48 protectors to oversee 523,000 square miles of the Territory: McMahon 1977: 25.

[94] Hess 1994: 67.

[95] Watson 1988: 221.

[96] Lawford 1988: 15.

[97] Mary C Stephenson 1982, *Interview with E. C. (Ted) Evans*, Darwin, April-June 1982, Northern Territory Archives Service, NTRS 266 (Oral history transcript) TS46 (Box3): 38 (Tape 2,Side A).

[98] *Report of Debates: Conference of Representatives of Missions, Societies, and Associations Interested in the Welfare of Aboriginals to Consider the Report and Recommendations submitted to the Commonwealth Government by J.W. Bleakley Esq.* Unpublished, Transcribed by the Commonwealth Attorney-General's Department, Melbourne, 12 April 1933, National Archives (Canberra), CRS A1 33/87,82: 24.

[99] Cited in Haebich 1992: 149.

[100] Anon 1935: 8.

[101] Berndt and Berndt 1987: 18; Stevens 1968: 16.

[102] Italics added. Pearson 1999: 23.

[103] Amin 1976: 15.

[104] Watson 1988: 208.

[105] Barnes 1988: 272.

[106] Italics added. AR Driver 1949, 'Correspondence to the Secretary, Department of the Interior', 6 July, National Archives (Darwin), CA1070, F1, 43/24.

[107] RK McCaffery 1953, 'Maintenance Payment to Dependants of Aboriginal Employees on Pastoral Properties: Circular Memorandum no.72 from Acting Director of Native Affairs to District Superintendent, Darwin, Acting Superintendent, Alice Springs, and patrol officers', 4 September, National Archives (Darwin), CRS F1 Item: 1953/307.

[108] HC Giese 1981, *Interview with Dr C. E. (Mick) Cook*, Darwin, 2 March 1981, Northern Territory Archives Service, NTRS 226 (Oral history transcript) TS179, 60 .

[109] Shandley 1988: 73.

[110] Mary C Stephenson 1982, *Interview with E. C. (Ted) Evans*, Darwin, April-June 1982, Northern Territory Archives Service, NTRS 266 (Oral history transcript) TS46 (Box3): 30-1 (Tape 2,Side A).

[111] Wilson 1952: 94.

[112] HJ Goodes (Director-General, Melbourne) 1960, *Child Endowment for Aboriginal Children on Cattle Stations in the Northern Territory*, Memorandum to the Minister, 17 March, 1960, NAA (Canberra): A885, B456, Part 2.

[113] LL Gillespie (Assistant NT Administrator) 1962, *Child Endowment for Aboriginal Children on Cattle Stations in the Northern Territory*, Memorandum to the Director, Department of Social Services, Adelaide, 31 October 1962, NAA (Canberra): A885, B456 Part 2.

[114] CR Lambert 1953, 'Employment and Payment of Aborigines in the Northern Territory: correspondence from the Secretary for Department of External Territories to the Administrator of the Northern Territory', 29 January, National Archives (Darwin), CRS F1 Item: 1953/307 .

[115] Bush 1996: 3.

[116] Rowse 1987: 84.

[117] Although the 1948 Berndt report on stations owned by Vestey's noted that spiritual and economic foundations of tribal life were fractured: Berndt and Berndt 1987: 208-10.

[118] JW Allen 1943, 'Aborigine Station Employees — Northern Territory: memorandum for the Minister for the Interior, Canberra from the Secretary, Northern Territory Pastoral Lessees' Association', 27 November 1943, National Archives (Canberra), A452/54; 1955/506.

[119] McGrath 1987: 174.

[120] Interview in Rose 1991: xxi.

[121] Shaw 1992: 17.

[122] Clark 1962: 5.

[123] Newton-King 1999: 124.

[124] Patterson 1982: 38.

[125] Turley 2000: 7.

[126] Wharton 1994: vii-viii; Albrecht 1957: 3.

[127] Patterson 1982: 311; Scully 1977: 19.

[128] Berndt and Berndt 1987: 9-10.

[129] Ann McGrath 1978, *Interview with Noel and Dorothy Hall*, Darwin, 28 August, Northern Territory Archives Service, NTRS 226 (Oral history transcript) TS230 (Box 14): 4.

[130] Wright 1960: 89.

[131] Marsh 1954: 1.

[132] Bird 1988: 101.

[133] Green 1988: 191.

[134] Elias 1982: 88.

[135] McGrath 1987: 64.

[136] Durack 2000a: 49.

[137] Sing and Ogden 1992: 68.

[138] Mary C Stephenson 1982, *Interview with E. C. (Ted) Evans*, Darwin, April-June 1982, Northern Territory Archives Service, NTRS 266 (Oral history transcript) TS46 (Box3): 43-4 (Tape 2,Side A).

[139] Yu 1994: 19.

[140] Lawford 1988: 23-4.

[141] Despite the *Land Rights Act (NT)* 1976, which resulted from the eight year Gurindji strike on Wave Hill, no land was granted to Aboriginal people on pastoral leases. See <http://www.nlc.org.au/html/land_comm_hist.html>, accessed September 2007.

[142] Altman and Whitehead 2003.

[143] Watson 1988: 250-1.

[144] Watson 1988: 248.

Dreaming the circle: indigeneity and the longing for belonging in White Australia

Jane Mulcock

In settler-descendant societies indigenous identity becomes a powerful and a fraught symbol of belonging to place. Multiple voices negotiate its meaning, make claims and counter-claims, extend invitations and deny access. One Australian says 'we are all indigenous to somewhere. My ancestors were Scottish'. He says 'here, in the bush, where I was born, where I grew up, I can feel the spirits watching me'.[1] Another says 'I am seventh generation Australian. I am indigenous. I am proud'.[2] In court, in a native title dispute, a White forester says 'My family has lived here for generations ... I have the right to camp, hunt and fish ... My father taught me how'.[3] Many voices challenge these statements of non-Aboriginal belonging, call them colonial, call out against the crime of appropriating identity. And then an Aboriginal custodian negotiating for land in another native title claim says to the Australian court: 'We have a gift we have been trying to give you ... We want to fill up your emptiness with meaning so that you can love us and our country. We want to teach all Australians about their belonging in this country ... before it's too late'.[4] The circle spins and spins, its constant grinding friction sets deep emotions aflame.

The concepts of indigeneity and belonging are intimately entwined, woven together in conversations about attachment to place, about nationalism and love of country, about 'soil, blood and identity'.[5] This meshing and merging leads to slippages of meaning, and to the raw and salty conflicts that sometimes flare out of contesting definitions. Most readers would probably agree that when it comes to land, indigeneity begets belonging. To be indigenous, is after all, to be autochthonous, to be born of the land. But what of ancestral connections? In settler societies like Australia or New Zealand or Canada not all of us born of the land can easily call ourselves indigenous. Our colonial histories have led to situations where descendants of the prior inhabitants, the peoples displaced by colonial incursions and settlements, have the first, and many argue the only, claim to indigenous status. However, as those settlements grow to be five or six or seven generations deep the concept of indigeneity is increasingly contested. Once a source of shame for some, it is now a source of pride for many of those who can claim it, a sign of resilience and embeddedness, a sign of deep belonging, desired more than discouraged, proclaimed more than disguised. At least among those for whom belonging to place is an important source of personal identity.

'So', some people ask, 'how many generations does it take to become indigenous to a chosen homeland?' Perhaps there is another term that those of us not descended from aboriginal inhabitants (in the general sense) might use to describe our particularly unsettled state of belonging and not belonging; the fact remains, however, that some settler descendants are increasingly trying on indigenous identities as a way of understanding and describing the strong feelings of attachment to place that they experience. This emergent indigeneity (with a lower case 'i') is usually described as different from or separate to Australian Aboriginal Indigeneity (with an upper case 'I' to denote its currency as a highly specific and politicised identity marker). Settler descendant claims to indigeneity usually seem to refer instead to the more generic category of being 'native-born'.[6]

In the course of undertaking ethnographic fieldwork that required me to participate in a range of workshops and events focused on Indigenous spirituality, I began to recognise patterns of identification amongst the other 'non-Indigenous' participants. These people typically expressed strong feelings of attachment to particular places, or to 'nature' in a more general sense. Many wanted to find ways of expanding those feelings of belonging through ritual. They looked to the traditions of Indigenous peoples as an obvious starting point, as a source of inspiration and guidance for the development of a personal, nature-based form of spiritual practice. While some Indigenous people themselves reject this interest, dismissing it as another form of colonisation, as theft, appropriation, rape,[7] others choose to work with it, to see it as an opportunity for education, for increased respect and understanding. In doing so, however, this latter group of individuals sometimes cross highly sensitive boundaries associated with the construction of politically powerful and exclusive Indigeneities. By deliberately embracing, engaging or encouraging 'non-Indigenous' interest in Indigenous spirituality they risk transgressing some of the borders that other Indigenous people and their supporters rigorously defend.[8]

The widespread idea, based both on myth and reality, that Indigenous peoples have an intimate (and) spiritual relationship with nature that White people living in industrial societies have lost, has a long history.[9] In North America and Europe, Native Americans especially have, often inadvertently, provided inspiration for White people trying to express their own feelings of attachment to nature and to land.[10] Since the early 1900s, North American children have been encouraged to learn about the natural environment by becoming 'Camp Fire Boys and Girls' and dressing as 'Indians'. In Europe, networks of 'hobbyist' groups have long allowed adults to enact their fascination with Native American indigeneity through costume and performance.[11] This Western intellectual tradition — based on widely accepted beliefs about entrenched differences (and hidden similarities) between the categories of White and Indigenous[12] — has led to instances where people born into the former category have claimed they belonged in the latter.[13] Perhaps the most famous of these is 'Grey Owl', an English-born man who adopted a Native American persona in the 1920s and achieved celebrity status as a public lecturer and writer, bringing Indigenous perspectives on nature, spirituality and the need for environmental conservation to White audiences in Europe and North America.

Over the last few decades these ideas about indigeneity and ecological wisdom have been enthusiastically embraced by the environmental movement[14] and by the alternative health and spirituality (or New Age) movement.[15] Contemporary Paganism and Shamanism bridge these two groups with their particular focus on the development of historically grounded nature-based religions that locate humans firmly within the natural world.[16] In these contexts Indigenous spiritual beliefs and practices have been widely represented as a way of entering into or becoming part of the natural landscape, a means of 'reconnecting' to the earth and to an imaginary pan-human, pre-Christian past when nature-based religion was the only religion and all people (supposedly) lived in harmony with their environments.[17]

Such representations of Indigenous people have been closely tied to processes of colonialism and to common-sense interpretations of evolutionary thought. But what of Indigenous peoples themselves? What of Indigenous agency? How might these stereotypical representations be reclaimed and re-written by representatives of the groups being depicted? How might they be utilised as teaching devices to provide interested White people with a more realistic understanding of contemporary Indigenous cultures? How might the deliberate and careful sharing of Indigenous spiritual traditions by Indigenous people themselves constitute a transgression of colonial relations?

* * *

In August 1996, I attended a day-long workshop in Perth, Western Australia, entitled 'The Ancient Wisdom of Aboriginal Women'. The participants were a group of 50 White migrant and Australian-born women aged somewhere between 20 and 70 years. The facilitator was Tjanara Goreng-Goreng, an Aboriginal woman from Queensland. The strong attachments to, or 'feelings for', land expressed during the day by several women who had lived in rural Australia for long periods of time struck me as particularly significant. These statements about emotional bonds to place reminded me of a workshop I had attended two months earlier called 'Belonging and Being in Australia'. In that instance, David Mowaljarlai, a senior Ngarinyin man from the Kimberley region of Western Australia, was the guest of honour, and the focus of the event was on the similarities between Aboriginal and non-Aboriginal identity in Australia. These two workshops provided the foundation for my study of ideas about indigeneity, belonging and spirituality among a selection of Australian-born people of Anglo-Celtic ancestry.[18] The varying, and often very active, contributions that

Aboriginal Australians made to the evolution of these same ideas played a key role in my interpretations of the material I collected.

The following stories, drawn from my fieldnotes, illustrate some of the ways in which the series of workshops run by the Aboriginal facilitator from Queensland challenge the boundaries of I/indigeneity by offering those of us who would usually be described as 'non-Indigenous' the opportunity to truly belong, to overcome the ambiguities of settlement and ancestry by adopting an Aboriginal framework of inclusivity, a framework that accepts and promotes the true belonging of all people living in Australia through beliefs about the all-embracing nature of ancestral spirits and of the land itself.

* * *

Jarrahdale, Western Australia, May 1997.[19]

White voices sing out into the dusk chill, sing in an Indigenous language, songs from Northeast Queensland. Feet dance on winter wet grass, on long settled Noongar soil. White feet. And one pair of Goreng-Goreng Waka-Waka feet. Women's feet. Women's voices.

White hands shake green branches, new growth pulled from eucalyptus trees. White bodies pass through eucalyptus smoke. Around eucalyptus fire. White minds drawn, seduced, liberated, discomfited by Indigenous ritual. Women's ritual. Women's songs. Women's dance. Women's company. Indigenous company.

This Aboriginal woman generously gives us permission to belong, because we were born here, because we have lived here. Courageously and with no apology, she asks us to belong.

By running workshops on Aboriginal spirituality for non-Aboriginal women around Australia, Tjanara Goreng-Goreng makes a particular contribution to processes of reconciliation. She welcomes the interest that participants express in Aboriginal beliefs and practices and she shares some of her own knowledge with them in return. Questions of belonging circulated around the room at each of her workshops, sometimes explicit, sometimes not. Closely linked to this topic was a kind of search for indigeneity, a desire to find points of connection or commonality with Aboriginal people at a spiritual or emotional level, usually through the prism of attachment to land.

Thirty-five women gathered together on a cold night, many of us strangers. Sitting in a circle in a small hall surrounded by tall trees. A little uncertain, a little hesitant, a little excited. Why are we all here? Our Aboriginal leader asks each one of us to tell the group why we have come: to learn about Aboriginal culture; for healing; for spiritual connection; because it felt right. These are our reasons.

Tjanara makes a circle on the carpet with white ochre. She sings in her traditional language and we copy her. She shows us how to dance and we dance. One woman describes a wailing ceremony that she has heard about. She has experienced much loss and asks if we will wail with her.

We are divided into three age groups. Twenty of the women present are older than forty years. Together they form the outer circle. They are the senior women. Thirteen of the remaining group are between forty and thirty. They form an inner circle. Only two of us are left, both 'babies' under thirty. We sit in the middle, in the embrace of our elders.

The group was also divided on another axis, those who had been to previous workshops led by this facilitator and those who had not. The weekend gathering described here was called 'Sacred Circles, Sacred Dreaming' and was promoted as a follow-up to 'The Ancient Wisdom of Aboriginal Women'. The implication was that those of us who had done the first workshop were ready to progress to the next level of knowledge. In an interview a few days before the Jarrahdale event, Goreng-Goreng told me that she felt non-Aboriginal women came to her workshops because of a desire for female companionship, for community and for the healing that can come from being in community. She also felt that they came out of an awareness that they were living on Aboriginal land and that part of her responsibility was to show them the positive aspects of Aboriginal culture. Ritual and ceremony were an important part of this process, and something that she felt was missing for women in (so-called) Western societies. She also incorporated more standard forms of learning in her programs.

We sit on the floor and listen to Tjanara's introduction to the workshop. She tells us that everyone born in Australia belongs to the land and to the Rainbow Serpent that travels through the land. She also explains, for those born overseas, that the Rainbow Serpent takes in whoever chooses to put down roots in this country. She tells us that Aboriginal people have a responsibility to teach non-Aboriginal Australians, to share some of their spiritual knowledge with us so that we will better understand our own place in the world. She tells us stories about the Dreaming, how the continent was formed, how Aboriginal law was passed down through generations. She talks about songlines and sorcery and love magic, about the power of women and their knowledge of childbirth, about the way that a child's spirit comes up through the land and into its mother's body. We listen quietly.

The night darkens. We hear about recent Aboriginal history, about missions and colonisation, about suffering and fear and disease and oppression, about brutality and surveillance, devastation and imprisonment. About traumatised children and suicide, assimilation, acculturation. Carefully, we ask questions.

Difficult, delicate, negotiations of belonging are under way in contemporary Australian society. The tensions surrounding these negotiations are rooted in the long histories of Aboriginal and European thought and in the shorter history of Australian colonisation. They simultaneously draw together, emerge from, and produce a set of highly contested feelings and beliefs about what it means for those of us who are not of Aboriginal descent to belong to a place that was once stolen from, and is now shared — at least officially — with, Aboriginal people. Belonging is a fraught topic in settler societies. While Indigenous peoples have moral rights to belong based on primary associations with place that stretch back to a vanishing point far in the distance, colonial power relations have ensured that their cultural, economic and political belonging in the nation state is much more tenuous. On the other hand, as willing citizens, settlers and their descendants usually have clear claims on the cultural, economic and political fronts, but their belonging to place, to the land they inhabit, cannot be taken for granted.

In the morning we make our way back to the hall. The air is still crisp but the sun is warm. Spirits have lifted. The room is very different in the daylight, bright and airy. We begin with singing and dancing. Tjanara does some healing work and draws us back into our circles of the night before. Some of the women wail and cry, releasing hidden grief, safe and comfortable in the company of the group. This outpouring of emotion runs its course. Our leader encourages and soothes us with a healing ritual when it is over.

After lunch we sit down again together, this time to sew. We make headbands from red fabric and have white ochre designs painted on our faces. Then we move outside.

We sit in two semi-circles on the grass, the older women separated from the younger women, facing each other but slightly apart. Tjanara, our leader calls us forward one by one. She ties our headbands on, embraces each of us and whispers the name of an animal totem. When the last woman has been embraced she asks us to re-group according to the totems she has given us. She lights a small fire on the ground and lays green eucalyptus leaves over the top for a smoking ceremony. Solemnly, she asks each of us to step through the smoke, promising to ourselves as we go that we will do no evil to others. By the time we finish, dusk is falling again, the evening chill is setting in. To celebrate we dance the Water Dreaming and Leaf dances that we learned the night before until the fire dies down. Finally we move back into our age-based circles and pledge to support and help the people around us by following the three rules of the Dreaming that Tjanara recited for us: respect yourself; respect others; respect the land. In the growing darkness we bow our heads and close our eyes while she sings a sacred song to complete our ritual.

Winter wet grass, bare feet, women's voices.

Figure 4.1: Face painting in the sewing circle

Photograph by J Mulcock

Figure 4.2: Our headband ceremony

Photograph by J Mulcock

Figure 4.3: Women dancing Water Dreaming

Photograph by J Mulcock

Figure 4.4: Evening meal in ochre

Photograph by J Mulcock

The communal meal that evening was marked by a certain euphoria. Every woman (except Tjanara) chose to leave her ochre face paint on. The atmosphere was one of excitement and release. A storytelling session after dinner kept many of women together until late in the evening.

The final day began with a minute of silence in recognition of the Noongar people upon whose land we were sitting. The morning session focused on Aboriginal spiritual healing practices and in the afternoon we made dancing belts which Tjanara tied around our waists in a ritual similar to that of the day before. She told us that the belts were symbols of achieving womanhood. She also emphasised that none of this was equivalent to initiation, a misinterpretation that had occurred at one of her previous workshops. We returned to the dancing ground for a farewell ceremony where we again formed into our totem groups and danced and sang together. Tjanara drew us into a circle for the last time and asked us to say good bye to each other silently, one by one, promising as we did so to look after one another forever because now we were sisters.

* * *

There is an important epilogue to the story of the Jarrahdale workshop. I always sensed that the workshop facilitator's acknowledgement of non-Aboriginal belonging was a much welcomed message at each of the gatherings I attended. When I later interviewed some of the other participants, a few of them confirmed this intuition by talking about the significance of this woman's input for the development or unfurling of their personal sense of belonging to place.

One participant, Susan,[20] went so far as to write 'Noongar' in brackets next to 'Australian' when asked to nominate her primary cultural identity on a form provided as part of the interview — even though she stated that her actual ancestry was, to her knowledge, all Anglo-Celtic. She told me that the Aboriginal workshop facilitator had helped her to recognise her own indigeneity and spoke with intensity about her sense of spiritual belonging in the south-west of Western Australia. Susan related strongly to Noongar author and artist Sally Morgan's account of 'discovering' her Aboriginality as an adult,[21] reporting that she too had long carried the feeling that 'something was missing' from her life.[22]

Susan became increasingly interested in Aboriginal culture and spirituality after she started to study the healing powers of Western Australian wildflowers. Her adult experiences of using bush flower essences to deal with stress and emotional trauma, combined with her vivid childhood memories of spending time in the bush around her outer suburban home in Perth, evoked what she described as an 'innate feeling of belonging' to the Australian landscape. Susan compared this feeling with the attachments to land described by Aboriginal Australians. She explained that using Western Australian wildflower essences had helped her to recognise her own attachment to place, and her desire 'to belong to the

Indigenous people' of the area where she was born and raised.[23] This search for an indigenous self[24] coincided with, or perhaps grew out of, Susan's search for her 'inner self', a search that took shape as part of her efforts to cope with the increasing pressures of a busy urban lifestyle and a difficult marriage. Susan believed that using and learning about Western Australian wildflower essences helped her to 'come full circle', to re-establish the connections that she had with 'the bush' during her childhood.

The night before our formal interview, Susan phoned to express some of her concerns about talking to me and to emphasise the importance of what she was going to tell me. One of the things she challenged was my conceptualisation of Indigenous and non-Indigenous cultures in Australia as two separate categories. She felt this distinction was unsustainable, given that many so-called 'non-Indigenous' people were also born in Australia and felt a strong attachment for the country. When I asked her to expand on this observation in the interview, she talked about feelings of belonging and not belonging to place, firstly by comparing her family's experiences of feeling 'at home' whilst travelling through the Australian desert with the unease of the American friends they were with, and secondly by referring to her own and other people's feelings of discomfort when living away from their countries of birth. Susan's interactions with the Aboriginal workshop facilitator from Queensland strengthened and justified her sense of belonging by providing an explanatory framework that she was receptive to.

Amber and Diane,[25] two of the other women I interviewed who had participated in the Jarrahdale workshop, spoke in similar ways about their desire to 'belong' to the land and the 'permission' to do so that they felt that the Aboriginal facilitator provided. Both in their late forties with teenage children, these women were close friends. They were also artists and liked to spend time together in the bush painting, working with textiles or taking photographs. Amber especially reported strong feelings of attachment to, or engagement with, some of the places that they visited. For example, she described a number of events that she believed were encounters with spirits in the landscape, suggesting that they were similar, 'in a way', to those reported by Aboriginal people she knew.[26]

Amber made several very clear statements about her understandings of the links between indigeneity and belonging to place when she articulated a strong desire to 'connect' with Aboriginal people as part of the process of connecting to Australian land. Here are her words.

> I think that it's important for me to make that connection with Aboriginality because I live in this land, I am here, through a whole set of circumstances that I don't know really anything about, but I'm here, I'm in this land and unless I make a connection with the people who are

connected with this part of the earth then I think I'm lacking something in my life.[27]

Amber suggested that at one point in her life she had hoped that she would find evidence that she was of Aboriginal descent, although the experience of working closely with Aboriginal people over several years eventually allowed her to understand and accept her difference. She made very strong associations between Indigenous people, spirituality and emotional or psychological involvement in the landscape. As I listened to her talk about her own spiritual experiences in the bush, I thought I heard an undercurrent of awkwardness, perhaps embarrassment, related to her non-Indigenous status — as if her feelings and perceptions were less believable or less valid because of her Anglo-Celtic ancestry.

Diane also reflected independently on the links between Aboriginality, non-Aboriginal identity and feelings of belonging in Australia. She told me that the more she learned about Aboriginal people the more uncertain she became about her own belonging in Australia. Diane expressed a kind of postcolonial guilt about European invasion of Aboriginal country alongside an assured statement about her right 'to live here'. This was followed by an acknowledgement of the significance that Tjanara Goreng-Goreng's inclusive approach to belonging held for her:

> Tjanara said to us ... 'if you were born here then you are part of the land'. I felt so happy when she said that, I really did, it was like relief.[28]

Amber and Diane also talked about a much earlier encounter with a Noongar women from Denmark in south Western Australia, who argued that all people living in Australia were part of the Aboriginal Dreaming regardless of ancestral background.[29] It seemed that this experience had also been formative in the development of Amber's and Diane's ideas about indigeniety and belonging. The workshop confirmed some of these ideas and further supported the notion that non-Aboriginal Australians could 'truly belong' to the Australian continent.

* * *

These desires for, or expressions of, a kind of non-indigenous indigeneity have not come out of the blue. They are not unique or even particularly surprising. Rather they are part of a bigger picture that encompasses two centuries of contact between settlers (i.e. invaders), their descendants, Aboriginal people, and the landscape itself. Related processes of indigenisation were evident, for example, in the 1930s in the poetry of the Jindyworobaks, a group of writers who advocated the development of a truly Australian literary tradition.[30] A similar theme pervaded the contemporaneous work of well known artist Margaret Preston who encouraged Australian artists to 'be Aboriginal' as a means of establishing a unique 'national art'.[31] More recent examples of Australian settler descendant claims to a kind of indigeneity have also been documented, often in the context of public conversations about national identity. Growing interest among non-Aboriginal Australians in native plants and animals, support for Aboriginal sporting heroes, and curiosity about Aboriginal spirituality, culture and identity have all been interpreted as part of a national process of indigenisation.[32]

Over the last decade or so anthropologists, historians and literary scholars have begun the task of documenting and analysing non-Indigenous feelings of belonging to land in Australia, New Zealand and the Americas.[33] These writers consider assertions of settler descendant indigeneity, the feelings of attachment associated with being 'native-born', as genuine, valid attempts to understand and communicate a particular kind of relationship to 'adopted' country. An important issue that becomes apparent through their work is the lack of descriptive language available for talking about these sensitive and often contested attachments to place. The words 'indigenous' and 'native' have become so embedded in political discourses about the rights of first nations that they can no longer be used — at least in settler societies — in a purely descriptive, apolitical sense.[34] As suggested earlier, these terms have become entwined in moral discourses about true (i.e. spiritual) belonging to land in such locations. This means that when someone, Aboriginal or non-Aboriginal, suggests that it is possible to truly belong to a place regardless of indigenous heritage, she or he steps across an invisible boundary that carries considerable political currency and is rigorously defended by those who would like it to be impermeable.

The stories recounted here of the workshops run by an Aboriginal facilitator, and the responses of some of the participants from those workshops, thus illustrate two transgressive movements around the idea of indigeneity, two attempts to renegotiate and destabilise the boundaries, to push the concept beyond its commonly perceived limits. The non-Aboriginal transgression is obvious.[35] By publicly identifying too closely with indigeneity or Aboriginality in the course of claiming a kind of spiritual belonging to place, the women participants I refer to above are breaching a highly politicised boundary that is marked out and defended through accusations of appropriation, theft and misrepresentation. These accusations, delivered by one sector of the Aboriginal community and their supporters, are heavily informed by a postcolonial politics of minority identity requiring the exclusion and denouncement of any 'inauthentic' claims to belonging — the (implicit) argument being (at least in part) that the unique moral status of the group will be eroded if membership is not strictly monitored.[36]

But there is another logic at play, a logic lodged in discourses of spirituality and belonging, particular discourses of affect or emotion that work against political rationalities, rubbing and niggling at them like uncomfortable clothing on sunburned skin. This is the logic promoted by individuals like the Aboriginal woman who ran the workshops described above, active cultural agents who might be thought of as 'border crossers'.[37] Goreng-Goreng's transgression lies in her willingness to allow, to even encourage, a kind of belonging to place that it is not tied to indigeneity — at least in the sense of Aboriginal ancestry. When she publicly states that anyone born in Australia belongs to the land, she subtly undermines another Aboriginal / academic narrative that tells us the only way to truly belong in Australia is to be of Aboriginal descent.[38] Others in the Aboriginal community share similar opinions on this issue.

Over several years I have collected quotes attributed to Aboriginal people from around Australia that support the idea of non-Aboriginal belonging to the land. I did not set out to look for such material and I did not even really notice it until I finally sat down to collate and synthesise the data I had gathered. The variety of concurring Aboriginal voices surprised me — and the quality that seems to unite them is a clear public focus on spiritual life. I relate some of these perspectives here.

Diana James, a white woman who has worked and lived for many years with Pitjantjatjara people quotes her Aboriginal teacher, Nganyinytj, as saying,

> [I]f we were born in this country, our spirits weren't sent in fast delivery post packs across from England or Yugoslavia or wherever else. They're from here and we might be standing up in white skin or looking like we come from Greece but, actually, our spirit is of here and this is what we have to acknowledge and we have to get in tune with. It's important that people really look below the skin and start to connect at the heart level, to work together for creating a new spirituality, a new sense of place and strength that is truly Australian, that wells up from the ground.[39]

Wenton Rabuntja, a Pitjantjatjara man, is quoted by a journalist as arguing that all Australians belong to the Dreaming in which they were born — no matter what their heritage might be. Rabuntja says that place of birth is most important for place of belonging.

> If our kids go over to America or some other place and Australian kid born there, well he's part of that one and that Dreaming and he's traditional where he was born. His borning place is number one.[40]

In each of these instances it is possible that the translations are imprecise or the people doing the translating are misinterpreting what they have been told. The following quote, however, comes directly from a speech that Ngarinyin elder David Mowaljarlai made to the Federal Court as a part of his native title claim over land in the Kimberley region of Western Australia. He said:

> We don't want to hurt you because you were born here in Australia, so you belong in Australia. But you have to learn about the culture of Australia so you know your own belonging, your naming and your identity. It's no good if you stay ignorant of the culture of this land, while your belonging is overseas. The Law for this land is recorded in the land. We can teach you that law. That way you won't be strangers in your birth country.[41]

I have also heard a senior Noongar man, Noel Nannup, tell audiences that everyone who has been in Australia for longer than six years belongs to the land. Finally, Wiradjuri woman Maisie Cavanagh reflected on this issue of belonging at a presentation I attended — although her comments were a little more cautious. She pointed out that Aboriginal people don't have a monopoly on a land-based spirituality and that *all* Australians can experience feelings of belonging to places. She also commented, however, that the feeling of belonging that comes from having generations and generations of extended family in one place is different from the feeling of belonging that one individual coming to a place from elsewhere can experience. Perhaps she is suggesting that attachment to place is not necessarily the same thing as belonging?

Together, these perspectives indicate that some Aboriginal people believe in the value of sharing part of their cultural knowledge about belonging to land with non-Aboriginal people. By extending some of their spiritual beliefs to incorporate Australians who are not of Aboriginal descent, these individuals provide a new framework through which to continue negotiations. By allowing for the possibility that non-Aboriginal people do truly belong to the land where they were born or where they have chosen to put down roots, and that this belonging doesn't have to undermine Aboriginal belonging in any way, they seem to be inviting new levels of engagement and mutuality in which they are the experts: they seem to be saying 'We are your teachers and this is your spiritual land too. Be in relationship with it. Accept responsibility. Care for it'.

* * *

The crossing of politically sensitive borders that mark off symbolically loaded social categories is a transgressive act. Tjanara and the women attending her workshop move across the borders of indigeneity and belonging in different directions. The former reaches towards the latter and vice versa. This movement can be interpreted in both positive and negative ways depending on whether the reader favours the logic of the 'border guards'[42] or the 'border crossers'. There are plenty of Aboriginal voices raised in opposition to non-Aboriginal belonging — these voices tend to be loud and strategic, they tend to be part of a strong and resistant public discourse overtly focussed on political and social injustice. (I am not suggesting that politics is without spirituality or vice versa, but that some people choose to privilege one over the other in their public lives.)

Other, quieter, voices also talk of injustice and ways of overcoming it by growing the respect that some non-Aboriginal Australians have for Aboriginal people. But I think they include an additional message — about the importance of also growing the respect that non-Aboriginal people have for themselves, for their attachment to the land that nurtures them, for their spiritual lives and the spiritual lives of others.

Like them or hate them, settler discourses of belonging and indigeneity are probably here to stay. Not only do they have a long history, but now the voices of Aboriginal people can also be heard in the public domain, some giving support through their own understandings of the importance of settler belonging, of spiritual belonging as a source of responsibility to land and people, blood and soil. Loose parallels can be drawn with the logic of nationalism and patriotism and, perhaps at the opposite end of the political spectrum, with the logic of deep ecology proposed by some environmental philosophers (often influenced in turn by their exposure to Indigenous philosophies).[43] These Aboriginal voices are being hungrily embraced by those non-Aboriginal Australians who are engaged in their own spiritual search for belonging to place, a search that is perhaps inevitable in settler societies with the kind of violent and dispossessing history of Australia, perhaps part of a deeper settling, a more thorough acceptance of place and history.

By opening our ears and minds to the stories that people tell about their spiritual encounters with Aboriginal people, in this case with Goreng-Goreng through her workshops for women, it is possible to detect something of the heartfelt 'longing for belonging'[44] present in Australian settler descendant discourse. Politically acceptable or not, it exists. This search, this quest, this process, and all its implications, should no longer be ignored or dismissed. The time to engage with it is now.

White faces, painted with white ochre. Queensland Ochre. Totems whispered, remembered. Over the warmth of a hot meal, the excited chatter of women renewed. White women. Indigenous woman. Australian women.

Acknowledgements

Thanks are due to Tjanara Goreng-Goreng for reading this paper at short notice and providing permission for her name and words to be used. Thanks also to each of the other anonymous interviewees referred to in this paper, all of whom contributed generously to my research.

References

Ashcroft, Bill, Gareth Griffiths and Helen Tiffin 1989, *The Empire Writes Back: Theory and practice in post-colonial literature*, Routledge, London.

Bauman, Zygmunt 1992, 'Soil, blood and identity', *The Sociological Review* 40(4): 675-701.

Behrendt, Larissa 1998, 'In your dreams: cultural appropriation, popular culture and colonialism', *Law: Text: Culture* 4(1): 256-279.

Bell, Avril 1999, 'Authenticity and the project of settler identity in New Zealand', *Social Analysis* 43(3): 122-143.

Bowman, Marion 1995, 'The noble savage and the global village: cultural evolution in New Age and Neo-Pagan thought', *Journal of Contemporary Religion* 10(2): 139-149.

Butel, Elizabeth 1985, *Margaret Preston: the art of constant rearrangement*, Penguin in association with the Art Gallery of New South Wales, Ringwood, Victoria.

Churchill, Ward 1994, *Indians Are Us? Culture and genocide in Native North America*, Common Courage Press, Maine.

Cuthbert, Denise and Michele Grossman 1996, 'Trading places: locating the indigenous in the New Age', *Thamyris* 3(1): 18-36.

Deloria, Philip 1998, *Playing Indian*, Yale University Press, New Haven.

Dominy, Michèle 1995, 'White settler assertions of native status', *American Ethnologist* 22(2): 358-374.

——— 2001, *Calling the Station Home: Place and identity in New Zealand's high country*, Rowman & Littlefield Publishers, Lanham.

Dyer, Richard 1988, 'White', *Screen* 29(4): 44-64.

Eggington, Robert 1996, 'Intellectual property rights: the question of cultural ownership: a Noongar perspective', *Noongar Karnadjil* 1: 14.

Ellen, Roy 1986, 'What Black Elk left unsaid: on the illusory images of Green primitivism', *Anthropology Today* 2(6): 8-12.

Elliot, Brian 1979, *The Jindyworobaks*, Portable Australian Authors series, University of Queensland Press, St Lucia, Queensland.

Feest, Christian (ed.) 1989, *Indians and Europe: An interdisciplinary collection of essays*, Alano Verlag, Aachen.

Francis, Daniel 1992, *The Imaginary Indian: The image of the Indian in Canadian culture*, Arsenal Pulp Press, Vancouver.

Frankenberg, Ruth (ed.) 1997, *Displacing Whiteness: Essays in social and cultural criticism*, Duke University Press, Durham, NC.

Goldie, Terry 1989, *Fear and Temptation: The image of the indigene in Canadian, Australian and New Zealand literatures*, McGill-Queen's University Press, Kingston.

Green, Rayna 1988, 'The tribe called Wannabee: Playing Indian in America and Europe', *Folklore* 99(1): 30-55.

Greer, Germaine 2003, 'Whitefella Jump Up: the shortest way to nationhood', *Quarterly Essay* 11: 1-78.

Hamilton, Annette 1990, 'Fear and desire: Aborigines, Asians and the national Imaginary', *Australian Cultural History* 9: 14-35.

Harvey, Graham 1997, *Listening People, Speaking Earth: Contemporary Paganism*, Wakefield Press, South Australia.

Hume, Lynne 2000, 'The Dreaming in contemporary Aboriginal Australia', in G Harvey (ed.), *Indigenous Religions: A companion*, Cassell, London: 125-138.

Ilcan, Suzan 2002, *Longing in Belonging: The cultural politics of settlement*, Praeger Publishers, Westport.

Jacobs, Jane 1994, 'Earth honouring: Western desires for Indigenous knowledges', *Meanjin* 53(2): 305-314.

James, Diana 1996, Recorded lecture, Australian Transpersonal Institute National Conference, Sydney.

Kehoe, Alice Beck 1990, 'Primal Gaia: primitivists and plastic medicine men', in J Clifton (ed.), *The Invented Indian: Cultural fictions and government policies*, Transaction Publishers, New Brunswick: 193-210.

Krech, Sheppard 1999, *The Ecological Indian: Myth and history*, Norton, New York.

Lattas, Andrew 1990, 'Aborigines and contemporary Australian nationalism: primordiality and the cultural politics of otherness', *Social Analysis* 27: 50-69.

—— 1991, 'Nationalism, aesthetic redemption and Aboriginality', *The Australian Journal of Anthropology* 2(3): 307-324.

—— 1992, 'Primitivism, nationalism and individualism in Australian popular culture', in J Arnold and Bain Attwood (eds), *Power, Knowledge and Aborigines*, La Trobe University Press, Bundoora: 45-58.

Luhrmann, Tanya 1994, *Persuasions of the Witch's Craft: Ritual magic in contemporary England*, Picador, London.

Maddock, Kenneth 1991, 'Metamorphosing the sacred in Australia', *The Australian Journal of Anthropology* 2(2): 213-232.

Mies, Maria 1993, 'White man's dilemma: his search for what he has destroyed', in M Mies and V Shiva (eds), *Ecofeminism*, Spinifex Press, Melbourne: 132-163.

Milton, Kay 1998, 'Nature and the environment in Indigenous and traditional cultures', in D Cooper and J Palmer (eds), *Spirit of the Environment: Religion, value and environmental concern*, Routledge, London: 86-112.

Miskimmin, Susan 1996, 'The New Age movement's appropriation of Native spirituality: some political implications for the Algonquian Nation', *The Papers of the Algonquian Conference* 27: 205-211.

Morgan, Sally 1987, *My Place*, Fremantle Arts Press, Fremantle.

Morton, John 1996, 'Aboriginality, Mabo and the republic: indigenising Australia', in Bain Attwood (ed.), *In the Age of Mabo: History, Aborigines and Australia*, Allen & Unwin, St Leonards, New South Wales: 117-135.

Morton, John and Nicholas Smith 1999, 'Planting indigenous species: a subversion of Australian eco-nationalism', in K Neuman, N Thomas and H Eriksen (eds), *Quicksands: Foundational histories in Australia and Aotearoa New Zealand*, University of New South Wales Press, Sydney: 117-135.

Mowaljarlai, David 1995, 'We have a gift', *Nova: Western Australia's Holistic Journal* 2(9): 29.

Mulcock, Jane 2001, '(Re)discovering our indigenous selves: the nostalgic appeal of Native Americans and other generic indigenes', *Australian Religious Studies Review* 14(1): 45-64.

—— 2002, 'Searching for our indigenous selves: belonging and spirituality in Anglo-Celtic Australia', Unpublished PhD thesis, University of Western Australia.

Mulcock, Jane and Yann Toussaint 2002, 'Memories and Idylls: Urban reflections on lost places and inner landscapes', *Transformations* 2, <http://transformations.cqu.edu.au/journal/issue_02/pdf/MulcockToussaint.pdf>

Neuenfeldt, Karl 1998, 'Aboriginal didjeriduists in Australian education: cultural workers and border crossers', *Journal of Intercultural Studies* 19(1): 5-19.

Paine, Robert 2000, 'Aboriginality, authenticity and the settler world', in A Cohen (ed.), *Signifying Identities: Anthropological perspectives on boundaries and contested values*, Routledge, London: 77-116.

Plumwood, Val 2000, 'Belonging, naming and decolonisation', *Ecopolitics: Thought and Action* 1(1): 90-106.

Probyn, Elspeth 1996, *Outside Belongings*, Routledge, London.

Read, Peter 1994, 'Joy and forgiveness in a haunted country', *New Norcia Studies*: 1-9.

—— 1996, *Returning to Nothing: The meaning of lost places*, Cambridge University Press, Cambridge, UK.

—— 2000, *Belonging: Australians, place and Aboriginal ownership*, Cambridge University Press, Cambridge, UK.

Richards, Dave 1995, 'Whitefella Dreaming', *HQ Magazine*, May/June: 60-67.

Root, Deborah 1996, *Cannibal Culture: Art, appropriation, and the commodification of difference*, Westview Press, Colorado.

Rose, Wendy 1992, 'The great pretenders: further reflections on white shamanism', in MA Jaimes (ed.), *The State of Native America: Genocide, colonization, and resistance*, Race and Resistance Series, South End Press, Boston: 403-421.

Sackett, Lee 1991, 'Promoting primitivism: conservationist depictions of Aboriginal Australians', *The Australian Journal of Anthropology* 2(2): 233-246.

Sowelu, Daniel 2001, 'Maxine Fumagalli dies', *Nova: Keeping Body and Soul Together* 8(5): 28.

Taylor, Bron 1997, 'Earthen spirituality or cultural genocide? Radical environmentalism's appropriation of Native American spirituality', *Religion* 27: 183-215.

Thomas, Nicholas 2001, 'Appropriation/appreciation: settler modernism in Australia and New Zealand' in Fred Myers (ed.), *The Empire of Things: Regimes of value and material culture*, School of American Research Press, Santa Fe: 139-163.

Torgovnick, Marianna 1997, *Primitive Passions: Men, women and the quest for ecstasy*, Alfred A. Knopf, New York.

Trigger, David 2002, 'Indigeneity, ferality and what "belongs" in the Australian bush: nature, culture and identity in a settler society', Conference paper presented at the International Sociological Association XV World Congress, Brisbane.

ENDNOTES

[1] Interview by the author, Leederville, Western Australia, 29 October 1996.

[2] Informal conversation with the author, Burrup Peninsula, 1 October 2002.

[3] Cited in Trigger 2002: 4.

[4] Mowaljarlai 1995: 29.

[5] Bauman 1992.

[6] Read 1994; Dominy 1995; Trigger 2002.

[7] For example Behrendt 1998; Miskimmin 1996.

[8] For example Eggington 1996; Rose 1992; Green 1988.

[9] Kehoe 1990; Francis 1992; Mies 1993; Deloria 1998; Feest 1989.

[10] Torgovnick 1997: 139.

[11] Deloria 1998.

[12] For discussion of 'Whiteness' (in contrast to 'Blackness') see for example Dyer 1988; Frankenburg 1997.

[13] For some contemporary Australian examples see Mulcock 2001.

[14] See Milton 1998; Ellen 1986; Sackett 1991; Jacobs 1994.

[15] See Deloria 1998; Root 1996; Torgovnick 1996; Hume 2000.

[16] For example Luhrmann 1994; Harvey 1997; Bowman 1995; Taylor 1997.

[17] See Krech 1999 for a historical critique of this idea.

[18] Mulcock 2002.

[19] Unless otherwise indicated, italicised text denotes loosely reconstructed descriptions based on my fieldnotes and my memories of attending these events.

[20] 'Susan' is a pseudonym.

[21] Morgan 1987.

[22] Interview by the author, Winthrop, Western Australia, 13 June 1997.

[23] See Mulcock and Toussaint 2002.

[24] Mulcock 2002.

[25] 'Amber' and 'Diane' are pseudonyms.

[26] Interview by the author, Mosman Park, Western Australia, 30 August 1997.

[27] Interview by the author, Mosman Park, Western Australia, 30 August 1997.

[28] Interview by the author, Mosman Park, Western Australia, 14 August 1997.

[29] Sowelu 2001.

[30] Elliot 1979.

[31] Butel 1985: 50; Thomas 2001: 141.

[32] Morton and Smith 1999; Morton 1996; Hamilton 1990; Lattas 1990, 1991, 1992; Maddock 1991; Goldie 1989.

[33] Read 1996, 2000; Morton 1996; Dominy 1995, 2001; Trigger 2002; Paine 2000; Bell 1999; Ashcroft, Griffiths and Tiffin 1989; Greer 2003.

[34] Paine 2000.

[35] Some Aboriginal commentators would also argue that Goreng-Goreng's actions are transgressive; as a teacher working alone rather than in the physical company of her community, as a Queenslander teaching in Western Australia, as an Aboriginal teacher willing to share cultural knowledge with non-Aboriginal students.

[36] For example Churchill 1994; Deloria 1998; Cuthbert and Grossman 1996.

[37] Neuenfeldt 1998; Mulcock 2002.

[38] For example, Interview with Aboriginal historian Jackie Huggins, Late Night Live, ABC Radio National 2003.

[39] James 1996.

[40] Cited in Richards 1995: 67.

[41] Mowaljarlai 1995: 29.

[42] Bauman 1992: 678.

[43] For example, Plumwood 2000.

[44] Probyn 1996; Ilcan 2002.

Resisting the captured image: how Gwoja Tjungurrayi, 'One Pound Jimmy', escaped the 'Stone Age'

Jillian E Barnes

A cultural courtesy

The language used in this story is quoted directly from tourism marketing material. These tourism images and the language used to create them are important historical records. They both reflect and help shape attitudes and aspirations. Some of these images are now considered unacceptable. My purpose is to highlight historical sensibilities. By referring to them I seek to critique rather than endorse their usage.

Aboriginal readers are warned that this paper includes names and images of deceased persons. I thank Gabriel Possum and Isobel Hagan for kindly granting their permission to reproduce images of their grandfather, Gwoja Tjungurrayi.

Figure 5.1: 'Definitive' Commonwealth stamp 1950.

Design Nicholas Freeman, Freeman Design Partners.

Figure 5.2: Bamboro-Kain 1839.

Navy Art Gallery, Naval Historical Centre, Washington DC, [detail, image reversed].

Figure 5.3: Photograph of Gwoja Tjungurrayi 1935.

Walkabout, September 1950 cover [detail]. Reproduced with permission from Tjungurrayi's granddaughters Gabriel Possum and Isobel Hagan.

A snapshot

A chance encounter took place in the remote, rocky desert-scape east of Alice Springs sometime in the 1930s between an ambitious young tourism executive from Melbourne and a young Warlpiri-Anmatyerre man.[1] The Melbourne man was touring Australia by car, searching for spectacular pictures and adventure stories for a new tourism magazine. The Aboriginal man was walking south to a large ceremonial gathering of clans with a senior companion. The tourism executive, Charles Holmes, could not believe his good fortune when a young, fit and handsome man named Jimmy appeared unexpectedly before him, naked, carrying a woomera, a spear and a boomerang. He immediately drew a mental link between the books he had been reading and the man he was looking at. Holmes was overcome by the belief that the man named Jimmy was the most magnificent specimen of Aboriginal manhood, a living example of Baldwin Spencer's 'Stone-Age' man and Charles Pickering's 'wild' 'original' hunter all rolled into one.[2] He felt compelled to capture Jimmy's image on film and instructed his cameraman to snap a series of photographs. The camera shutter whirred as the photographer launched into action, stage-managing poses, expressions and settings and freezing for posterity scores of static portraits and action shots. During the following 30 years these captured images played a significant role in the definition of Australian Aboriginality. Holmes later admitted he had used them repeatedly to present Jimmy as a 'symbol of a vanishing race'.[3] These images also enmeshed both men in a complicated relationship, an understanding of which provides a rare insight into the dynamics of Australian race relations and the power of tourism as an agent of social control and change.

Figure 5.4: Indian Detour on The Chief, 1929 Grand Canyon Line, Santa Fe Railroad.

Reproduced with permission from Burlington Northern Santa Fe Railway Company, Texas.

Introduction

Representations of Indigenous people have long been used to promote tourism to remote regions by colonising powers. The Santa Fe railroad's romanticisation of Native Americans or 'Indians' and its glorification of western expansion are legendary (Fig 5.4).[4] Pictures of Indigenous Australians or 'Aborigines' have been likewise used for tourism marketing purposes. Even before the first train rattled through Heavitree Gap into Alice Springs in 1929, tourism interests created images to entice travellers to the 'Dead Heart',[5] which the government had earmarked for speedy development. This story reveals how Gwoja Tjungurrayi or Jimmy escaped from a narrow definition of Aboriginality imposed on him by tourism image-makers like Holmes, which identified him as the remnant of a vanishing 'Stone-Age' race. It shows how he developed relationships, created an environment and took advantage of unusual opportunities to produce counter-images and create a new understanding of Aboriginality.

This paper begins by surveying Holmes' use of the captured images of Tjungurrayi to render Central Australia into a tourist site/sight and make it attractive to three target market groups by educating them to see and relate to place and people in particular ways while they were there. It then draws a biographical sketch of Tjungurrayi and sets his lived experiences against the stereotypical views promoted by Holmes. The story concludes with a saga of a stamp, in which Tjungurrayi's identity and life were revealed to tourists, and a series of articles generated by a new regime of image-makers. These latter writers included Tjungurrayi in their production of images to create a new understanding of Aboriginality.

The birth of Central Australian tourism

The earliest tourism marketing campaigns for Central Australia drew inspiration from Charles Holmes' *We Find Australia*,[6] Baldwin Spencer and Frank Gillen's *Arunta: A study of a Stone Age People*[7] and Charles Pickering's *Races of Man*.[8] The newly established Australian National Travel Association (ANTA) drew from these literary sources and compiled a vast image bank, which it referred to, exhibited and made available to travel writers and advertisers.

Shortly after Holmes commenced his management of ANTA,[9] he toured Australia with a photographer to survey tourist sights and collect interesting stories for the association's forthcoming tourism magazine, *Walkabout*. Holmes published an account of his adventures in *We Find Australia* the following year.[10] This book provides invaluable insights into the mind of the man who steered Australia's most powerful tourism image-making institution for thirty years.

Holmes presented himself as a prophetic publicity man hunting for stories about settler Australians who had shaped the destiny of the new nation. His hero was John Macarthur, the man he claimed 'blew the trumpet ... on this country's capacity to grow wool'.[11] *We Find Australia* described a modern industrious white race conquering primeval land, wrestling it into a promised land and replacing 'Stone-Age' savagery with British civilisation. He presented the inland as the 'Real Australia' where the wealth of the nation was being discovered and developed, and the period as the 'breaking of a new dawn'.[12]

Holmes supported the principle of 'White Australia'. He sought to foster the belief that the Australian population was already 97% white British stock and the 'effacement' of the remaining 62,000 'full-bloods' or 'wild savages' was assured.[13] His chapter '"Stone-Age" People' divided settlers and 'the Aruntas' into two separate groups inhabiting two distinct worlds: one 'modern', the other 'primitive'.[14] The book promoted two distinct types of masculinity: white 'manliness' which was progressive, courageous and virile, and brutish Aboriginal hunter-warriorship which was innately 'childish', warlike, monstrous, purposeless and moribund. Echoing Baldwin Spencer, Holmes identified 'blacks' as archaic, static subjects who were incapable of change, and vanishing scientific curiosities that were worth studying before they died out.[15]

Whilst this was Holmes' dominant view of Aboriginality, he occasionally slipped into a contradictory position by evoking romantic literature and describing 'primitive' Aboriginal men as the virile remnants of a 'wild' 'original hunter state'. This was the case when he revived a description coined by Charles Pickering in 1851.[16] Holmes quoted Pickering verbatim to describe Jimmy as 'the finest model' of 'human proportions I have ever met', combining 'perfect symmetry, activity and strength' with a head like 'the antique bust of a philosopher'.[17] His cameraman, Roy Dunstan, likewise framed his photographic images of Jimmy in conventional eighteenth century romantic language. A striking resemblance exists between a Dunstan photograph (Fig 5.3) and a sketch of 'Bamboro-Kain of the Newcastle Tribe', the man Pickering identified as the ideal Australian Aboriginal (Fig 5.2).[18]

The language of tourism

We Find Australia exemplifies Dann's claim that tourism marketing professionals have created a distinctive language that glorifies modernity, promotion and consumerism.[19] So too did a Commonwealth Railway's poster designed by the talented graphic artist, Percy Trompf.[20] This applied the Santa Fe railway aesthetic (Fig 5.5) to Central Australia and replaced 'Indians' of North American pueblos with 'Arunta' men (Fig 5.6). Trompf likewise contrasted modern, energetic white explorer-travellers with 'primitive' 'native' men. He assigned a set of formulaic positions and postures to the groups. Colonial figures and their modern conveyance occupied centre stage and were orientated towards the right to symbolise the future. Aboriginal men were relegated to servile positions, diminished in scale and located towards the rear to represent the past.

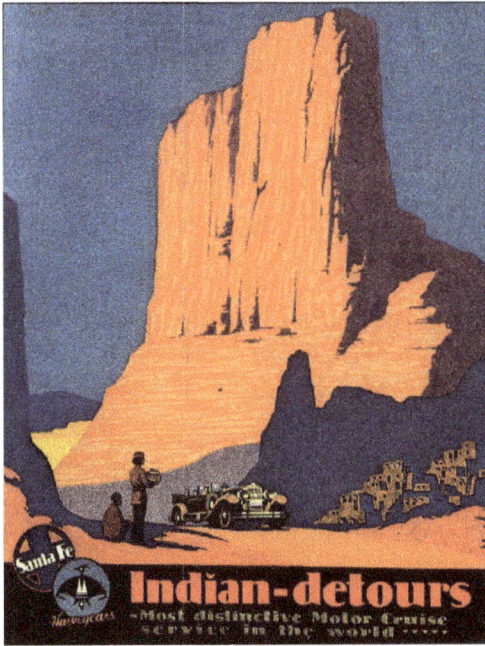

Figure 5.5: (L): Indian-Detours 1920s Santa Fe Railroad/Harveycars.

Reproduced with permission from Burlington Northern Santa Fe Railway Company, Texas.

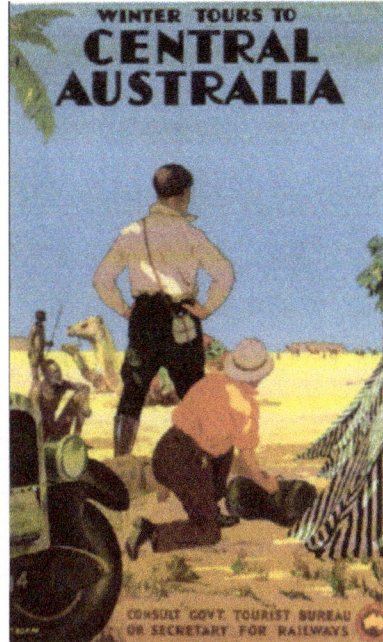

Figure 5.6: (R): Poster: Winter Tours to Central Australia.

Percy Trompf, 1930, Commonwealth Railways, National Library of Australia, nla.pic-an21530848.

Such were tourism representations of Central Australia when ANTA launched *Walkabout* in November 1934. During the next quarter century, Holmes used captured images of Jimmy to promote ANTA's corporate goals. In the process Jimmy became a celebrity and a symbol for Australian colonisation, modernisation and Aboriginality.

Before Holmes catapulted Jimmy into international fame, however, he cast him in a position of national infamy whilst seeking to educate tourists to see the inland from three overlapping perspectives. Drawing upon the language of tourism, I have called these the 'Imperial', the 'pioneer' and the 'anthropological' tourist gazes.[21]

The 'Imperial' tourist gaze

The first way of seeing constructed by Holmes promoted an 'Imperial' tourist gaze. This celebrated British discovery and territorial annexation. Holmes mobilised a range of writers to associate the inland with a history of exploration, danger and the mastery of a hostile wasteland, and to identify explorers as heroic trailblazers: the founding fathers of the nation. Through image juxtaposition, writers promoted belief in settler and Indigenous Australian alterity, or difference, and demonised the Aboriginal men encountered by explorers during expeditions.

Holmes used photographs of Jimmy to illustrate a major series on inland exploration by Russell Clark[22] and Frank Clune. This ingeniously reinscribed the Leichhardt,[23] Kennedy,[24] and Burke and Wills[25] 'tragedies' of thirst, tortured agony and failure as glorious, intrepid and purposeful successes. Articles never named or individualised Jimmy. Rather, they promoted the idea that he typified all 'natives' who had interacted with explorers through time and space. Despite having connections to particular clans and country, Jimmy was said to be the same as any Aboriginal man encountered by explorers between Lake Eyre and Arnhem Land during the previous century.

This series presented the inland as an unknown, uninhabited and untracked wilderness. Authors organised explorer action into a theme of 'to strive, to seek, to find and not to yield', and a sequence of clashes against natural obstacles. This included Aboriginal men. Clark used a language of violence, sacrifice and domination to describe explorers hacking their way across the continent, being speared by Aboriginal men and giving way only to death.

Interaction with Aboriginal men and natural terrains was described in adversarial terms. Clark compared jagged mountain peaks to the sharpened teeth of savages and divided Aboriginal people into two categories: 'semi-civilised' allies like Kennedy's faithful guide Jacky Jacky and 'primitive' tribal enemies. The latter were presented as either wandering marauders or treacherous cowards. Holmes used images of Jimmy that emphasised his weaponry and watchful, defensive positioning. Captions identified him as either a passive element of the natural environment: 'The Aboriginal … as … seen by early explorers' (Fig 5.7),[26] or as an active foe: 'as primitive today as were the natives who slew Kennedy' (Fig 5.8).[27]

Figure 5.7: 'The Aboriginal ... as ... seen by early explorers'.

Walkabout, January 1936. Photo Roy Dunstan.

Figure 5.8: 'As primitive today as were the natives who slew Kennedy'.

Walkabout, March 1936.

Images of Jimmy functioned as a foil to add lustre to explorer action. This literary device has been called the construction of 'cultural distance' or Indigenous alterity.[28] In tourism literature it worked to simultaneously glorify explorers and deride Aboriginal people. Holmes used photographs of Jimmy to perpetuate a stereotype of the 'ignoble savage'. In so doing, he presented twentieth century Aboriginal men as brutish elements of malevolent nature, marauding, treacherous foes and aimless roamers in a virginal and available inland. This 'Imperial' gaze selectively ignored contemporary knowledge about Aboriginal connections to land. For example, anthropologists Donald Thomson and Norman Tindale were revealing that complex networks of travel routes existed throughout the continent for intertribal ceremonial and trade purposes. They showed that clans were connected to ancestral territories within which they ranged and camped according to customary laws.[29] Ignoring this work suggests that *Walkabout* may have encouraged their writers to present an understanding that privileged stereotypes rather than Aboriginal ways of mapping and occupying the land.

The 'pioneer' tourist gaze

ANTA was equally strategic in its use of Jimmy's image to construct a 'pioneer' tourist gaze. This associated Central Australia with colonial development, modern civilisation and bewildered 'primitive natives'. Whilst the 1930s has been identified as a time when Alice Springs still had one foot planted in the 'bad old days of the frontier' and another in 'the beginning of modernity',[30] *Walkabout* reflects a government determination to jettison the frontier associations by granting tax exemptions to primary producers and additional lands for leasehold.[31]

Holmes mobilised writers to educate tourists to view modern development as national 'progress'. Each contributed stories about battles waged and won by inland pioneers to convert a dead wasteland into a productive promised land, and a disorientated 'Stone-Age' race into useful workers. Holmes used images of Jimmy to construct this gaze. This included a full-length portrait of Jimmy,[32] which was quickly appropriated and used by other fledgling tourism entrepreneurs.[33]

This portrait was influenced by both an eighteenth century European painterly tradition and a pre-existing set of stereotypical poses of Aboriginal warrior-hunters (see Fig 5.7). Dunstan adopted the language of a sub-genre of portraiture developed to portray Indigenous peoples throughout the New World. Sir Joshua Reynolds' portrait of Omai has been identified by London's Royal Academy as its exemplar of this sub-genre because it embodied the idea of the 'noble savage', fused classical sculptural and romantic painterly aesthetics, and influenced generations of image-makers.[34] This included William Blake,[35] who was one of the first artists to apply this neo-classical style to the representation of Indigenous Australians (Fig 5.9). This genre also influenced anthropologists including Baldwin Spencer and his partner in science, Frank Gillen. Spencer had undertaken formal drawing classes at the Manchester school of art.[36] He modelled portraits of Aboriginal warrior-hunters on a set of four stereotypical poses that were in circulation among scientific groups from the 1880s.[37] These were popularised in public lantern lectures and publications from the 1890s (Fig 5.10).[38]

Dunstan's photographs of Jimmy often appeared with obscure captions. One simply stated 'Aborigines examining a motor-car' (Fig 5.11).[39] In these instances a range of stimuli influence reader interpretation. These include proximate stories and personal preconceptions. This issue of *Walkabout* featured an article on the problems and possibilities of developing Central Australia.[40] Its author discussed labour options and called for intelligent economic planning rather than whimsical, outdated optimism.[41] He concluded 'coolie labour' was 'inappropriate', tribal Aboriginal men were unreliable and modern scientific methods would enable white men to compete for international markets. One interpretation of the combination of image, caption and narrative is that *Walkabout* sought to present Jimmy as an itinerant, unreliable worker and modernity as a purely Anglo-Australian preserve.

Figure 5.9: (L): 'A Family of New South Wales' 1792 by William Blake (1757-1827) after sketch by Governor Phillip Gidley King (1758-1808).

From John Hunter, An Historical Journal of the Transactions at Port Jackson and Norfolk Island, London, 1793, etching and engraving (NGV 40), P8-1974, National Gallery of Victoria, Melbourne, (detail).

Figure 5.10: (R): 'Arunta Man', FJ Gillen 1896.[42]

South Australian Museum Archives. Reproduced in Aboriginal Australia Arts and Culture Centre 2003: 1, [image reversed].

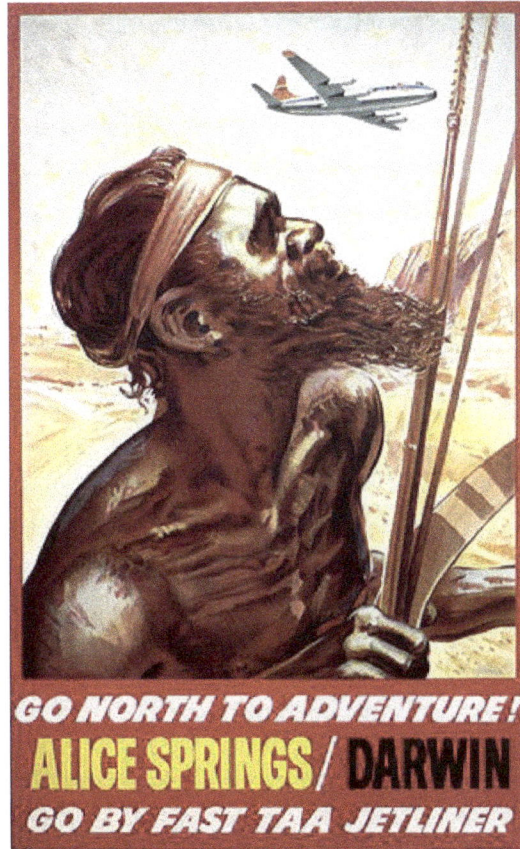

Figure 5.11: (L): 'Aborigines examining a motor car'.

Walkabout, February 1937.

Figure 5.12: (R): 'Go North to Adventure! By TAA Jetliner'.

Stylised poster by Warner 1958, National Archives of Australia, M2459.

The positioning of people from pre-modern societies alongside symbols of modern 'civilisation' is a ploy common to tourism image-makers. Their juxtaposition of 'primitivity' and 'modernity' provides tourists with a measure for 'western' progress. Here are three striking examples. Firstly, TAA used a stylised image of Jimmy looking at an aeroplane flying over Uluru to promote it as a tourist site where tourists could see 'Stone-Age' men gazing awestruck at modern technology (Fig 5.12). Secondly, a lavish book celebrating South Australia's centenary drew on ANTA's image-bank to glorify the achievements of a 'Great White Nation'.[43] A portrait of Jimmy appeared adjacent to a map of the Australian continent on the title page. It was coloured solid black. This montage of black man and black map symbolised the point from which white colonisation began: a blank slate waiting to be inscribed by an industrious colonising people.

Finally, Holmes ran Jimmy's portrait on the cover of *Walkabout* to mark the progress made by settler Australians during the first fifty years of federation.[44]

Holmes first published Jimmy's portrait on *Walkabout's* cover in 1936.[45] Tourist interpretation of his uncaptioned picture may have been conditioned by contemporary publications on 'pioneer conquest' and 'the Aboriginal problem' by Ursula McConnel.[46] She identified herself as a university trained social 'scientist' who was using her professional knowledge to advance colonisation by managing the development of Aboriginal capabilities and helping bewildered 'primitive' people rise to a higher level of civilisation.[47] Within the context of intense ideological ferment and debate about Australian race relations, McConnel advocated the use of 'intelligent control' rather than violent repression, which she stated, had provoked murderous Aboriginal discontent and inhibited colonisation. She presented Aboriginal people as incapable of self-directed change and valuable in chiefly scientific and labour terms.

Photographs of Jimmy were regularly used to promote the interlinked goals of inland development and Aboriginal 'reconstruction'. These included the Aboriginal program at the newly established Haast Bluff reserve to convert subsistence food gatherers into surplus economy food producers.[48] Local government patrol officer VC Hall described how he had 'arrested' 'the drift' of disorientated tribespeople between white settlements, missions and cattle stations; and 'broken' 'passive resistance' campaigns led by 'tribal' elders. He presented Aboriginal capitulation as enlightened acceptance and progress in the governance of Aboriginal people. An image of Jimmy was used to illustrate the new category of hunter-producer. It identified him as a 'fine hunter' who was 'still a man': able to engage with the modern economy and free to go 'back to nature' when he wished to do so.

McConnel and Hall had vested interests in 'reconstruction'. Both presented Jimmy as a symbol — or successful product — of their respective professions. Holmes' use of the image of Jimmy may be seen as an attempt to quieten humanitarian protest against 'reconstruction' and to belie other interpretations. These included authoritarian regimes seeking to break the spirit of Aboriginal people and Aboriginal elders capitulating because they were dependent on settler society for their survival.

A comparison of official articles and commercial advertisements provides another insight into the racial inequities and contradictions of tourism marketing. For example *Walkabout* and tourism entrepreneurs used images of Jimmy to serve opposite ends. Whilst *Walkabout* endorsed patrol officers' attempts to muster Aboriginal people onto reserves and curb their freedom of movement, Ansett Travel Services and Bond's Motor Service told tourists they could 'Go Walkabout *anywhere*' to see tribespeople in their 'natural surroundings'.[49] This included restricted areas like the Haast Bluff ration depot.

Figure 5.13: 'Aborigines Seeking Food and Knowledge'.

ANTA, Australian Scene, 1955.

Holmes later used images of Jimmy for contrasting ends in two lavish annual publications. Both reported on Australian social policy. One presented Jimmy as a failure rather than a success of assimilation policies. It used a montage to set Jimmy and his companion disappearing into the distance against Aboriginal children looking forwards within a modern classroom (Fig 5.13).[50] The other conflated Aboriginal depopulation with inadequacy.[51] Aboriginal people lacked, it argued, capacities to adjust to new 'social and moral codes'. It is possible to identify three categories of Aboriginality in this article: those who belonged to the past (tribespeople with 'forlorn attitudes' resigned to 'extinction'); those who were useful in the present (workers); and those who were being prepared for the future (educated, assimilated children). This montage can be interpreted as an attempt by Holmes to condition tourists to see men like Jimmy as innately incapacitated, static remnants of an archaic culture who accepted their own demise.

This official 'pioneer' tourist gaze did not receive universal support from tourism image-makers. Both nature-writer Charles Barrett[52] and tourism entrepreneur AG (Bert) Bond used images of Jimmy to challenge the ideas fostered in *Walkabout*. They romanticised Aboriginal primitivism and identified 'tribal' Aborigines as an integral part of wild nature rather than a culture positioned at the bottom-most rung of human civilisation. Barrett drew on Spencer and Gillen to promote the inland as 'another world' where nature remained 'unspoilt' by progress. He identified this world as 'Larapinta Land', associated it with 'cultural purity' and divided Aboriginal people into two groups: 'authentic' 'Stone-Age' Aborigines and partially 'civilised' 'natives' who were 'spoilt' because they wore clothing and looked 'grotesque'. Barrett denigrated the corroborees Aboriginal people staged for tourists and contrasted them with the sacred ceremonies formerly witnessed by Spencer and Gillen, classifying the former as 'entertainment' and the latter as 'authentic' cultural rituals or the 'real thing'.[53] The emergence of this alternative viewpoint suggested a 'naturalist' tourist gaze was gaining momentum in opposition to the developmentalism fostered by the 'pioneer' tourist gaze.

Both Barrett and Bond encouraged tourists to visit the Haast Bluff reserve to see 'ancient' Aborigines in their natural hunting grounds and take photographs whilst they were there.[54] They sought to educate tourists to see reserves as tourist sites where they could study warrior-hunters moving 'quietly through the scrub' carrying spears, boomerangs and shields, practising 'Stone-Age' customs and performing 'weird corroborees' in 'ochre, pipeclay and ... feathers'. A full-page advertisement for *Walkabout* magazine appeared adjacent to Barrett's article. It featured an uncaptioned full-length portrait of Jimmy. This juxtaposition of image and romantic narrative of Aboriginal primitivism, can be interpreted as an attempt by Barrett to associate Jimmy with the idea of the pristine 'noble savage' and to encourage tourists to travel to 'Larapinta Land' to see Aboriginal people living harmoniously within nature far beyond the reach of modern conditions.

The 'anthropological' tourist gaze

McConnel's publications reflected a philosophical shift in the governance of Aboriginal people and a controversial development in anthropological practice. She represented the viewpoint held by 'functional' anthropologists. They believed 'uncivilised' Aboriginal people should be absorbed into Anglo-Australian society, whereas their more 'traditional' counterparts argued that 'primitive' Aborigines were a 'wonder of the world' and should be preserved in reserves for scientific research.

Both standpoints were accommodated in the resolutions of the 1937 Aboriginal Welfare Conference. They were predominantly based on a new set of assumptions that Aboriginal people could be 'elevated' to 'white standards', the Aboriginal 'race' could be 'absorbed' into the dominant white population, and Aboriginality should be expunged. Whilst the conference proceedings assigned to three categories of Aboriginal people the 'destiny' of 'elevation' within white society,[55] it prescribed 'Uncivilised Full-Bloods' should be preserved for 'sentimental reasons' and 'scientific study'.[56] This exception reinforced a similar recommendation made by Baldwin Spencer a generation earlier.[57] Holmes reinvigorated Spencer's ideas to promote an 'anthropological' tourist gaze.

Spencer's biographer, John Mulvaney, has stated that his viewpoint as a biologist and anthropologist was shaped by his 'crude evolutionary bias' and staunchly traditionalist anthropologist interests.[58] This combination of scientific theory and professional preference led to extraordinary contradictions. For example, social Darwinism shaped Spencer's identification of Aborigines as a monolithic 'Stone-Age' race determined by a set of static social structures and beliefs. He attributed Aboriginal cultural change to external pressure rather than internal dynamism, and believed this incapacity to adapt would result in Aboriginal extinction. His professional interest, however, led to his valorisation of 'pristine' Aboriginality and his dismissal of voluntary Aboriginal adoption of new influences as racial 'degeneration'.[59] Spencer held the doctrines of progress and utilitarianism to be a totally European preserve.

Spencer's ideas had a powerful impact on tourism image-makers. His public lectures were celebrated Melbourne entertainments and his *Arunta: A study of a Stone Age People* was recommended reading for travelling men of science during the heyday of scientific field research.[60] These ideas however did not go unchallenged. Professor JW Gregory argued that these 'old' ideas 'must be abandoned' and identified Aborigines as a race in flux and a 'specialised adaptation' to challenging desert conditions.[61] Gregory's respect for a pre-modern society's capacity to sustain itself in a harsh environment, however, held no appeal for Holmes. He sought to educate tourists to appreciate the government's ideal of modern science remaking Central Australia into a wealth-producing region suitable for Anglo-Australian colonisation and civilisation. He mobilised Spencer's ideas to produce an 'anthropological' tourist gaze that presented desert Aborigines as Australia's equivalent to European 'Stone-Age' cavemen. Whilst he occasionally slipped into contradiction, Holmes predominantly used images of Jimmy to present a viewpoint contrary to romantic naturalism and primitivism.

Walkabout articles identified Aborigines as the 'lowest' and earliest form of mankind that was closer to brutes than human beings.[62] Articles by Philip Crosbie Morrison[63] and William Charnley[64] included echoes of maritime explorer William Dampier[65] and anthropologists Spencer and Gillen.[66] They drew links between desert Aborigines and European 'Stone-Age' men of 200,000 years ago,[67] and itemised their incapacities from a modern Eurocentric perspective. Both claimed 'Stone-Age' Aborigines did not work metals like Europeans, nor wear clothes, build homes, worship, display inventiveness or cultivate the soil.[68] Crosbie Morrison also disparaged Aboriginal cultural practices — including initiation rites to manhood like scarification and teeth knocking — as savage, blood-curdling self-mutilations.[69] Holmes used three uncaptioned photographs of Jimmy to illustrate these articles. In so doing, he implied Jimmy was a living remnant of a barbaric 'Stone-Age' race that lacked any capacity to adapt to modern conditions.

Holmes also drew on Spencer's evolutionary thinking to create a sense of urgency and stimulate tourist demand. He stressed that isolated, 'full-blooded' Aborigines were in limited supply and urged tourists to travel to see them before they disappeared.[70] This was not, however, a new practice. The Santa Fe railway had made similar claims to entice tourists to the American west to view Native Americans.[71] Further, both the American railway and Holmes shared a common problem. Whilst their publications romanticised development, both had vested interests in the preservation of 'primitive' peoples and their traditions because they were valuable tourism 'products'. This was one of the many contradictions of Holmes' position. Another was the imperative to simultaneously promote the official ideal of assimilation and meet tourists' preferences for 'primitive' culture. Holmes wove his way through these complexities by mobilising Spencer's claim that Australian Aborigines were the world's last surviving remnants of a Stone-Age race to promote tribal Aboriginality as a distinctively Australian tourist attraction with a limited product lifecycle. This 'anthropological' tourist gaze encouraged tourists to divide Aboriginal people into two polarised groups: 'authentic' Aborigines who were 'full-blooded', 'primitive', 'tribal' men like

Jimmy;[72] and their 'inauthentic' counterparts who were so-called 'detribalised', 'mixed-blooded' and 'semi-civilised' 'degenerates'.

All of these travel writers used images of Jimmy over an extended period to glorify British exploration, colonial development and Aboriginal 'reconstruction', as well as to either romanticise or disparage Indigenous men. As a general rule they promoted belief in Aboriginal alterity. This solidified social barriers by dividing settlers and Aborigines into two imaginary polarised worlds: modernity and primitivity. Three overlapping tourist gazes used images of him to typecast or symbolise 'tribal' Aboriginal men as being either murderous adversaries of explorers; unreliable and incapable workers who were of no value to a pioneering nation; majestic vanishing hunters who were part of wild nature; or barbaric remnants of an archaic culture who posed a problem to a modern civilised nation. All of these characterisations were part of a pre-existing set of images of Indigenous people that had circulated throughout European colonies from the eighteenth century[73] and within all levels of Australian society from the earliest days of colonisation.[74] Whilst travel writers did not create them, it is clear they evoked and reinvigorated a range of colonial discourses and stereotypes to promote tourism to the inland.

Gwoja Tjungurrayi: the man behind the image

Such were the stories of Jimmy as told by tourism image-makers. We might well ask, however, how do these relate to the life lived by the man whose images were captured by Holmes and Dunstan. This question is not easily answered. Vivien Johnson's work with Jimmy's — or more correctly Gwoja Tjungurrayi's — adoptive son, the well-known Western Desert artist Clifford Possum Tjapaltjarri, provides a helpful starting point.[75] The following biographical sketch of Tjungurrayi's life has been compiled from many tiny morsels of information gleaned from a broad range of published, archival and oral sources.

Displacement and massacre

Tjungurrayi was born into a Warlpiri-Anmatyerre descent group a decade before pastoralists began to 'lease' vast runs of his ancestral country, take possession of scarce water supplies, and develop herds that depleted native vegetation and drove away native game. The timing and location of Tjungurrayi's birth remain unclear.[76] Most probably he was born during the 1890s at or near a large rockhole soakage known as Ngarlu to Anmatyerre, or Red Hill to English speakers.[77] Even though this was in Anmatyerre country, Tjungurrayi had a Warlpiri skin name and strong affiliations with Warlpiri country. He therefore had crossover connections with Warlpiri and Anmatyerre clans and country.[78]

His birthplace lies at the heart of Tjungurrayi's ancestral estate, approximately 200 kilometres north-west of Alice Springs. The latter ranges from Central Mount

Wedge in the south, through Napperby to Coniston in the north-east, and north-west through Mount Denison to just above Yuendumu (Fig 5.14).[79] This inheritance was based on a Tjungurrayi/Tjapaltjarri patrilineal system that incorporated Tjungurrayi into a richly interwoven system of custodianship. This spiritual, economic and social system bestowed upon him a range of custodial rights and ritual obligations with 28 sites in the region, each of which was associated with historical or mythological events and travels of the Tjukurrpa, or 'Dreaming'.[80]

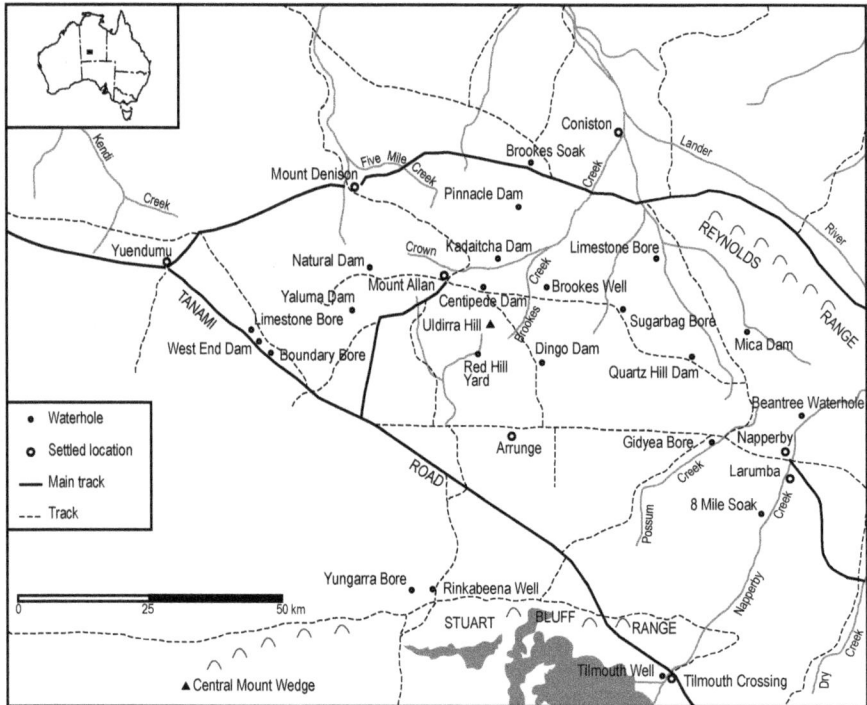

Figure 5.14: Tjungurrayi's Ancestral Estate.

Based on Carto Tech Services, Clifford Possum Tjapaltjarri's Estate, Art Gallery of South Australia, and Vivien Johnson (2003: 21-2), redrawn by G.Hunt.

The usual form of address in Western Desert society is by skin name, or one of eight kinship subsection names.[81] Gwoja's skin name of 'Tjungurrayi' was determined by the names of his parents. It in turn determined the skin(s) he should marry and those of his children. His given name of 'Gwoja' was an old orthography and an Arrernte word for 'water'.[82] This was possibly because Tjungurrayi's personal 'totem'[83] was the water spirit and his principal sacred site was Watulpunya, a water Tjukurrpa site near Central Mount Wedge.

During the late nineteenth century, however, pastoralists increasingly encroached upon, and pastoral leases began to re-territorialise Tjungurrayi's ancestral country (Fig 5.15). This fuelled animosities between the two groups of people. The 1920s drought intensified competition between cattle, pastoralists and Anmatyerre for precious supplies of water and food. This sometimes led to violent relationships. Accounts differ about the murder of the white dingo trapper Frederick Brooks at Brooks' Soak or Yurrkuru in 1928 by a local Aboriginal man known as 'Bull frog'. It is now generally accepted that a punitive expedition comprising many local pastoralists,[84] authorised by the local government resident[85] and led by Mounted Constable Murray, resulted in the massacre of many Aboriginal men, women and children near Coniston. This was one of many skirmishes when Warlpiri-Anmatyerre were shot while resisting arrest[86] and scenes of death now called 'the killing times'.[87] All this contributed to the decimation and migration of Anmatyerre-Warlpiri groups.[88]

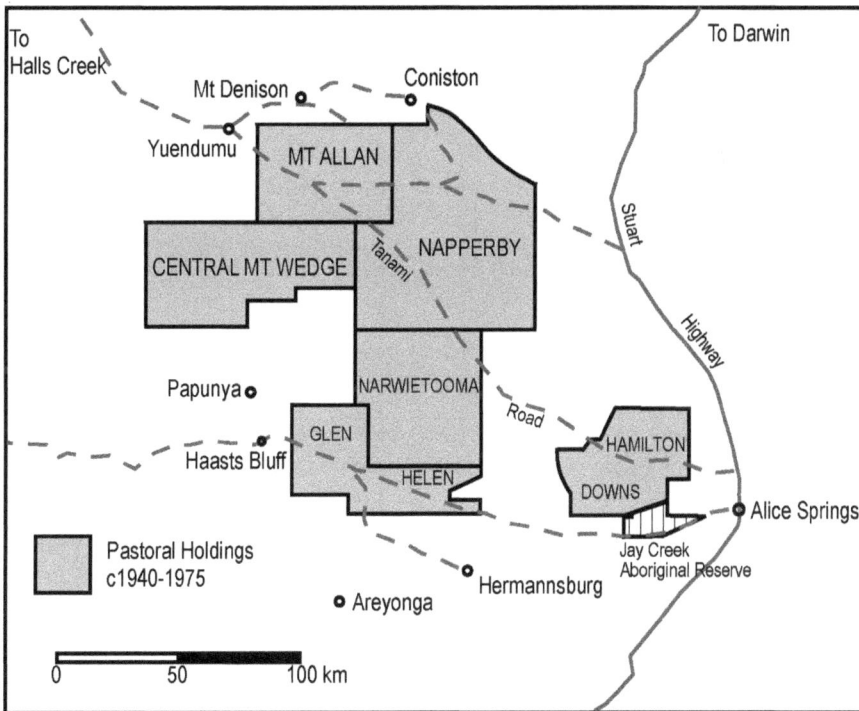

Figure 5.15: Pastoral Holdings re-territorialise Ancestral Country.

Based on Carto Tech Services, Clifford Possum Tjapaltjarri's Estate, Art Gallery of South Australia, and Vivien Johnson (2003: 36), redrawn by G.Hunt.

Explanations also differ for Tjungurrayi's experiences during the 'killing times'. One claimed his father was taken prisoner by Constable Murray, escaped and fled with his family to the Arltunga region east of Alice Springs.[89] Another described Tjungurrayi 'worm[ing] his way out from among the dead and dying' at Yurrkuru to 'narrowly escape death from a hail of rifle fire poured at him by whites'.[90] Clifford Possum's oral account of his father's capture and evasion records that a mounted policeman arrested and chained him up before 'carry him 'round to show'm every soakage. They leave him ... tied up on a tree, big chain ... they put leg chain too ... Then everybody go out and shoot all the people ... They come back and see him — nothing! This chain he broke'm with a big rock and he take off ... to mine ...'.[91] We know from official inquiries that Tjungurrayi was not the perpetrator of the killing. It is possible that this oral account describes Tjungurrayi being transferred to Alice Springs for questioning. It documents that Tjungurrayi escaped the killings, fled to the Arltunga region and avoided capture.[92] Tjungurrayi was therefore a survivor of a traumatic 'killing time' that decimated Anmatyerre-Warlpiri clans and a man violently displaced from his ancestral country.

Tjungurrayi's real encounters with 'trail blazers' were sharply different to those attributed to him by travel writers. *Walkabout's* representation of him as a marauding foe was totally misrepresentative of his lived experience as a violated, seemingly non-offensive, dispossessed Warlpiri-Anmatyerre man.

Survival and adjustment

An Alice Springs newspaperman, Alan Wauchope, marvelled at Tjungurrayi's ability to 'bury' this traumatic experience 'deeply within himself', and work 'amicably and well for whites'.[93] Tjungurrayi's behaviour may suggest he decided selective cooperation rather than retaliation would help to ensure his survival and ongoing presence in Warlpiri-Anmatyerre lands. Fragmentary comments reveal Tjungurrayi 'proved himself' as a good worker in three fledgling industries between the 1920s and 1950s.

It is not apparent if Holmes knew Tjungurrayi was a miner when they met. Tjungurrayi worked for several years in the Arltunga goldfields and the eastern Harts Range mica mines,[94] earning a reputation as a hard worker and 'good miner'.[95]

After this period of asylum in distant Alyawerre country, Tjungurrayi spent most of his life working for pastoralists within or near his ancestral country, including at Napperby,[96] Hamilton Downs[97] and Mount Wedge stations.[98] During the mid-1930s, Tjungurrayi settled on Napperby station,[99] joined an extended family group, and met and married Long Rose Nangala in the late 1930s. His wife was a widowed Warlpiri woman, a mother of three children and an adoptive mother to two more who were orphaned during the 'killing times'.[100] Through his marriage, Tjungurrayi became the adoptive father of four sons and one daughter ranging from three to ten years old.

He then worked a hard and dangerous life as a stockman and station hand for twenty years, mustering, branding and driving cattle, sinking bores and helping pastoralists develop their cattle leases into vast empires. Aboriginal men like Tjungurrayi played an essential role in the development of the Central Australian cattle industry. They were a cheap source of labour, being paid primarily 'in kind' or with essential goods that were necessary for their survival rather than cash wages.[101] For long hours of hard toil he received a yearly issue of cotton working clothes, a weekly ration of flour, tea and sugar and occasional pieces of butchered bullock.

The pattern of Tjungurrayi's life as a working family man during the cattle season, and a traditional custodian who fulfilled his ritual obligations during the off-season, came to an abrupt halt shortly after his marriage. His family was involuntarily 'centralised' into a new government reserve at Jay Creek in Northern Arrernte country, after a change to the system of governance for Aboriginal people. Tjungurrayi's son Clifford Possum likened this enforced upheaval of people from every station and soakage to the 'mustering' of cattle and 'imprisonment' by VC Hall, the patrol officer with 'Native Welfare'.[102] Tjungurrayi had to readjust once more to dramatically changed conditions to provide for his family and maintain connections to Warlpiri-Anmatyerre country.

He took advantage of new opportunities at Jay Creek, by adapting his traditional skills and knowledge to the needs of the tourism industry, and engaging in the cash economy. Scientists and tourists passed through Jay Creek en route to Hermannsburg mission and its resident pastor, FW Albrecht, encouraged Aborigines to make artefacts for sale to tourists.[103] This included a range of plaques, coat hangers and carvings. Albrecht also hired camels and supplied Aboriginal camelmen as guides.[104] Tjungurrayi carved and sold wooden artefacts to tourists.[105]

Clifford Possum has recorded that his father created a niche for himself as a guide for 'Aboriginal enthusiasts' even before the family moved to Jay Creek. He remembered people like TGH Strehlow[106] asking his father to guide him after hearing of his 'encyclopedic knowledge' of his 'Dreaming' country. He described his father 'working as a show'm-round-countries', being asked to explain 'what this one [Dreaming] mean?', and 'show'm round every … place' including Mt Wedge so people could 'take picture'.[107]

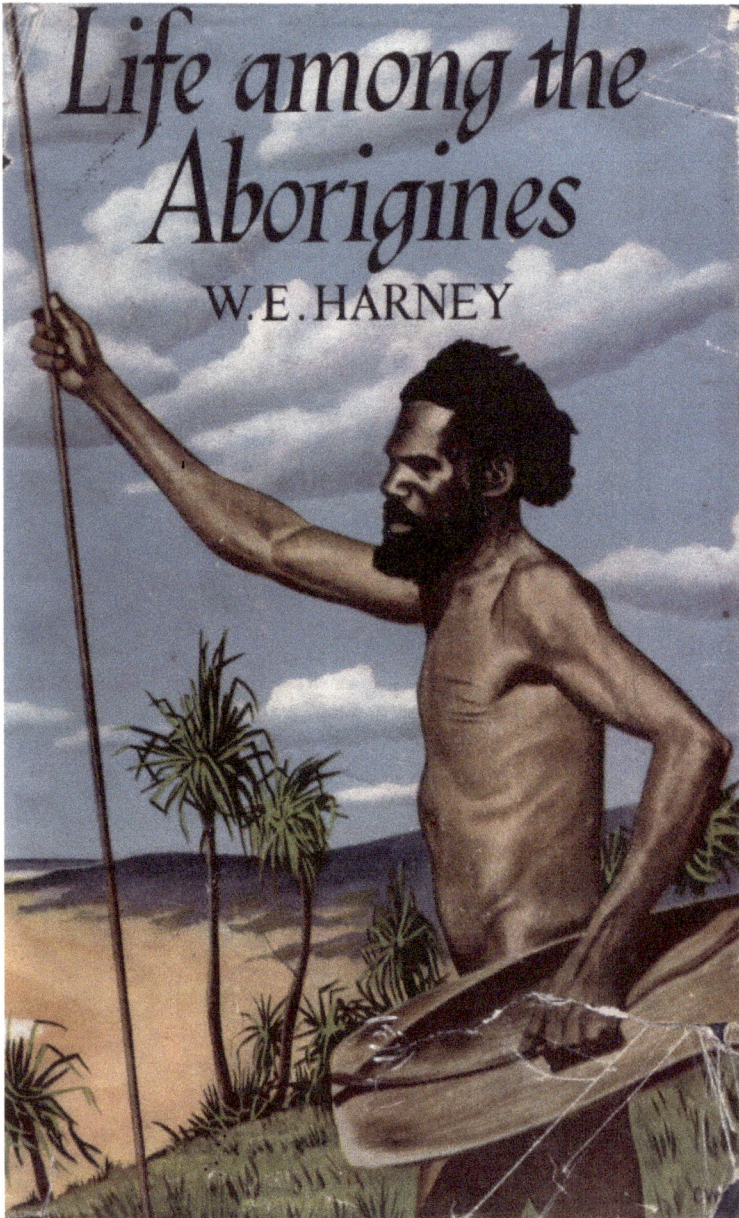

Figure 5.16: 'A mark of respect'.

Harney 1957, cover.

References in Strehlow's diary[108] and Albrecht's biography[109] suggest Tjungurrayi may have accompanied them through Warlpiri, Anmatyerre and Alyawerre country during the 1930s. Unfortunately Albrecht did not name the men who accompanied him to Central Mount Wedge in 1936, but historian Dick Kimber suggests it may have been Tjungurrayi who guided him.[110] We know from diaries that Tjungurrayi was a regular visitor at Strehlow's field camp near Arltunga in 1935. It is probable Tjungurrayi assisted Strehlow during the period when he witnessed many 'totemic acts' and 'made himself' professionally.[111]

A range of leading scholars and writers sought out Tjungurrayi during the next two decades to gain access to his 'unsurpassed' knowledge of Warlpiri-Anmatyerre country.[112] This included Charles Mountford and Bill Harney. Both these men featured images of Tjungurrayi on the covers of their publications as a mark of their respect and gratitude for his guidance and generosity in sharing his ancestral knowledge (Fig 5.16).[113] Mountford has identified the men who guided him as 'possess[ing] great dignity', 'proven integrity' and 'profound philosophical knowledge'.[114]

Transmission of knowledge to the next generation

Working within the pastoralist and tourism industries enabled Tjungurrayi to fulfil a personal compulsion. He was one of the few living keepers of 'totemic' sites and caretakers for the 'Dead-fella Dreaming' upon whom the responsibility to pass on knowledge to future generations weighed heavily. His life was largely dominated by the drive to pass on the Law in its perfect form.[115]

After the 'absorption' policy was adopted in 1937 and whilst assimilative institutions were discrediting Aboriginal practices, knowledge and authority, Tjungurrayi sought to transmit ancestral knowledge to the next generation. Johnson acknowledges the crucial role Tjungurrayi played in the education of his sons in 'totemic landscapes' and 'Dreamings'. She describes Tjungurrayi telling stories to his sons around the evening campfire about his daily travels with anthropologists and recounting the names and 'Dreamings' associated with his 'totemic landscape'. Johnson explains that his job as a 'show'm round countries' enabled him to pass on his knowledge of country and Law to his sons, and demonstrate to them how they could earn respect from settler society for competence in their own culture.[116] This had significant implications for the revival of desert culture after three of Tjungurrayi's sons became leading figures in the Western Desert art movement which defied assimilative forces and adapted the visual language of Warlpiri-Anmatyerre culture to new expressive forms (Fig 5.17).[117]

Tjungurrayi's real response to colonial development was dramatically different to that portrayed by travel writers. Stories in *Walkabout* identifying him as a dysfunctional inhibiter of development were grossly misrepresentative of his lived experience. Tjungurrayi repeatedly adapted to changed circumstances. He broke down cultural barriers by firstly developing a reputation as a hard and effective worker in three industries, and secondly building respectful working relations with non-Indigenous knowledge-makers to promote a more realistic understanding of Aboriginality.

Unwanted celebrity?

Whilst Tjungurrayi lived his complex life, Holmes continued his unrestricted and uninformed use of his photographs. This situation changed abruptly in the early 1950s however, after Holmes was instrumental in having one of his portraits mass-produced on a stamp and Tjungurrayi was inadvertently catapulted into an international symbol of Australian Aboriginality.

Figure 5.17: Clifford Possum Tjapaltjarri with daughters, Gabriella and Michelle (left to right).

Photograph: Peter Los 1989, (reproduced with permission from Los and Johnson 2003: 143).

On 14 August 1950, the postal authorities released two 'definitive' Australian stamps featuring a stylised image of Tjungurrayi. They were in circulation for 16 years until 1966. This resulted in the sale and worldwide dissemination of 99 million portraits of Tjungurrayi. Newspaperman Alan Wauchope marvelled at the response to the stamps by international philatelists.[118] For example, Malcolm MacGregor[119] was determined to 'hunt' down and gain an autographed stamp from the unnamed man whose head adorned the latest addition to his vast stamp collection. He enlisted Holmes in his search.

Tjungurrayi, however, had other ideas. Thus began a four-year stamp saga in *Walkabout* during which Tjungurrayi's name and personal circumstances were first revealed to tourists.

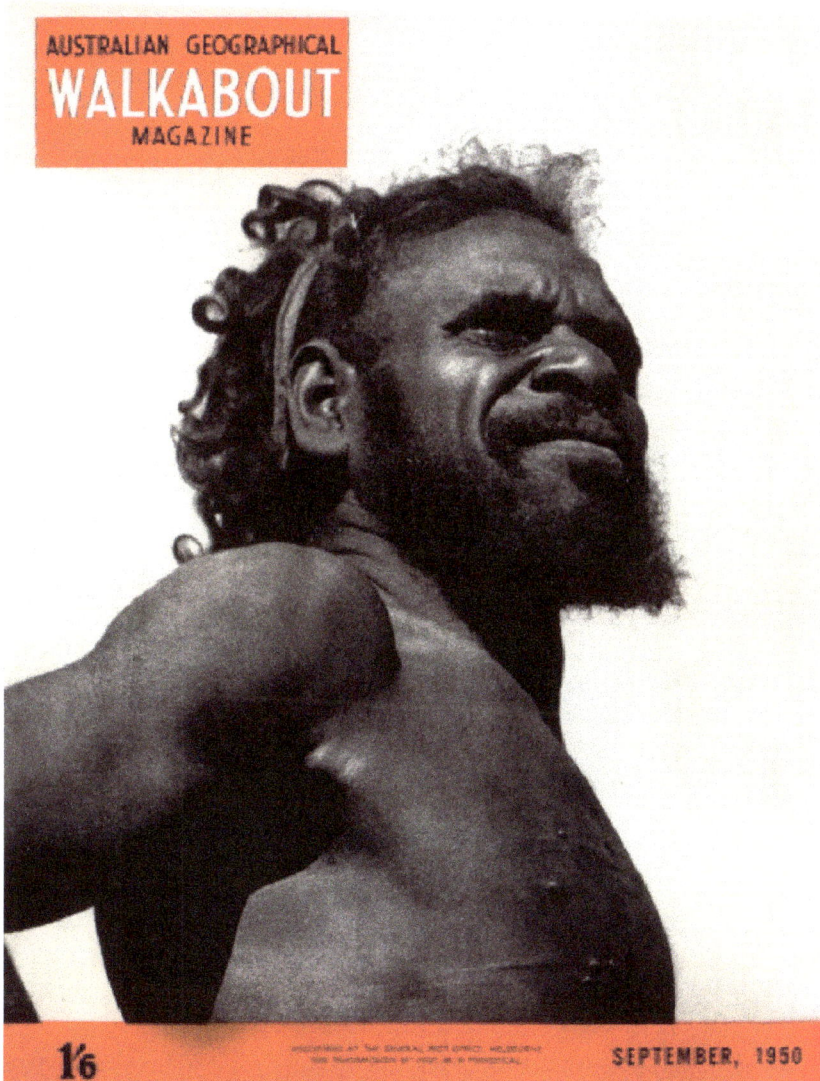

Figure 5.18: 'The most publicised [A]boriginal in Australia'.

Walkabout, September 1950, cover and p. 9.

One month after the stamp release, Holmes re-ran Tjungurrayi's photograph on the cover (Fig 5.18) and advised tourists he was trying to locate Jimmy and send him a gift to commemorate his appearance on a stamp. Holmes also outlined the details of their first and only meeting, recounted his first impressions of the statuesque Aboriginal man, provided a biographical sketch and attributed a personalised identity to Jimmy. With lasting echoes of Pickering, Holmes described 'Jimmy' as a 'fine...specimen of [A]boriginal manhood ... [t]all and lithe, with a particularly well-developed torso, broad forehead, strong features and the superb carriage of the unspoiled primitive native'.[120] The article identified him as a 'member of the Wailbri [sic] tribe' with a 'group name of Djungarai' [sic] (Tjungurrayi), and an anglicised name of 'One Pound Jimmy'. Holmes also referred to Jimmy's terrifying ordeal in the Coniston Massacre, typifying him as a living 'reminder of a black page in the history of native affairs' rather than a remnant of a 'vanishing race'. Given the governance orientation of this biography, it is probable Les Penhall, the local patrol officer responsible for the location of Jimmy, was the source of this information.

Holmes also asserted a form of intellectual ownership over Jimmy by advising readers ANTA was the copyright holder of his images. The issue of legal right became a burning one after Holmes and *Walkabout* subscribers discovered 'One Pound Jimmy' statues were being made, sold and displayed without ANTA's approval,[121] and publications failed to acknowledge ANTA's role in the discovery and promotion of 'its' Aboriginal celebrity.[122]

Holmes kept tourists updated on the status of the hunt for Jimmy and MacGregor's stamp collecting quest. A triumphant article finally announced 'One Pound Jimmy' had been 'located'. Its details must have surprised readers familiar with former representations of him. Holmes advised tourists that Jimmy was 'nowadays' a gardener on a cattle station, a husband and a father. He illustrated this article with a cropped version of a fresh photograph taken by Penhall of a much older Jimmy standing naked in a pose reminiscent of the one used to portray him as the classical native warrior (Fig 5.19).[123] An uncropped copy of this photograph has recently been found in the Smithsonian archives in Washington DC. It suggests Penhall may have asked Jimmy to strip to the waist for the photograph to assist tourist recognition and comparison with the stamp portrait (Fig 5.20). Despite the reference to Jimmy's work on a cattle station, it is clear Holmes reworked this photograph for publication, removing any evidence of Jimmy's clothing and engagement with contemporary pastoral life (Fig 5.19). Further, whilst Holmes used Jimmy's international celebrity as the basis for his observation that 'One Pound Jimmy' had finally 'emerged from the Stone-Age' into modernity, his cropping of the image accentuated his nudity and scarification — or 'primitive' qualities — and reinvigorated the eighteenth century conventions embodied in Dunstan's original images.

COMMONWEALTH 8½d. STAMP

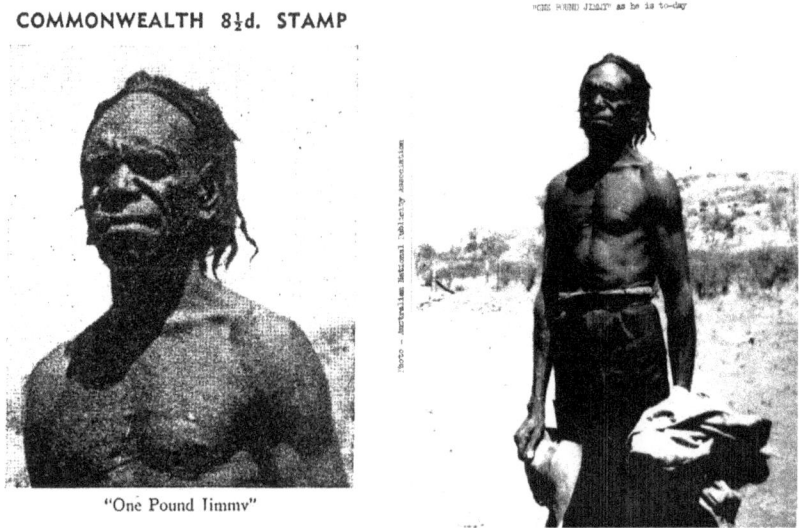

"One Pound Jimmy"

Figure 5.19: (L): Cropped image of 'One Pound Jimmy'.

Walkabout, December 1951.

Figure 5.20: (R): Uncropped photograph taken by Penhall and sent to MacGregor by Holmes.

Smithsonian Institution, 1951-4.

The themes of game hunting, specimen collection and conquest permeated an article by the stamp collector Malcolm MacGregor.[124] He identified himself as a 'hunter of big game' who collected signatures of living 'notables' holding 'positions of power and authority' and some 'unusual items'. The American philatelist explained his decision to include 'One Pound Jimmy' was due to his 'magnificent' physical appearance rather than his honourable deeds. MacGregor stressed the difficulty of his hunt, acknowledged Jimmy's attempts to avoid him and identified his quarry as a 'wary native' who had suspected there was 'trouble afoot', decided he 'wanted nothing of it' and 'gone bush'. Further, he applauded those who helped him 'secure' his autographed stamp, expressing admiration for Holmes' 'discovery' and Penhall's capture of Jimmy. Holmes illustrated this article with a photograph of MacGregor's prized new collectible: a thumb-printed set of 'One Pound Jimmy' stamps (Fig 5.21). This quest however, inadvertently set in chain a series of events that led to *Walkabout's* production of a new way of seeing Tjungurrayi and Aboriginality.

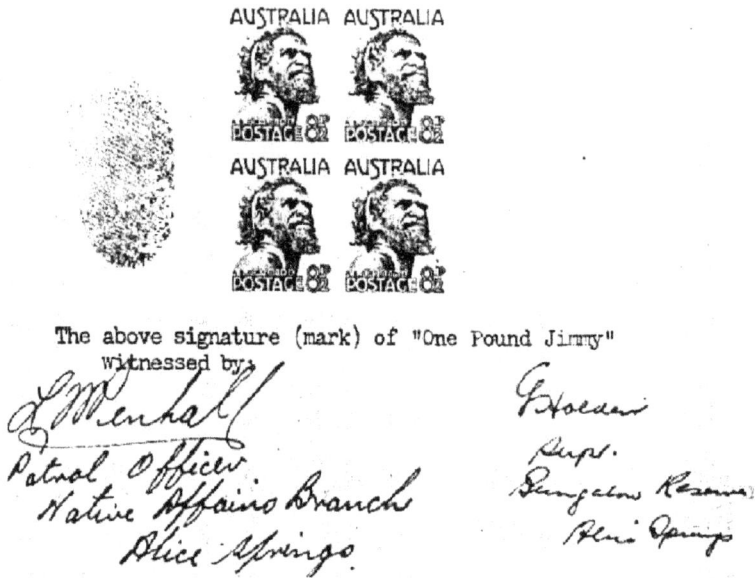

The above signature (mark) of "One Pound Jimmy"
witnessed by:

[handwritten signatures]

Thumb-print of "One Pound Jimmy" witnessed by officials of the Native Affairs Branch.

Figure 5.21: 'Latest addition to MacGregor's stamp collection'.

Walkabout, September 1950.

Holmes: discoverer or myth-maker?

The meeting

A contradiction unfolded during the stamp saga, which raises questions about Holmes' 'chance encounter' with Tjungurrayi. In September 1950 Holmes advised he had met Jimmy in 1935. After the stamps had created an international sensation and Jimmy became an icon of the quintessential 'authentic' Australian Aborigine, Holmes and MacGregor settled on a common meeting date of 1931. This was used in many local and international publications.[125] This modification may appear like an insignificant lapse of memory or slip of the pen. The reason, however, may lie elsewhere.

Strehlow's records provide a valuable clue. A footnote made by the linguist in Woritarinja's genealogy — also known as Jim Utjeba or 'Goggle-eye' — identifies him as Tjungurrayi's older companion in tourism photographs (Fig 5.22). Strehlow claims Dunstan took these photographs near his camp at Arltunga on 14 July 1935.[126] His diary records interaction between the man 'connected with ANTA', the 'official photographer' and Aboriginal men. It describes the arrival of a 'party' of 'tourists' in a Bond Tours' lorry and their 'demands' that Strehlow organise a photo session of 'natives posing at the Rock Holes' and a corroboree for the following day. Despite his indignation at being treated like the so-called 'cheap proprietor of a cheap monkey-show', Strehlow persuaded an older man named 'Jim' (probably Jim Utjeba) to organise the men to perform for the tourists and Dunstan's camera.[127] Many of these photographs now form part of the collection of the State Library of Victoria.[128]

Figure 5.22: Hale River men Tjeria and Woritarinja (left and right), TGH Strehlow (centre), Arltunga, 1935.

Strehlow Research Centre, Alice Springs 05572.

It appears Holmes preferred his readers to believe he encountered Jimmy under less contrived circumstances and revised the date to suggest Tjungurrayi was the 'Jimmy' he described in his *We Find Australia* of 1932. During his 1931 travels to gather stories and images for *Walkabout*, Holmes had preconceived ideas of 'authentic' Aboriginality and searched for living specimens of Pickering's 'wild' 'original' hunter and Spencer's 'Stone-Age' man. These ideas were tainted from the beginning and Holmes' use of Tjungurrayi's images perpetuated this flawed preconception. We may never know the truth about the meeting between Holmes and Jimmy. The contradictory explanations offered by Holmes and Strehlow raise important questions: why did Holmes permit 1931 to become the accepted date of their meeting when Dunstan started working for *Walkabout* in March 1935 and Bill Howieson[129] was the photographer who accompanied Holmes during the travels recorded in *We Find Australia*.[130]

The name

Writers have long meditated on the origin and meaning of Tjungurrayi's anglicised name. Holmes stated that Jimmy 'rejoiced' under the name 'One Pound Jimmy' when he captured his images.[131] Johnson suggests Tjungurrayi may have adopted this name in an attempt at anonymity, given that he was wanted by the police after his escape from custody following the Coniston massacre.[132] Holmes' claim is questionable. Tjungurrayi's biographical information appears to have been supplied to Holmes later, during the stamp saga by Les Penhall from Native Affairs. 'One Pound Jimmy' is the racy kind of language Holmes liked to use. I believe he would have used it in publications before 1950 had he known it.

Also questionable are the suggestions made by newspaper, biographical and obituary writers that this name was bestowed on Tjungurrayi because he asked for the standard rate of one pound sterling for odd jobs or single handicrafts. Given this was equivalent to a week's accommodation at Hermannsburg,[133] two months work as a stockman in the Napperby area,[134] or four weeks 'regulation wages' for companion/camel-man/guiding work for anthropologists,[135] it is unlikely Tjungurrayi would have asked for or been given one pound for a single job he performed or a single carving he sold.[136] For example, *The Sun Travel Book* confirms that two shillings was the 'standard price for boomerangs, womeras [sic], and pitchies' at Jay Creek.[137]

Amadio and Kimber offer another solution. They suggest this name was given to Tjungurrayi during the stamp saga.[138] This is also misleading because evidence records that this name was used much earlier. Clifford Possum states he addressed his father as 'One Pound Jim' from early childhood and Strehlow's diary identifies him by this anglicised name in September 1935.

There is another possibility. It is not clear if Tjungurrayi assisted Strehlow as a 'camelboy', 'informant' or guide during the periods he was not required elsewhere for mining or pastoral work. It is probable Tjungurrayi witnessed or heard about an incident that occurred at Strehlow's camp on 18 August 1935 when respected elders were held to ransom by Strehlow for their cultural knowledge. A diary entry describes Strehlow withholding 'speech stew' from hungry, elderly men for 24 hours during a drought because they would not give him songs when he wanted them. Even though Strehlow's Aboriginal camel-man 'broke down' and 'pleaded' for the hungry men, they remained unfed until Strehlow 'acquired' his 'sacred songs'.[139]

It is possible that this experience, like the Coniston massacre, provided Tjungurrayi with a hard lesson. Given that he had a record of overcoming adversity and turning negative events into positive outcomes, Tjungurrayi may have vowed never to let himself be exploited like this and placed an exceptionally high price on his time and capabilities when travelling scientists were arriving and his expertise was in demand. This may have been an attempt by Tjungurrayi to negotiate a degree of economic autonomy through the commodification of his culture, during which he could at least set the terms and price.

Collaboration and escape

During the stamp saga a new image-making regime was gaining prominence in *Walkabout*. This group of writers and photographers was united in a belief that relationships with Aboriginal people were a necessary component of more respectful and realistic representational practices.[140] They sought to convince tourists that Aboriginal people were not 'naked, howling savages' eking out a dull and brutal existence,[141] but a 'cultured and courageous people, living in harmony with their environment and with a spiritual and moral way of life that the Western world could well envy'.[142] The contributions of Bill Harney[143] and Ainslie Roberts[144] combined to discredit earlier representations of Tjungurrayi and promote a new understanding of him. They identified Tjungurrayi as an extraordinary man who was capable of leading a complicated life and juggling multiple identities. These included the celebrity 'commemorated on a stamp', a cattleman, a cultural intermediary, a Warlpiri-Anmatyerre lawman/custodian, and a committed family man. Harney incorporated Tjungurrayi's personal voice and standpoint into *Walkabout* for the first time, and Roberts presented him pictorially as he wished to be seen.

Both Bill Harney's *Life Among the Aborigines* and Charles Mountford's[145] journal — documenting an anthropological expedition undertaken with Roberts and guided by Tjungurrayi — record an awareness of Tjungurrayi's commitment to his cultural inheritance and desire to assert his lawman/custodian identity.[146] These men promoted the idea of human mutuality rather than racial alterity and Harney in particular, sought to reverse the former *Walkabout* focus on Aboriginal difference and inferiority. Two of his articles sought to show how Tjungurrayi was working with settler Australians to overcome shared concerns and advance common aims and interests.

Harney described his travels with 'Djugadi' [sic] (Tjungurrayi) near Central Mount Wedge in a writing style that was new to *Walkabout*. He told stories of cooperative cohabitation rather than the segregation of two discrete worlds and organised them into two major themes: the resolution of the common problem of accessing water resources, and the belief systems used by both groups to explain the origins, rituals and taboos associated with them. Harney gave equal measure to rationales used by desert 'blackfellows' and pastoralists: Tjungurrayi's explanation of rainbow serpents, culture heroes, rituals and visitation rites was interwoven with geographic explanations given by Bill Waudby, the station lessee. Harney demonstrated Tjungurrayi and Waudby were conversant with each other's logic, and explained both combined to form one chapter in the book of humanity dealing with the means to survive in arid conditions.

Both Harney and Roberts first hooked tourist attention by highlighting the fact that Tjungurrayi was the man known as 'the head on the stamp'. It is also possible these references to the stamp saga were an editorial flourish by Holmes himself.[147]

Harney outlined how Warlpiri men, including Tjungurrayi, used 'traditional' knowledge of country to help Waudby 'open up' Central Mount Wedge for pastoralism. He recounted how they had eventually led Waudby to their sacred wells after acting 'dumb' for months with statements like 'nothing water longa this land', and had only revealed them after they were satisfied Waudby was a worthy recipient of the knowledge. Harney described Waudby and Warlpiri working together digging wells, sinking bores and erecting windmills to establish cattle runs and the homestead. He identified Tjungurrayi as Waudby's valued gardener who cared for the precious lawn and garden-beds in challenging desert conditions.

Harney highlighted Tjungurrayi's acumen in acting as an agent of understanding between two cultural groups. He described him resolving cross-cultural misunderstandings, grounding new relations on positive footings by making appropriate introductions, and translating English into Warlpiri and vice versa for people living on the station and travelling through it.

Both writers acknowledged Tjungurrayi's skills as a custodian of knowledge and teacher who could make sense of a 'place of misunderstanding'. Harney drew on Tjungurrayi's teachings to explain how desert men located native soaks, sank wells, maintained ritual relationships that bound them to their country, interpreted the sound of wind droning around Mount Wedge as the 'singing of a ritual chant of the Dreamtime' by the 'Earth Mother', and read landmarks as symbols of the ancestral creation figures. These included Kumalba (Emu Springs) as a 'dreaming place' that commemorated the 'legend of the Buk Buk owl', Mount Wedge as a 'symbol of the culture hero' 'Kurinya', and engraved circles on flat sandstones at Kumalba as symbols of women's breasts. Harney explained how Tjungurrayi taught him to imagine 'scenes of ochred black men grinding spears for hunting, chanting their [Kumalba] … song, and rubbing hands over the symbolic circles of the women's dreaming'. Further, he included the following English translation of a chant used by Warlpiri to teach young males about women's business: 'a woman's breast is like the Witaraga tree that grows on the hill'.[148] In so doing, Harney used Tjungurrayi's lore to educate tourists to see Aboriginal men as sensual rather than brutish beings and Warlpiri practices as a '[f]ar cry from the old days of cave-man getting his girl with a knotted club'.[149]

Harney identified Tjungurrayi as a senior lawman committed to the continuity of tribal law and introduced tourists to the Warlpiri philosophy of custodianship. He recalled Tjungurrayi's statement that 'true ritual [was] the will to live' and explained his stories set out how 'desert blackmen' should use the things 'nature or tribal heroes' placed on ancestral lands for them in a disciplined and orderly fashion that was both life sustaining and respectful of all living things. Harney identified contemporary Warlpiri station life as a continuation of traditional ways, in that it sought to both maintain ancestral culture and devise survival strategies to cope with changed circumstances. Further, Harney relayed the despair experienced by Tjungurrayi when new conditions prevented him from living according to 'true tribal law', and sacred sites were desacralised by cattle or reduced to 'just nothing'.[150] It is possible the latter reference was Tjungurrayi's response to a trend amongst young Warlpiri men to reject the mores of desertmen, resist tribal authority and adopt modern cowboy culture.

Finally, writers presented Tjungurrayi as a family man with cross-cultural family networks. Harney described the 'chanting of contented natives' coming from the 'Aboriginal camp at night'. This was unusual given Barry Hill's observation that 'many station owners' had, by this time, 'banned the old ceremonies'.[151] Roberts however introduced a further note of loss and despair. He described Tjungurrayi as a grieving father seeking solace from his extended Warlpiri-Anmatyerre family in the desert for sorry business after his daughter Joycee died of pneumonia.[152] This occurred after Harney recorded Waudby's baby son 'Jim' being taught the bush lore of desert people. References to Tjungurrayi's constant proximity to the homestead garden and Waudby's choice of his son's name, suggest that Tjungurrayi may have been the boy's namesake and teacher, plus a member of his employer's extended family network.

While Harney's articles reflect a shift in *Walkabout's* image-making practices, it is evident there were still constraints on what writers could say. A comparison of Harney's accounts of Tjungurrayi published in *Walkabout* and elsewhere suggest that either Holmes or Harney deemed some issues were unprintable in the former. This includes Harney's discussion of Indigenous elders' selective acceptance and rejection of attempts to assimilate them. For example his London published *Life Among the Aborigines* explained that attempts by Native Affairs to re-settle Warlpiri in modern houses were met with Warlpiri preferences for 'grass-thatched shelters among the bushes'. It also recounted struggles between colonial missionaries and Pintupi over the education of their children. Harney described how Pintupi elders were thwarting missionary attempts to teach their children 'hackneyed' Arrernte on mission stations by ensuring they learned Pintupi from family networks and English in government rather than mission schools. Harney told tourists that elders had decided this would best ensure their children gained an understanding of the colonising culture.[153] In his commercially published book — rather than in government-supported tourism literature — Harney felt free to describe Tjungurrayi translating Pintupi songs sung by desertmen as they travelled from Areyonga mission to the Yuendumu government settlement via Mount Wedge station. Tjungurrayi relayed the happiness both he and Pintupi experienced in the knowledge that these chants were reinvigorating Pintupi language and their cultural connections to ancestral homelands.

"ONE POUND" JIMMY AND "OLD BILLY"

Figure 5.23: 'One Pound' Jimmy and 'Old Billy'.

Walkabout May 1958. Reproduced with permission of the artist's son, Rhys Roberts.

After Holmes retired in 1957, *Walkabout* published a letter and photograph submitted by Roberts.[154] His contribution departed from the conventions embodied in the images captured by Dunstan and mobilised by Holmes to reinvigorate old ideas of Aboriginality. This contested the former presentation of Tjungurrayi as a 'Stone-Age' man (Fig 5.23). Gone were the classical warrior-hunter pose, the faraway look and the suggestion of Aboriginal extinction, the boomerang, the spear and the woomera, the pristine natural environment and the nakedness. Roberts' photograph presented him as a Warlpiri cattleman in a cowboy shirt, gazing intently at the camera. He was laughing energetically in the presence of a friend. His mouth was wide open revealing a gap between his front teeth, which was possibly the outcome of a tooth removal ritual and a marker of his passage to manhood. In sending this photograph to *Walkabout*, Roberts sought to re-educate tourists about Tjungurrayi's complex identity. He presented him as an aging black man who had adapted to station life, maintained his connections to country and family networks, and advanced through levels of Warlpiri manhood.

Conclusion

There is still much to learn about the life of Tjungurrayi. This includes his possible participation in three cultural movements. Firstly, there is evidence to suggest he may have played a role in an Aboriginal resistance movement to revive native law that began in the Kimberleys and arrived in Central Australia near Mount Wedge whilst Jimmy worked there.[155] Secondly, we know from Clifford Possum's life stories that Tjungurrayi's family knew Albert Namatjira at Jay Creek and was familiar with the European style of landscape painting this Arrernte artist had learnt from Rex Battarbee. Jimmy's influence on his artist sons — three of whom participated in an alternative Indigenous arts movement at Papunya — is yet to be considered. After all, Mountford and Roberts encouraged Tjungurrayi to sketch on paper his 'totemic landscapes' from an aerial viewpoint. This provided Tjungurrayi with a means other than travelling and guiding to maintain, diffuse and promote respect for Western Desert cultural knowledge. Finally, Tjungurrayi or 'One Pound Jimmy' was a harbinger of Aboriginal economic independence through participation in Aboriginal cultural tourism. These concerns, however, are beyond the scope of this enquiry and beckon further work.

Holmes mobilised travel writers to guide the choices of tourists and educate them in particular ways of seeing Aboriginality, cross-cultural contact, and connections to land. Their articles used images of Tjungurrayi to support their claims. These narratives did not reflect Tjungurrayi's lived reality or personal qualities until the 1950s. They constricted understandings of Aboriginality to a narrow European idea of 'primitive' man. Holmes used these images to present desert men as 'Stone Age people' doomed to extinction. This legitimated dispossession and soothed troubled consciences. Image-making was a powerful form of self-justification for colonisation.

Tourism image-makers created three overlapping tourist gazes. Each shaped tourism rituals. They directed tourists to seek out 'Stone-Age' men, capture their likeness in photographs and display them upon their return home. This created a vicious circle. Aboriginal men became entrapped by a stereotype when tourists asked them to pose, take off their clothes, and act like a 'Stone-Age' man just like 'One Pound Jimmy'.

Despite this institutional power, Jimmy managed to challenge this myth and escape from its confines by developing relationships with a new regime of image-makers. The combined efforts of Harney, Roberts, Mountford and Tjungurrayi destabilised cultural barriers. They disproved the idea of 'two polarised worlds', promoted human mutuality rather than racial alterity, produced counter-images that fostered respect for desert culture and tribal law, and created a complex identity for Tjungurrayi.

Tjungurrayi moved from a disempowered to an empowered position. He was able to influence how he was presented to mostly Anglo-Australian tourists and some Aboriginal people. Holmes shifted from having unrestricted use of his photographs to being constrained by counter-images produced by Tjungurrayi in collaboration with others. Shortly after Tjungurrayi's passing on 28 March 1965, Roberts reworked his photograph into a painting for the cover of *The Dreamtime Book* (Fig 5.24).[156] This was possibly a response to the *Walkabout* cover. It commemorated the life of Tjungurrayi and asserted the ongoing presence of his spirit force in Warlpiri-Anmatyerre country. It shows him as a water spirit calling water to the earth to give life and renewal to a parched country, a thirsty people and all living things. This is a far cry from Holmes' presentation of him as a passive 'Stone-Age' man who willingly accepted his own extinction and dispossession.

Figure 5.24: 'Mamaragan, the Thunder-man'.

The Dreamtime Book, cover, 1973 [detail]. Reproduced with permission from the artist's son, Rhys Roberts.

The relationship between Tjungurrayi and Holmes provides many insights. The young tourism executive brought to his work a desire to present stories about Anglo-Australian pioneers shaping the destiny of a new white nation and a set of misconceptions about Aboriginal people. These revealed more about the aims and fears of his colonising culture than the people he claimed to represent. They blinded Holmes to the individual circumstances and lived experiences of men like Tjungurrayi. This is not a purely theoretical matter because images educate tourists how to see and relate to others. Images create effects. In this instance, they reinforced negative stereotypes of Aboriginal men and fostered a belief in British superiority/Indigenous inferiority when tourists were first being encouraged to travel to the inland. This limited tourists' capacity to imagine how to relate to Aboriginal people while they were there.

Tourism is a powerful agent of social change and identity construction. Whilst the extent to which travel images determine tourist attitudes and behaviour is a topic of much debate, it is generally accepted images do exercise intellectual force. Tourism image-makers hold positions of power in contemporary society. This story is one from which we can draw lessons and inspiration. It reveals the dangers associated with the indiscriminate combination of ideas and photographs drawn from tourism image-banks. It also shows how cross-cultural collaboration produced images to foster new ways of seeing that incorporated Tjungurrayi's lived experiences, preferred identities, alternative rationale and contribution to the history of Central Australian cohabitation.

Figure 5.25: Roy Dunstan, photographer as he preferred to be seen.

Smithsonian Institution, 1951-4 [detail].

Figure 5.26: Charles H Holmes as he wanted to be identified.

Smithsonian Institution 1951-4.

Figure 5.27: Woritarinja and Tjungurrayi as never portrayed by Holmes.

[detail, cropped to respect cultural markings of the men], Roy Dunstan, 1936-1938, 'Two Old Aboriginal Hunters with Weapons', Australian Aborigines at the Devil's Marbles area north of Alice Springs, Northern Territory, Charles Weetman collection, State Library of Victoria, H92.342/215, <http://www.slv.vic.gov.au/pictoria/b/2/6/doc/b26630.shtml>

A postscript

The legacy of the relationship between Holmes and Tjungurrayi lives on. Ever since Holmes first published Tjungurrayi's portrait in *Walkabout*, official institutions have adopted it for their own instrumental and transformative purposes. For example, the Aborigines Welfare Board (NSW) used a stylised version of it on the masthead of their monthly magazine, *Dawn* (Fig 5.28).[157] This was published for an Aboriginal readership as part of the Commonwealth government's policy of Aboriginal 'uplift', assimilation and 'progress'. This began the process of using Tjungurrayi's image to encourage Aboriginal people to give up their 'old' ways and embrace 'new' 'tasks and responsibilities' within Anglo-Australian society. It also marked the beginning of the reception and re-appropriation of his image by Aboriginal people for new effects. For example, the Australian Institute of Aboriginal and Torres Strait Islander Studies has recently digitalised and re-published *Dawn* in an electronic format on DVD.[158] This reinterprets the practices of the 'welfare' regime as 'patronising', 'paternalistic' and 'authoritarian'. It also seeks to provide Aboriginal people with a valuable resource to re-trace their family histories and promote pride in

Aboriginal survival and identity. The progeny of Charles Holmes and Gwoja Tjungurrayi continues to shape race relations in unexpected forms.

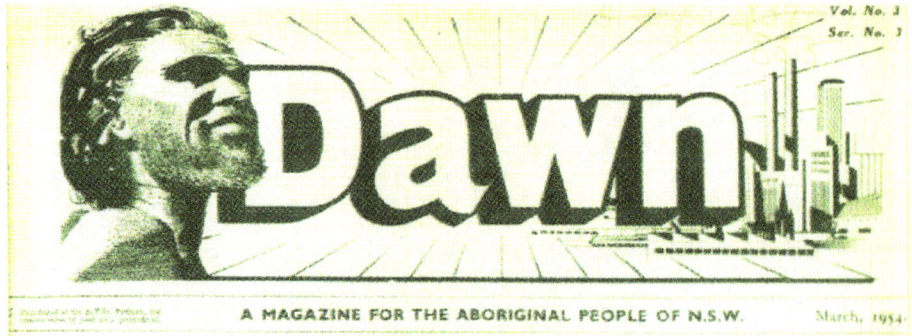

Figure 5.28: Tjungurrayi on *Dawn's* masthead, *Dawn* magazine cover, 1952 and *Dawn* digitised DVD cover, 2004.

Australian Institute for Aboriginal and Torres Strait Islander Studies.

References

Aboriginal Australia Arts and Culture Centre 2003, *Brochure: Aboriginal Desert Discovery Tours: Experience the Land & Experience Our Culture*, Alice Springs.

Agate, Alfred 1839, Artist, 'Bamboo [sic] Kain of the Newcastle Tribe', Navy Art Gallery Exhibit: 'The Alfred Agate Collection: The United States Exploring Expedition 1838-1842', Ref 98-89-GJ, Department of the Navy, Naval Historical Center, Washington DC, <http://www.history.navy.mil/ac/exploration/wilkes/wilkes1.html>, accessed 8 February 2004.

Amadio, Nadine and Kimber, Richard 1988, *Wildbird Dreaming: Aboriginal Art from the Central Deserts of Australia*, Greenhouse, Melbourne.

Anonymous 1937, 'Cameraman's Walkabout', *Walkabout*, February: 55.

Anonymous 1947, 'Albert Namatjira: Alice Springs Exhibition', *Centralian Advocate*, 20 September: 7, Alice Springs Library.

Anonymous 1965a, 'Obituary', *Northern Territory News,* 28 April: 2, Northern Territory Library, Darwin.

Anonymous 1965b, 'One Pound Jimmy is Dead', *Centralian Advocate*, 29 April: 1, Alice Springs Library.

Ansett Travel Services 1949, 'Go "Walkabout" Anywhere with Ansett Travel Service', *Walkabout*, August: 45.

Anthony, Thalia 2004, 'Labour Relations on Northern Cattle Stations: Feudal Exploitation and Accommodation', *Drawing Board* 4(3), March: 117-136.

ANTA 1950, *Walkabout*, September: cover.

ANTA 1955, *The Australian Scene*, ANTA, Melbourne.

ANTA 1956, 'Aborigines and Whites', *Australia Handbook*, ANTA, Melbourne.

Art Gallery of South Australia 2003, *Clifford Possum Tjapaltjarri Education Kit*, Art Gallery of South Australia, Adelaide.

Australian Institute of Aboriginal and Torres Strait Islander Studies 2004, *Dawn and New Dawn* 1952-75: a magazine for the Aboriginal people of New South Wales, digitised by AIATSIS, Canberra.

Barnes, Jill 2006, 'The House that Tourism Built: *Walkabout*, Captured Images of Aboriginality and Colonisation', *History in Global Perspective: Proceedings of the 20th International Congress of Historical Sciences,* University of New South Wales, Sydney.

Barrett, Charles 1939, *Central Australia*, Sun Travel Book No. 1, State Library of Victoria.

Bond Motor Service 1946, *Northward Adventure: Bond Awaits You: Travel to Central Australia by Bonds*, Commonwealth Railways, Series B300, Control 7161, CR150, Tourist Traffic Central Australia Railway, NAA (South Australia).

Brady, EJ 1918, *Australia Unlimited*, George Robertson, Melbourne.

British Association for the Advancement of Science 1929, *Notes and Queries on Anthropology*, Royal Anthropological Institute, London.

Butler, Roger 1993, *Poster Art in Australia: The Streets as Art Galleries — Walls Sometimes Speak*, National Gallery of Australia, Canberra.

CATA (Central Australia Tours Association) 1969, *Tour the Australian Outback*, CATA, Alice Springs, private collection.

Charnley, William Campbell 1930-1934, 'Stories by W. Charnley published in *Life Magazine*', Battye Library Collection, Perth.

—— 1947, 'The Antiquity of the Aboriginal', *Walkabout*, February: 29-32.

Clark, Russell 1936a, 'The Unveiling of a Continent: Impressions of the Exploits of Ludwig Leichhardt', *Walkabout*, January: 12-17.

—— 1936b, 'The Unveiling of a Continent: The Kennedy Expedition, Cape York Peninsula, Queensland', *Walkabout*, March: 18-21.

Clune, Frank 1938, 'With O'Hara Burke to the Gulf: A Brief Outline of the First Australian Transcontinental Crossing', *Walkabout*, March: 13-19.

Commonwealth of Australia 1939, *Aboriginal Welfare: Initial Conference of Commonwealth and State Aboriginal Authorities held at Canberra 21-23 Apr 1937*, Commonwealth Government Printer, Canberra.

Commonwealth Railways 1938, Series B300, File: Central Australia: Winter Holidays, NAA (South Australia).

Crosbie Morrison, P 1940, 'Among the Stone-Age', *Walkabout*, March: 51-2.

Dann, G 1996, *The Language of Tourism: A Sociolinguistic Perspective*, CAB International, Oxford.

Dilworth, L 1996, *Imagining Indians in the Southwest: Persistent Visions of a Primitive Past*, Smithsonian Institution Press, Washington DC.

Dunstan, Roy 1936a, Photographer, Image captioned 'The Aboriginal, as seen by the early explorers: a study of a Central Australian aboriginal with spear, shield, and throwing-stick', *Walkabout*, January: 12.

—— 1936b, Photographer, Image captioned 'Central Australian Aboriginal', *Walkabout*, September: cover.

Edwards, Elizabeth (ed) 1992, *Anthropology and Photography, 1860-1920*, Yale University Press/Royal Anthropological Institute, New Haven/London.

Ellingson, T 2001, *The Myth of the Noble Savage*, Berkeley, University of California Press.

French, Alison 2002, *Seeing the Centre: The Art of Albert Namatjira 1902-1959*, National Gallery of Australia, Canberra.

Gregory, JW 1909, *The Dead Heart of Australia: A Journey Around Lake Eyre in the Summer of 1901-1902*, John Murray, London.

Haines, AB 1937, 'Peopling Australia's Northern Territory', *Walkabout*, February: 22-30.

Hall, VC 1948, 'Trading Post of the "Never Never"', *Walkabout*, July: 31-32.

Harney, Bill 1950, 'Roads and Trade', *Walkabout*, May: 42-45.

—— 1952, 'New Lands from Old', *Walkabout*, June: 17-20.

—— 1953, 'Desert Pilgrims', *Walkabout*, July: 41-42.

—— 1957, *Life Among the Aborigines*, Robert Hale, London.

Henson, Barbara 1992, *A Straight-Out-Man: FW Albrecht and Central Australian Aborigines*, Melbourne University Press, Melbourne.

Hill, Barry 2002, *Broken Song: TGH Strehlow and Aboriginal Possession,* Knopf, Sydney.

Holmes, Charles H 1932, *We Find Australia*, Hutchinson & Co, London.

—— 1933, *We Find Australia (Illustrated)*, 4th impression, Hutchinson & Co, London.

—— 1950, 'New Commonwealth Stamp', *Walkabout*, September: 9.

—— 1951, 'Commonwealth 8.5d stamp', *Walkabout*, December: 9.

—— 1952, 'Mail Bag: One Pound Jimmy', *Walkabout*, November: 46.

Isaacs, Jennifer 2000, *Hermannsburg Potters: Aranda Artists of Central Australia*, Craftsman House, Sydney.

Johnson, Vivien 1994, *The Art of Clifford Possum Tjapaltjarri*, G&B Arts International/Craftsman House, Sydney.

—— 2002, 'Master of the Desert Dreaming', *Sydney Morning Herald*, 3 July, <http://www.smh.com.au/articles/2002/06/26/1023864605233.html>, accessed 10 September 2004.

—— 2003, *Clifford Possum Tjapaltjarri*, Art Gallery of South Australia, Adelaide.

Jones, PG 1995, 'Norman B Tindale: an obituary', *Records of the South Australian Museum*, December: 159-76.

Kreczmanski, Janusz B and Stanislawska-Birnberg, Margo 2002, *'The Tjulkurra': Billy Stockman Tjapaltjarri*, JB Books, Adelaide.

Loos, Michael 1996, 'Gwoja Tjungurrayi (One Pound Jimmy)', *Northern Territory Dictionary of Biography*, vol 3, Northern Territory Press, Darwin: 314.

MacGregor, Malcolm 1954, '"Big Game Hunter" in Autographed Stamps', *Walkabout*, August: 28-31.

McConnel, Ursula H 1936a, 'Cape York Peninsula: (1) The Civilised Foreground', *Walkabout*, June: 16-19.

—— 1936b, 'Cape York Peninsula: (2) The Primitive Background', *Walkabout*, July: 11-15.

—— 1936c, 'Cape York Peninsula: (3) Development and Control', *Walkabout*, August: 36-40.

McInnes, J 1953, 'Mail Bag: One Pound Jimmy', *Walkabout*, July: 46.

McLuhan, TC 1985, *Dream Tracks: The Railroad and the American Indian, 1890-1930*, Abrams, New York.

Mountford, Charles 1956, 'Journal 2/60, Expedition to Central Mount Wedge', Mountford-Sheard Collection, State Library of South Australia, PRG 1218/2/59.

—— 1967, *Australian Aboriginal Portraits*, Melbourne University Press, London.

Mulvaney, DJ and Calaby, JH 1985, *So much that is new: Baldwin Spencer, 1860-1929, a biography*, Melbourne University Press, Carlton, Victoria.

NSW Aborigines Welfare Board 1952-1969, *Dawn: A Magazine for the Aboriginal People of NSW*, Sydney.

Pickering, Charles 1851, 'The Australian Race', in *Races of Man and Their Geographical Distribution*, HG Bohn, London: 139-146.

Pioneer Tourist Bureau 1938, 'The Friendly Aboriginal ... You can witness corroborees and colourful ceremonials', *Walkabout*, May: 57.

Pioneer Travel Service 1939, 'Travel Interstate on a Holiday Motor Tour with Pioneer', *Walkabout*, March.

Pioneer Tours 1948, 'Darwin and Central Australian Tour', *Walkabout*, June: 38.

Roberts, Ainslie 1958, 'Mailbag: One Pound Jimmy', *Walkabout*, May: 40.

Roberts, Ainslie and Mountford, Charles 1973, *The Dreamtime Book*, Rigby, Adelaide.

Schoolcraft, Henry R 1847, *Notes on the Iroquois: or, Contributions to American history, antiquities, and general ethnology*, EH Pease, Albany.

Smithsonian Institution 1951-4, 'Press Clippings, Photographs and Correspondence' in File: Malcolm MacGregor Autograph Collection, National Postal Museum, Smithsonian Institution, Washington DC.

Spencer, Baldwin 1904, 'Totemism in Australia: Presidential Address to Ethnology and Anthropology section', Paper presented at the Report of the Tenth Meeting of the Australasian Association for the Advancement of Science, Dunedin.

—— 1913, 'Preliminary Report on the Aboriginals of the Northern Territory', *Bulletin of the Northern Territory* 7: 7-28.

Spencer, Baldwin and Gillen, Francis 1899, *The Native Tribes of Central Australia*, Macmillan, London.

—— 1912, *Across Australia*, Macmillan, London.

—— 1927, *Arunta : A study of a Stone Age People,* Macmillan, London.

Strehlow, TGH 1935, Book VII: Diary. Central Australia 1935, Strehlow Research Centre Archives, Alice Springs.

Strehlow, TGH c1950, 'Footnote 21' in Family Tree V 1, Strehlow Research Centre Archives, Alice Springs.

Sullivan, Milanka 2002, 'A Dying Wish based on an Ancient Culture Sabotaged by Contemporary History', <http://www.artspeak.com.au/Essay%20Clifford%20Possum%20A%20Dying%20Wish%20Sabotaged.htm>, accessed 15 September 2007.

TAA 1958, *Poster: Go North to Adventure! Alice Springs/Darwin: Go by Fast TAA Jetliner,* NAA, Series M2459.

Tennent, George J and Hay, William O 1945, *Early Australia in Photographs*, Savvas Publishing, Adelaide.

Thomson, Donald F 1934, 'Across Cape York Peninsular with a Pack Team: A 1000 mile Trek in Search of Unknown Native Tribes', *Walkabout*, December: 21-31.

Tindale, NB 1937, 'Native Songs of the South East of South Australia', *Transactions of the Royal Society of South Australia* 6: 107-20.

Tuit's Overland Tours 1949, 'Explore the Colourful North with Experienced Territorians', *Centralian Advocate*, 3 June: 10.

Urry, John 1990, *The Tourist Gaze*, Sage, London.

Vanderwal, Ron (ed) 1982, *The Aboriginal Photographs of Baldwin Spencer*, introduced by John Mulvaney, selected and annotated by Geoffrey Walker, Curey O'Neil, Melbourne.

Wauchope, Alan 1965, '"One Pound Jimmy" joins immortals', *Centralian Advocate,* 13 May, Alice Springs Library.

Weathersbee, RDJ 1979, 'Dr C P Mountford: A Personal Tribute', *Anthropology in Australia*, Proceedings and Tribute to the Life and Works of the Late Dr CP Mountford: 49-51.

Wilson, John 1954, 'Kurungura: Aboriginal Cultural Revival', *Walkabout*, May: 15-19.

Wolfe, Patrick 1991, 'On Being Woken Up: The Dreamtime in Anthropology and in Australian Settler Culture', *Comparative Studies in Society and History* 33(2), (April).

Woolmington, Jean 1973, *Aborigines in Colonial Society: 1788-185: from 'Noble Savage' to 'Rural Pest'*, Cassell, Sydney.

ENDNOTES

[1] Holmes 1951; MacGregor 1954: 29.

[2] Spencer and Gillen 1927; Pickering 1851: 139.

[3] Holmes 1950.

[4] See generally Dilworth 1996.

[5] Gregory 1909.

[6] Holmes 1932.

[7] Spencer and Gillen 1927. The preferred spelling for 'Arunta' is now Arrernte.

[8] Pickering 1851.

[9] Holmes was the son of British parents and a recently returned AIF captain from the Great War. He left his position as Chairman of Victorian Railways Betterment and Publicity Board to establish ANTA in 1928/29.

[10] Holmes 1932.

[11] Holmes 1932: 153.

[12] Holmes 1932: 29.

[13] Holmes 1932: 87, 131-2, 206-7.

[14] Holmes 1932: 118-132.

[15] Holmes 1932: 122-3.

[16] The medical doctor and naturalist Charles Pickering accompanied an American scientific exploring expedition to Sydney in the 1830s (Pickering 1851: 139).

[17] Holmes 1932: 125; Holmes 1951; MacGregor 1954: 29.

[18] Agate 1839.

[19] See Dann 1996.

[20] Butler 1993: 19.

[21] See Urry 1990.

[22] Clark also published under the pen name of Gilbert Anstruther.

[23] Clark 1936a.

[24] Clark 1936b.

[25] Clune 1938.

[26] Clark 1936a: 12.

[27] Clark 1936b: 21.

[28] Edwards 1992: 9.

[29] Thomson 1934; Tindale 1937; Jones 1995.

[30] Kimber in Hill 2002: 284.

[31] Johnson 2003: 35.

[32] Dunstan 1936a.

[33] This included bus operators AA Withers of Pioneer Tours and Len Tuit of Tuit's Overland Tours, as well as aerial operator Trans Australia Airlines. See Pioneer Tourist Bureau 1938 and Pioneer Tours 1948; Tuit's Overland Tours 1949; TAA 1958.

[34] The Tahitian prince, Omai, returned to England with Lieutenant James Cook. The portrait by Reynolds is in a private collection, see image at <http://www.tate.org.uk/britain/exhibitions/reynolds/roomguide8.shtm>.

[35] The prominent English poet, William Blake, was an engraver and book illustrator, trained at the Royal Academy.

[36] Mulvaney and Calaby 1985.

[37] Personal communication, Dick Kimber, Alice Springs, 22 March 2004.

[38] Mulvaney and Calaby 1985: 181; Vanderwal 1982; Spencer and Gillen 1899; Spencer and Gillen 1912; Spencer and Gillen 1927.

[39] Anonymous 1937.

[40] Haines 1937.

[41] For an influential literary work that inspired some of this optimism see Brady 1918.

[42] Identification of photograph, personal communication, John Mulvaney, Canberra, 16 March 2004 and Philip Jones, South Australian Museum, Adelaide, 2 April 2004.

[43] Tennent and Hay 1945.

[44] ANTA 1950.

[45] Dunstan 1936b.

[46] Ursula McConnel was then employed by the new Anthropological Research Fund of the Australian National Research Council.

[47] McConnel 1936a, 1936b, 1936c.

[48] Hall 1948.

[49] Ansett Travel Services 1949; Bond Motor Service 1946.

[50] ANTA 1955: 58-9.

[51] ANTA 1956: 51.

[52] Charles Barrett authored the *Sun [newspaper] Travel Books* and was a natural history journalist for *The Herald [Melbourne]*.

[53] Barrett 1939: 3.

[54] Bond Motor Service 1946; Barrett 1939:3.

[55] These categories included children of 'Mixed Bloods', 'Detribalised Full Bloods', and 'Semi-Civilised Full-Bloods' living in tribal areas (excluding pastoral workers) who would receive 'benevolent supervision on reserves' whilst being elevated to white standards (Commonwealth of Australia 1939).

[56] See Commonwealth of Australia 1939.

[57] In his then capacity of special advisor to the Commonwealth government for Northern Territory Aboriginal policy, Spencer prescribed two destinies for Aboriginal people: town workers/'cultural degenerates', landless charity cases/'Wandering Outcasts', and pastoral/'Useful Workers' would be 'phased out' when 'white settlers took up the land'; and 'Vanishing Wild Natives' would be segregated and preserved on reserves. Underlying Spencer's recommendation was the assumption that Aborigines would always be rejected by white society. Whilst he did not explain the expression 'phased out', it has evolutionary overtones of racial extinction. See Spencer 1913.

[58] Mulvaney and Calaby 1985: x, 206.

[59] Mulvaney and Calaby 1985: 212.

[60] See recommended reading in British Association for the Advancement of Science 1929.

[61] Gregory 1909: 202-8.

[62] See Charnley 1947; Crosbie Morrison 1940.

[63] Nature-writer Crosbie Morrison was a recipient of the Baldwin Spencer prize for practical zoology.

[64] Charnley became a professional writer of popular frontier adventure stories after sustaining an injury at work at the Kalgoorlie goldmines. See Charnley 1930-1934.

[65] Charnley 1947: 30.

[66] Charnley 1947: 30; Crosbie Morrison 1940: 52.

[67] Crosbie Morrison 1940: 52.

[68] Compare Charnley 1947: 30 and Crosbie Morrison 1940: 51 with Spencer and Gillen 1912: 6-7.

[69] Crosbie Morrison 1940: 52.

[70] Holmes 1932: 122, 125 and 131-2.

[71] Dilworth 1996: 51-65.

[72] Holmes 1950.

[73] Ellingson 2001.

[74] Woolmington 1973: 4-59.

[75] Johnson 1994, 2002, 2003.

[76] By the time Johnson completed her 2003 book, she had learnt additional information about Clifford Possum's life and family. This publication corrected an earlier assumption made by Johnson that Tjungurrayi was Clifford Possum's biological father. It is unclear whether Clifford Possum was referring to his biological or adoptive father when he stated his 'father' was born at Ngarlu in 1895. See Johnson 1994: 42-4; Art Gallery of South Australia 2003: 5; and revisions in Johnson 2003: 34 and 212. Personal communication, Vivien Johnson, Sydney, 3 March 2006. For another less likely suggestion relating to Tjungurrayi's birth see Amadio and Kimber 1988: 66.

[77] Tjungurrayi's authority in land and law knowledge for this country suggests he had a birth connection to it.

[78] Personal communication, Dick Kimber and Michael Cawthorn, Strehlow Research Centre, Alice Springs, 8 March 2004.

[79] Johnson 1994, 2002, 2003.

[80] 'Dreaming' is a variation on the term 'dreamtime' which was coined by Frank Gillen in 1894, introduced into the British anthropological canon by Baldwin Spencer in 1896 and popularised by Australian writer Langloh Parker in 1904. See Wolfe 1991.

[81] Johnson 2003: 16.

[82] Personal communication, Dick Kimber and Michael Cawthorn, Strehlow Research Centre, Alice Springs, 8 March 2004.

[83] The term 'totemic' was first used in North America to explain the connection Native Americans had with their land. See Schoolcraft 1847: 79. The word was first transmitted to Australia and used to explain Aboriginal relationships with their ancestral land in Spencer 1904.

[84] Kreczmanski and Stanislawska-Birnberg 2002: 13-14.

85 Henson 1992: 38.

86 Hill 2002: 153.

87 Sullivan 2002.

88 Amadio and Kimber 1988: 59-63.

89 Loos 1996.

90 Wauchope 1965.

91 Johnson 2003: 34.

92 Personal communication, Dick Kimber and Michael Cawthorn, Strehlow Research Centre, Alice Springs, 8 March 2004.

93 Wauchope 1965.

94 Personal communication, Dick Kimber and Michael Cawthorn, Strehlow Research Centre, Alice Springs, 8 March 2004.

95 Amadio and Kimber 1988: 66.

96 Loos 1996; Amadio and Kimber 1988: 66.

97 Wauchope 1965; Loos 1996; Johnson 2003: 35.

98 Amadio and Kimber 1988: 66; Harney 1952; Mountford 1956.

99 Loos 1996.

100 Long Rose Nangala was the mother of Clifford Upamburra (Possum) Tjapaltjarri, Immanuel Rutjinana Tjapaltjarri and Lily Tjapaltjarri and adoptive mother to Tim Leura Tjapaltjarri and Billy Stockman Tjapaltjarri.

101 Anthony 2004: 129.

102 Johnson 1994: 19.

103 Isaacs 2000: 31.

104 Henson 1992: 78.

105 Loos 1996.

106 The then newly graduated linguist TGH Strehlow was an avid collector of Aboriginal sacred songs and artefacts.

107 Johnson 1994: 16-17.

108 Hill 2002: 168-70; personal communication, Michael Cawthorn, Strehlow Research Centre, Alice Springs, 19 March 2004.

109 Henson 1992: 101.

110 Personal communication, Dick Kimber and Michael Cawthorn, Strehlow Research Centre, Alice Springs, 8 March 2004.

111 Hill 2002:149-50.

112 Amadio and Kimber 1988: 66; Loos 1996.

113 Harney 1957: cover; Roberts and Mountford 1973: cover.

114 Mountford 1967: 1.

115 Amadio and Kimber 1988: 59-60.

116 Johnson 2003: 17-18, 28; 2002.

117 They were Clifford Upamburra (Possum) Tjapaltjarri, Tim Leura Tjapaltjarri and Billy Stockman Tjapaltjarri.

118 Wauchope 1965.

119 MacGregor was a senior partner in the New York office of the American public accounting firm Peat, Marwick, Mitchell.

120 Holmes 1950.

121 Holmes 1952.

122 McInnes 1953.

123 Holmes 1951.

124 MacGregor 1954.

125 See media clippings in Smithsonian 1951-4.

126 Strehlow c1950.

[127] Strehlow 1935.

[128] State Library of Victoria 2006. 'Pictures Catalogue' by 'Artist/Creator' Roy Dunstan, <http://www.slv.vic.gov.au>, accessed 19 September 2007.

[129] Howieson was a 'committed pictoralist' and exhibiting member of the Melbourne Camera Circle and Victorian Salon of Photography. Personal communication, Alan Elliott, Archivist, Melbourne Camera Club, 22 October 2004.

[130] See acknowledgement of Howieson's contribution in Holmes 1933, opposite preface.

[131] Holmes 1950.

[132] Johnson 2003: 45.

[133] Commonwealth Railways 1938.

[134] Johnson 1994: 23.

[135] Hill 2002: 151.

[136] Wauchope 1965; MacGregor 1954: 30; Loos 1996; Anonymous 1965a.

[137] Barrett 1939.

[138] Amadio and Kimber 1988: 66.

[139] Hill 2002: 168.

[140] See Harney 1950, 1952, 1953.

[141] Spencer and Gillen 1912: 6.

[142] Weathersbee 1979: 49.

[143] Bill Harney was a former Native Affairs patrol officer, advisor to scientific/anthropological expeditions led by Charles Mountford and AP Elkin, and a writer of popular works on Aboriginal life and cross-cultural encounters.

[144] Ainslie Roberts was an internationally acclaimed photographer who left a career in advertising to foster respect for Aboriginal culture through painting the 'Dreamtime'. He collaborated with Charles Mountford on a number of publications.

[145] Charles Mountford was an ethnologist, photographer/film-maker and leader of ten expeditions to Central Australia. He had close working relationships with Roberts and Harney, having conducted fieldwork with both of them on numerous occasions.

[146] Harney 1957; Mountford 1956.

[147] Harney 1952; Roberts 1958.

[148] Harney 1952: 20.

[149] Harney 1953: 42.

[150] Harney 1952: 20.

[151] Hill 2002: 167.

[152] Roberts 1958.

[153] Harney 1957: 214, 216.

[154] Roberts 1958.

[155] See Wilson 1954.

[156] Roberts and Mountford 1973.

[157] NSW Aborigines Welfare Board 1952.

[158] AIATSIS 2004.

On the romances of marriage, love and solitude: freedom and transgression in Cape York Peninsula in the early to mid twentieth century

Jinki Trevillian

Romance and rebellion

Our romances are lived as much in our imaginations as in reality. Always included in our experiences are the thoughts and feelings that expand beyond the given situation, the things not said or done. These romantic relationships extend boundaries, and are met with repression. Rebellious relationships that break the laws of a society question the values of that society. People desire to protect their intimate stories precisely because of the possibility of public conflict and censure. Theodore Zeldin writes that:

> For most of history, love has been considered a threat to the stability of the individual and of society, because stability was usually valued more highly than freedom.[1]

Social attitudes to sex and relationships are internalised. In our cultivation of these values, however, it is our individual take on them that allows for the possibility of change. Social and moral laws define relationships as acceptable or transgressive, and yet there is always room for innovation and exploration when we create a specific intimate and personal space. Each of our intimate relationships has its rich history. In this way it is possible to start revolutions in the bedroom.

* * *

Fiction and truth in Cape York Peninsula romances

This article is based on my oral, archival and literary research into the history of Cape York Peninsula. In working with these oral histories I have become convinced that we need to approach the relation of truths and fictions in our histories as an open-ended and complex issue. To 'read' history as literature helps us to understand the complexities and ambivalences of human history as it is experienced and lived. Jon Simon asks, with reference to the work of Michel Foucault:

Can we tell, not lies, but different truths about ourselves that will become 'true' ... Parallel to an ethic of permanent resistance is an ethic of perpetual rewriting of the truth of our limits.[2]

There are inescapable fictions in our stories of romance. As in literature, our imagination is invoked to help us make sense of our experiences. As in literature, the use of fiction gives us access to other truths. 'It seems to me that the possibility exists for fiction to function in truth, for a fictional discourse to induce effects of truth, and for bringing it about that true discourse engenders or 'manufactures' something that does not yet exist.'[3] I would suggest that fiction's access to truth is also a way of bringing to light the emotional and psychic truths so often denied in rational discourse.

Reading history, or more accurately and broadly, reading our past, then becomes an act of 'rewriting'. This opening of the possibilities of our understanding of the past to the imagination is akin to the 'perpetual rewriting' described by Simon as parallel to the ethic of permanent resistance.[4] Interpretations of the past explore our ethical being and reality, both for individuals and collectively. This attempt at a deeper understanding of human history is what I am engaged in as an oral historian when I tell stories. The particular histories of the people of Cape York Peninsula are connected to shared human experiences of love and relationships, through the universalising themes of philosophy and poetry and the empathic identification of the reader.

Singing songs of love

Prevailing ideas about love and romance are explored in story and song. Aboriginal laws on sex, marriage and adultery on Cape York Peninsula were traditionally strict but open to challenge. In the south-west, at Pormpuraaw, infatuation of women with men was seen as the result of the men 'singing' the women and was accepted as inevitable.[5] The virtues of faithfulness were praised but 'sweethearts and extra-marital liaisons were celebrated in myth, ceremonies and increase rites'.[6] Forbidden love received especially devoted attention, while involving tragic consequences.

A traditional romance of illicit love was given a modern (1930s) telling in Ion Idriess' story of the 'runaways'.[7] Idriess and his mates assisted runaway lovers, even though they knew that the warriors chasing them were justified in the pursuit and the execution of the law-breakers, if they were caught.[8] The dangers and suffering that the young couple endured were, in this as in other literary romances, proof of the strength of their love. Forbidden love changes the world from how we are told it should be, but also confirms the rules.

Aboriginal myths and stories showed 'old-time' love and relationships, with their complex symbols of family and kin, food and environment. New possibilities in relationships needed new romances to describe them. Missionary and teacher

George Taplin (1889-1979) said of some songs that the Ngarrindjeri of South Australia 'will learn it with great appreciation if it seems to express some feelings which theirs does not'.[9] Christianity could offer a different marital ideal; Western culture had other romances, in fiction, films and songs.

Stories can disrupt the moral judgement of binaries of good and bad,[10] opening up other possibilities of how to live and love. History is adept at looking at the social and legal contexts of relationships but the existence of the romances themselves remain disruptive. It is the difference between a musical and a documentary; both forms tell a story about people and the world but in the musical the story is augmented by emotional outbursts of song.

Love disrupts our own storylines. We think we know what we want, how things are going to be, then all of a sudden we feel something we were not expecting. Gwen Molony, from Thursday Island, was an avid reader of romances.

> When I was growing up y'know I read these love stories; the blond was the bad girl and the nice dark-haired girl she was the heroine.
>
> I said 'When I grow up I'm going to marry a tall dark-headed man with curly hair'. My hero, y'know.
>
> I married a big blond Irishman![11]

So oral histories are like musicals; narratives are 'disrupted' by songs, poetry and emotion. Sometimes the speaker will literally break into song, or it may be a vignette; a story that sits outside the bigger story but nonetheless adds to it through feeling and colour and detail. The oral histories are also like songs; evocative and haunting. They can be incorporated into other histories but they remain an essentially different way of telling stories of the past.

This paper tells some of these stories at the points where romance runs through them, as marriage or its avoidance, as forbidden love, as songs.

Tradition and the separation of men and women

Mission dormitories separated boys and girls; the children fished, hunted, ate, bathed, slept and collected wood and water separately. Traditionally, their family and marriage regulated relationships between the sexes. Relationships defined by difference and rigid separation could nonetheless be intimate. Jean George grew up on the Mission at Aurukun but returned to her father's country and the Weipa Mission when she married. Hers was a traditional marriage, which brought Jean into the heart of her extended family.

Jean's husband was injured at Thursday Island during the war and was partially incapacitated. Both her husband's brothers lost their wives, so they shared food with her family. But her brothers-in-law would never speak to Jean.

> And he [my brother-in-law] was a real good hunting man, good hunting
> man. Go and get fishes for me, and especially big barra, so lovely. And
> dig wild yams for me, and I have wild yams, he cook it and bring it
> cooked one for me. He really good, he fed me a lot with different things.[12]

The relationship between food and love is seen here in both a general story of
family and community and a personal relationship between two people. Within
the boundaries of defined relationships, exchanges of food allowed people to
express deep love and affection.

> Like our customs, our in-laws they don't talk to us ... he talk to Annie,
> say 'Take it and share it with mum'. Or sometimes he cook it in the bush
> and bring cooked one, fish or yam, he wrap it, tie it up with grape-vine,
> all the yams. And then he shoot birds; geese or brolga, ducks, he bring
> them, even the inside part, he clean it and cook it and bring it cooked.[13]

It is a gift direct from her brother-in-law to Jean that gives her so much pleasure.
'After his wife die, he give everything to me. And I really enjoyed it!' 'He was
really good looking after me ... The other brother too, his wife died. So we were
looking after them all, the two brothers and my husband.'[14]

Although both Aboriginal 'bora' tradition and missionary rules controlled sexual
relations, the missionaries' ideas of appropriate relationships for young women
differed greatly from that of the elders. Conflict resulted from the white men's
abhorrence of marriages between young women and men who were much older
and/or had other wives. The vehement anti-sexual attitude of missionaries meant
that relations between male and female were deeply associated with sex and
wrong-doing. At Old Mapoon the separation of the sexes was given a powerful
symbol in the almond and other trees that were planted there. These were
designated as girls' and boys' trees. It is said that the girls' fruit was always
sweeter, a knowledge which reveals illicit comparison.

The segregation of the sexes affected adult relationships. Punishments for 'talking
to girls', as well as being psychologically damaging, created a charged atmosphere
around communication between the sexes. Women were largely absent from
working environments with cattle, on boats and in mining camps. Sailors' folklore
warned against female presence on boats as 'unlucky' and accidents were often
blamed on men having keepsakes from their girlfriends.[15] The culture of men's
work romanticised loneliness and the longings of solitude, in the images of
cowboys, sailors and bushmen.

The permission of family and church, or marriage as freedom

Aboriginal marriage laws were severely disrupted through European invasion
and the introduction of the Christian religion, despite continued efforts by the

old people to force adherence to traditional law. Stories (and punishments) of a 'west coast man' taking an 'east coast woman', have their roots in the Dreaming,[16] but the dislocation of invasion and settlement increased the possibility of new relationships and conflict. Just the presence of the white people offered an alternative. A significant element in Idriess' story of the runaways is that in leaving their land and people, the couple had an alternative place to go because of the Europeans. Taylor tells of an eloping couple that took refuge on a cattle station to escape punishment.[17] Cautionary stories of 'runaways' may have lost some of their power once new freedoms were glimpsed.

Family opposition was a test to the strength of feeling and commitment of young couples. Objection to prospective sons-in-law was considered a healthy tradition even when it involved threats and violence. Though romantic love was not disregarded, marriages served other purposes. Bound to tradition and an intricate network of kinship, spirituality, land and languages, marriage laws could not be treated lightly.

Gladys Williams' family at Pormpuraaw fought over her husband. The couple weren't 'married' in a State marriage, but living together. They had two boys.[18] The family did not approve Gladys' choice and her mother had arranged a traditional marriage with another man. The fighting got so bad that Government and Mission authorities sent Gladys and her husband to Palm Island after her husband speared her uncle.[19] When the couple returned after five years of exile, Gladys' husband and her brother-in-law had to fight and 'talk for him' before they could 'settle down'. The couple were married the Christian way.[20] Conversion to Christianity made Gladys' marriage possible by giving it an authority that was counter to traditional law, though the social consequences remained formidable.

While some young people rebelled against it, the main objection to traditional marriages came from the Churches.[21] Missionaries were clearly opposed to the marriage of young women to old men and to polygamy. Ina Hall of Weipa, and from the earlier established site of 20 Mile Mission, describes the enclosure of girls in dormitories by the missionaries to control marriage.[22]

> That's when Missionary said 'No, no, no ... God say no more, only one wife' ... [Aboriginal men said] 'No, no, no. You can't take that another woman from me. No, that's my wife!' (they spoke language). [Missionary said] 'Only one woman, you only allowed to have one woman'. They fight over it.[23]

Objection to multiple wives was inherent in European/Christian traditions. The cross-generational issue would seem to be related to more romantic values, culturally expressed in literature. The European sentiment exemplified in stories such as Tristan and Isolde, Romeo and Juliet, or novels such as Charles Dickens'

Bleak House or George Eliot's *Middlemarch*, idealised a romantic love based on youth. The patriarch or old man, whether the arranger of marriages or the promised groom, is figured as an obstacle. Young — similar aged — love was a relatively modern European ideal and although incorporated into 'Christian values' can hardly be seen as Biblical. European romantic feeling had been through its own revolution against 'traditional' values, and it is worth noting that these 'mythic' European romances were often tragic, involving social and civil conflict.

Geraldine MacKenzie compared herself and her husband favourably with earlier missionaries who objected to arranged marriages.[24]

> With the proviso made at Aurukun in the late twenties that the bridegrooms chosen for mission girls should be single and reasonably young, marriages backed by the agreement of all relations of both bride and groom, lasted happily. Early missionaries, before they had time to realise this, had tried to foster a freer, more romantic order of things, understandable to our European way of feeling.[25]

The MacKenzies realised that attachment to 'right' arranged marriages was so strong that a complete objection to them would only increase community turmoil. A 'freer, more romantic order of things' led to conflict, violence, social upheaval and instability.

Christian marriage, and its association with romantic love, freed Aboriginal men and women from traditional arranged marriages. As a child, Dulcie Costello used to hide when her betrothed, an old man, came to visit. Dulcie was immensely relieved when he died: 'Oooh, terrible! Imagine being happy 'cause someone dies, but I was that scared'.[26] Gordon Pablo explained the system of promising and initiation at Injinoo, which ensured that young men and women were ready for marriage.[27] But Gordon did not marry his promised wife.

> Well, I had promised one but — after that coming Christianity coming now everything changed. Christianity was there now.
>
> And, ah, promised one, like I don't know, I got no feeling for that promised one.
>
> So she married another man, I married another woman.[28]

The introduction of Christianity and a different set of laws could be personally liberating, allowing young men and women to follow their hearts.

New ways seemed to provide new freedoms but entailed a lack of choice as access to the old ways was denied. The new freedoms came with new rules and limitations that were set and policed at the discretion of the missionary, Church and State. An increase in individual freedom was thus connected to a cultural loss and a decrease in observance of tradition.

Making a song and dance about it

Just as traditional love was related to the power to 'sing', modern love is strongly articulated in song. During the war Gwen Molony played the accordion for the troops at Iron Range: 'Everyone would sing songs. One fellow asked for "You're the only star in my blue heaven", he was a long way from home. I felt sorry for him, he was thinking of someone.'[29]

Flo Kennedy was hula dancing with an American show company based at a military camp. Her group consisted of Thursday Island men who played guitar and sang: 'I had my own boys play for me … One day nobody turn up, I don't know what happened.' A white man from another band offered to play for her.

> I said, 'You don't play guitar?'
>
> He said, 'No, but I play drums'…
>
> I said 'Alright'. So I do that and he got his band to play and I danced to his drums … I was pleased with myself, to find out that I can dance to a white man's drum.[30]

Singing and dancing are not only romantic, they are also spiritual. Flo's family were from Badu Island although she grew up at Lockhart River Mission and Thursday Island. Flo learnt to dance from her Polynesian grandfather.

> It's lovely, hula dancing done properly is really nice, with meaning y'know, tell stories … And it speaks lovely words, y'know the action speaks lovely words.
>
> And it's got to come from inside to make it really meaningful, y'know.
>
> I guess anything has to come from inside, otherwise it means nothing.[31]

Aboriginal and Islander people came from a tradition of spiritual observance through song. John Coleman remembers how the old people used to sing while they worked,[32] and though the songs changed (Gordon Pablo fears in some cases they are lost altogether[33]) the singing continued. Church singing was important for many people; Royce Lee praises a family of singers from Hopevale,[34] Jean George recalls the fine baritone of her uncle.[35] Aboriginal people were learning 'popular' songs too. Peter Costello's favourite is a sentimental tune about a man missing his mother. The boys on the trochus boat used to sing 'When it's spring-time in the Rockies' and cry for their girlfriends.[36] Vivien Gostelow and Geraldine MacKenzie recall the Aboriginal stock workers singing to the cattle through the night.[37] The drovers sang, soldiers sang, men on boats sang.

The women at Weipa used to wait for their men to come home on the boats. As they arrived the men would be singing songs about the islands and the sea: 'Every little thing they make songs about; the wind and the rain, and brother and sister.'[38] The song influences from Thursday Island incorporated Islander traditions, modern popular music and Indigenous sentiment.[39] While the expressions are diverse, the preoccupations remain the same: the main subject of these songs is love, of place, home, family and beloved. Country music is popular to this day with its concentration on rural subjects and the misfortunes of love.[40]

Relationships and community

Bowie Gostelow's mother, Rose, had to get permission from the Department of Native Affairs to marry her husband, a white pastoralist, as she was under the *Aborigines Protection Act*. Rose was raised at Silver Plains Station. Her father was an Irishman named Patrick Fox. Her mother died when she was only a week old, and Bowie is unsure about her ancestry, despite her being considered Aboriginal by the government. There was reluctance to talk about Rose Gostelow's origins. In a book written by Bowie's wife she is described as 'Polynesian', but Bowie recognises the possibility of Aboriginal ancestry.[41]

A preference for marrying within the community is apparent throughout Cape York Peninsula. Many people met their spouses through family and local connections. Bowie's wife to be, Vivien Bell, was the daughter of an Endeavour River farming family and went to the same Cooktown school as Bowie, but was six years younger.[42]

In her memoir, Vivien Gostelow took a romantic view of her marriage. An episode on the journey to her new home at Violet Vale, when Vivien's horse bolted, exemplifies her image of Bowie: 'My wonderful sun-bronzed bushman, in his moleskins and legging, blue shirt and battered sombrero, rescued me so effortlessly, just as cowboys did in the movies.'[43] It is not surprising then that Vivien and Bowie fell in love through a shared interest in Westerns. Bowie was ill with his tonsils in Cooktown hospital, where 15-year-old Vivien was working: 'When matron was not around, I slipped in to talk to him, found he liked reading Westerns, and took him some books on my afternoon off. That is how our romance began.'[44]

The romance in Vivien's story is not only the love of a cowboy,[45] but the idealisation of pastoral life. Vivien describes a rural idyll of the station with its fruit trees, fresh milk and wholesome self-sufficiency, and of cattle droving with night-fires and singing. A central image in Vivien's pastoral romance was her mother-in-law, the picturesque matriarch of a pioneer family.[46] The uncertainty around Rose's heredity is interesting in this respect, for the pioneer woman is always contrasted against the 'wild blacks' and Rose Gostelow is no exception.[47] In Jon Simon's terms: 'Power relations should always be analysed in terms of adversarial struggle and confrontational strategies.'[48] While the construct of racial conflict remains in place, individuals slip through the gaps.

Illicit love and illegal relationships

Queensland law was quite clear on the illegality of sexual relations between Aboriginal people under the *Aborigines Protection Act* and white, coloured or exempt people not under the Act. The enforcement of this segregation was, as Walter Bowen of Hopevale explains, largely directed at keeping Aboriginal and white men and women apart.

> Them days see it's a different law altogether. The Australian law, see, if I were to put a hand on a white girl like this, I'm finished. The police just pick me up, put me up, lock me up ... I can't even go and talk to a white girl, as long as they see me that's it. Whether you're a half-caste or full blood don't make any difference.[49]

The legislation prohibiting inter-racial sexual relationships had been framed as protective, with reference to white men cohabiting with black women, which was seen — and it sometimes was — to be exploitative. In practice, Aboriginal women, as the 'victims', were the ones punished. Attempts by Aboriginal people to enforce their own laws in response to white men's transgressions, particularly through individual spearings in the early period of invasion, were met by the armed force of the settlers. Whole communities could be 'punished' because of allegations of illegal relationships between Aboriginal women and white men.[50] Numerous women were removed from Cape York Peninsula in the first half of the twentieth century, including 'VD suspects', considered as a category of immoral behaviour.[51] Concerns over the spread of infectious diseases in Aboriginal and non-Aboriginal populations were valid but greatly exaggerated in the interests of moral and social control, accompanied by issues of 'racial purity'.

European resistance to miscegenation was manifest also in the treatment — usually removal and institutionalisation — of 'half-caste' children. When Nancy Ross married she already had a child to a white man. Nancy had been taken from her own family, near Alice River, because her biological father was white. White pastoralists, who knew her father, raised her. As a young single mother Nancy was sent to a dormitory at Yarrabah Mission.

> I wasn't used to mission, you know, I wanted to get out.
>
> My husband came down ... I told him I wanted to get out, you know.
>
> We wrote a letter to him, to tell him to come down ...
>
> I was happy in a way, I had a lot of girlfriends there you know.
>
> I just wanted to get out of there, so I got married.[52]

Nancy wanted out of the dormitory but she only agreed to marry when her prospective husband promised to adopt her son as his own.[53]

Bamboo Friday and Wampoo Keppel married women to stop them from being removed by the police. These were arranged marriages, agreed to by family and following traditional laws: 'Gotta be right man, any close to family won't let her marry.'[54] Ruby Friday would have been sent to a government settlement or mission because her father was white. Ruby was born in 1942 but married at only 14 years of age to stop her from being taken away. Her husband Bamboo Friday was 19 years older.[55] Wampoo gives a more general reason for removing young unwed women from the bush: 'If any woman [don't] get married send 'em to Palm Island ... They didn't want any young girls walking around bush, outside, white man making trouble with them.'[56]

The cohabitation of white men with black women was commonly tolerated throughout the Cape.[57] Some men enjoyed the freedom from social (and legal) restraints of living in isolation. They were not legally married. Many had more than one de-facto wife. Those men who wanted to marry their chosen companion had to apply to the Department of Native Affairs for permission, which was sometimes, though not always, granted.[58]

The gendered focus of the Act reflects the cultural assumptions of Europeans about the likelihood of white women having relations with black men. A wife's social standing was determined by her husband, and a white woman could not be placed under the Protection Act. For an Aboriginal man to marry a white woman, it was necessary for him to be exempt from the Act. Authorities appeared reluctant to liberate men on the basis of affection formed with a woman. Exemption was more readily granted to 'half-caste' women to marry non-Aboriginal men.[59]

Aboriginal men who did have relationships with white women were subject to violent beatings by white men. Some are even now uncomfortable about how they might be judged. The guilt associated with these relationships is so strong that men fear being criticised. Many accounts of personal relationships and conflict, though spoken about openly, were specified as not to be made public. One man spoke of his 'best friend' as a white woman he was unable to get permission to marry.

Peter Costello experienced beatings motivated by racial discrimination and sexual jealousy; a beating he received from American soldiers left him with a broken jaw and ribs.[60] An Italian farmer he worked for agreed to Peter marrying his daughter, but he shied away from marrying a white woman: 'I was shy, you know, shy to come near because of racial, heavy racial ... She had it in mind too, but I wasn't ready.'[61] Claiming poverty, he left.

Marriage is not only about partnership but one's place within a community. Where communities are divided, the bond of marriage challenges that division.

In some cases spouses are accepted within closed communities but in times of conflict the couple may just as easily be isolated and excluded.

Censorship and homosexuality

Opposition can lead to silence. Reluctance to talk about 'inter-racial' relationships on Cape York Peninsula is not as absolute as the lack of comment on same-sex relationships. According to Alberto Manguel the desire to remain unlabelled (and uncensored) is an attempt to protect the limitless possibilities of human expression. Writing about the distinctions of homosexual and heterosexual, Manguel argues: 'our sexual affinities need only declare allegiance and define themselves under duress'.[62]

Perhaps the failure of language is not entirely related to demands for a forced declaration, but indicates a cultural poverty resulting from a 'modern' suppression of the language of non-heterosexual love. In a world 'without' women, the many single men living and working together on Cape York Peninsula suggest different domestic relationships to traditional gender roles, whether they were homosexual or not.[63] Writing of the masculine environment of colonial Queensland, Clive Moore suggests that male-to-male sex was highly probable but also talks of a culture of mateship as non-sexual romantic friendship.[64]

A Gugu-Yalanji myth, recorded by Ursula McConnel at Bloomfield, tells how Gidja the moon makes a woman out of a younger man.[65] McConnel's interpretation of the story relates it to the Eve myth of Genesis, comparing a world without women to one defined by their presence.[66] Nicola Henningham uses this myth as a theme in her discussion of male/female relations. The story also possesses other images, including homosexuality. Gidja, who was often in trouble for having wrongful sex — with close relations for example — is punished for 'making' the young man into a woman. The story has no active feminine principle and the child born from the union dies, showing the marriage to be infertile. I am not claiming this is the 'right' reading but suggesting possibilities inherent in the details of this version of the myth.

Family pressures to marry and produce offspring have plagued homosexual men throughout history. As Jon Simon describes it: 'gay friendship is the proliferation of new forms of relations between people beyond those currently sanctioned, namely marriage and the family'.[67] Waiu Whap, whose family were from Badu, taught and lived at Injinoo and Thursday Island. Waiu's arranged marriage left her in much the same situation as if she had remained single: 'He not really like a man, he a sissy. When I was at Thursday Island, he leave me with my people … When they want us to live together again, he run away from me … If I knew I should find another man.'[68] It was unfortunate for Waiu that her husband felt it necessary (probably due to his own family) to go through with their marriage although he had no desire to be with a woman.

Reluctance to wed: the love of solitude and independence

Marriage as an institution of family and state requires permission from parents, from missionaries, from the government. Sometimes it is not the obstacles to marriage but the pressure to wed that ruins romances. On Dulcie Costello's wedding day she had second thoughts: she hid under the bed-covers and the community policeman came several times to fetch her to church. Dulcie didn't feel she had any choice but to marry: 'signed the paper, I don't know what I'm going to do'.[69]

Reluctance to marry was not an exceptional experience for young men (and women) on the Cape. In his youth George Musgrave preferred solitude and independence. After 'running away' from an Islander girl on Thursday Island he was finally convinced to marry by the Laura police.

> Police ask 'George, you like to get married?'
>
> I said 'No way!' ...
>
> He said 'Why not?'
>
> I said 'No, I like to be by myself, can please myself, you can go any way, anywhere you wanted to go' ... 'If you married', I said, 'Soon as you get married, you gonna get a lot of order about, 'do this and do this'. When you by yourself you just roll your swag, pack up and you're gone.[70]

George describes being married as tying one to a place. The Laura police wanted George to stay in the district rather than be sent back to Coen to work on the stations. George's marriage worked not just as an administrative ploy, as through marrying the right woman George had a claim to stay in Laura. His relationship to the land changed from stranger/foreigner to one of belonging: 'Yeah that's why I stop here then ... I was bad up with police. They say "If you get married you'll be tracker ... Then you'll be policeman here". I had mind different way. Police job is really bad.'[71]

George was reluctant both at the prospect of marriage and at being coerced into the police force, which he described as dangerous work.

Although Willie Lawrence had doubts, everyone in the community was pleased when he finally wed. They even held a big dance in the Coen hall, usually reserved for white people's functions:

> I reckon everybody happy that I got married, they seen me walking around single for the rest of my life ...
>
> Oh dear, made me sorry that time when I got married hey [laugh].
>
> I like single life, you know, good.
>
> Well you can get about hey, you can get lots about.

You can go anywhere you want to go.

But when you get married, well you never know where you are.

You get a rope around your neck, and you never move ...

They tell you 'Oh you can't go over there!'[72]

Solitude has its own romance: the colourful image of the cowboy, the masculine superiority of the lone bushman, the self-sufficiency of the sailor. The Australian ideal of masculinity, and the images of American westerns value the solitary individualist. Women were not insignificant but they were often absent from the day-to-day working and social lives of men.

Willie and the other men were deeply influenced by Westerns and images of cowboys in books and magazines that reached the remote cattle properties. Movies seen in the towns were also powerful purveyors of modern culture. Most elusive of all in a predominately oral culture was popular song, passed on over campfires and along the road: 'Just give me land, lots of land and the starry skies above — *Don't fence me in.'*

Being a flash dresser and admired by the women wasn't so bad either. As one man said: 'I was a young man at that time, good rider, and well dressed'.[73] Men made careful note of their clothing: 'Them white moleskins, them kind we used to wear, and old tweed you know, tight ones you know, look nice too'.[74]

Going one's own way, not being tied down, is such an appealing prospect that even some who married chose this course. Peter Fischer got married because his mother wanted to protect him from jealous husbands and fathers.

> Too many women were chasing me. And my mother think world of me, he didn't want 'is son to get in any trouble like ... I had married women all chasing me, I was a beautiful looking young man. My mother growled [at] me then, 'You have to get married'. So she picked me out one there
> ...
> I should have picked one out for meself ... I reckon I'd have been much happier you know.[75]

Peter and his wife raised a large family, seven boys and seven girls, but his wife left him in later life: 'But it was sad, she walked out on me'. Peter Fischer may have been the object of sexual jealousy but he eschews the sentiment: 'I'm not a jealous man, I'm not a woman fighter'. Peter believes it is better to allow people their freedom, even if it means losing them: 'I think maybe better life for her, that she go the way she want to go and I go my way. And that's how we come parted.'[76]

Expressions of a 'lost love', and jokes about finding another husband or wife, acknowledge that one's choices are determined by circumstances as much as by individual will. But merely raising the possibilities inherent in these regrets is an act of 'rewriting', an act of permanent resistance, intimating not just the possibility of different choices but a different world in which to make them. This questioning of past actions and experiences examines not only individual moral and personal choices but also the definition of those choices by society and community. The modern cultural emphasis on individual freedom has opened up possibilities of multiple partners and non-sanctioned liaisons, but it should be recognised that — as in the romantic epics — these freedoms have also contributed to social and individual turmoil and uncertainty.

End note

While many of the lovers in these stories form the Cape York Peninsula found happiness, in and out of marriage, none of the stories describe freedom from the presence of family, community, laws and external forces. Perhaps, like Waiu Whap's husband or Idriess' lovers, true escape means running away to 'somewhere else'. Somewhere else is the stuff of songs: 'Over the rainbow'/ 'There's a place for us'. The stories themselves, however, express a freedom to feel and to imagine which is not limited by actual circumstances.

Foucault writes 'The soul is the prison of the body'[77] and Blake argues that 'Man has no body distinct from his soul'.[78] While Blake may accept the soul as prison, in the same sense that 'reason' is the bounded or outer circumference, he would also question this inherent duality. The inside and outside are not merely mutually dependent but more fluid. And, as Simon would have it, 'neither the soul nor the body can be privileged as sites of freedom or the grounds of revolt'.[79]

Songs of love are our insides coming out, as the songs in turn penetrate us. Sometimes our loves are rejected, opposed, disregarded, even despised. We can hide our vulnerability in the language of a mythic story, someone else's words which become our own. Expressions of love in songs and stories can be independent of actions and circumstances. Songs express our experiences both real and imagined. Like love itself they tell the oldest stories newly lived.

The freedom to feel is not the freedom to do, and yet as an expression of our humanity it is essential. If our desires reach their limits then our imaginations take them beyond those limits and make possible an alternative. Our imaginings also show us the ways in which we are constrained. Potential 'transgressive' relationships may not be realised but remain a force for introducing new possibilities.

Acknowledgements

I wish to thank the people of Cape York Peninsula who made invaluable contributions to my oral history research, without whose time and generosity none of my subsequent work would have been possible. In particular, this article has referred to the histories of the following participants, who have given permission for the material to be published:

Walter Bowen, interview tape 29/6/1999.

John Coleman, interview tape 5/7/2000.

Dulcie Costello, interview tape 30/6/1999.

Peter Costello, interview tape 25/6/1999.

Peter Fischer, interview tape 26/6/2000.

Bamboo Friday, interview notes 6/7/1999.

Jean George, interview tape and notes 2/8/2000.

Bowie Gostelow, interview tape 9/11/2000.

Ina Hall, interview tape 12/8/2000.

Flo Kennedy, interview tape 21/9/2000.

Wampoo Keppel, interview tape 7/10/2000.

Willie Lawrence, interview tape 5/10/2000.

Royce Lee, interview tape 19/6/2000.

Gwen Molony, interview tape and notes 16/9/2000.

George Musgrave, interview tape 30/6/2000.

Gordon Pablo, interview tape 23/9/2000.

Nancy Ross, interview tape 12/7/2000 and interview notes 13/7/2000.

Bruce Yunkaporter, interview tape, 28/8/2000.

Waiu Whap, interview notes 4/9/2000.

Gladys Williams, interview notes 19/10/2000.

Silas Wolmby, interview tape 22/8/2000.

References

Primary sources

Department of Native Affairs Records, 'Register of Removals 1908-1936', 'Administration Missions — Removals 1941-44' File Series A/64786 & A/69465, Queensland State Archives, Brisbane.

Security Service Report 2/12/49, 'Survey Cape York Peninsula (within shire of Cook)', A/9108/3 Roll 17/47, National Australian Archives, Canberra.

Thursday Island State High School 1988, 'Torres Strait at War: a recollection of wartime experiences Thursday Island', Thursday Island State High School.

Secondary sources

Bell, Diane 1998, *Ngarrindjeri Wurruwarrin: a world that is, was and will be*, Spinifex, Melbourne.

Blake, William 1790, 'The marriage of heaven and hell', in MH Abrahams et al (ed.), 1986, *The Norton Anthology of English Literature*, 5th edn, vol 2, WW Norton & Co., New York and London.

Gostelow, Vivien 1988, *Sunshine and shadow*, Pinevale Publications, Mareeba.

Henningham, Nicola 2000, 'A different story: gender and the history of white settlement in north Queensland, 1840-1930', PhD thesis, Department of History, University of Melbourne.

Idriess, Ion (1932) 1955, *Men of the Jungle*, Angus and Robertson, Sydney.

McConnel, Ursula 1933, 'The moon legend from the Bloomfield River, North Queensland', *Oceania* 3: 9-25.

MacKenzie, Geraldine 1981, *Aurukun Diary: 40 years with the Aborigines*, The Aldersgate Press, Melbourne.

Manguel, Alberto 1999, *Into the Looking-Glass Wood*, Bloomsbury, London.

Moore, Clive 1998, 'Colonial manhood and masculinities', in C Moore and K Saunders (eds), 'Australian masculinities: men and their histories', *Journal of Australian Studies*, special issue volume 56: 35-50.

Parker, David 1994, *Ethics, theory and the novel*, Cambridge University Press, Cambridge.

Pearson, Noel 1998, 'Guugu Yimidhirr history: Hopevale Lutheran Mission 1900-1950', in Kociumbas (ed.), *Maps, dreams, history: race and representation in Australia*, Sydney Studies in History 8, Department of History, Sydney University: 131-236.

Read, Peter 2000, *Belonging: Australians, place and Aboriginal ownership*, Cambridge University Press, Cambridge.

Rigsby, Bruce 1994, 'Review of literature: Coen and Port Stewart', in B Rigsby and D Hafner, *Claim Book; Lakefield National Park Land Claim*, Cape York Land Council, Cairns.

Simon, Jon 1995, *Foucault and the political*, Routledge, London.

Taylor, John 1984, 'Of Acts and Axes: an ethnography of sociocultural change in an Aboriginal community, Cape York Peninsula', Phd thesis, James Cook University, Queensland.

Trezise, Percy 1969, *Quinkan Country; Adventures in Search of Aboriginal Cave Paintings in Cape York*, AH & AW Reed, Sydney.

Zeldin, Theodore 1998, *An Intimate History of Humanity*, Vintage, London.

ENDNOTES

[1] Zeldin 1998: 83.

[2] Simon 1995: 93.

3 Foucault cited by Simon 1995: 92.

4 Simon 1995: 93.

5 Taylor 1984: 268.

6 Taylor 1984: 268.

7 Idriess 1932: 21-30.

8 Idriess 1932: 34.

9 Bell 1998: 155 citing Taplin 1873.

10 Parker 1994: 50.

11 Gwen Molony, interview tape 16/9/2000.

12 Jean George, interview notes 2/8/2000.

13 Jean George, interview notes 2/8/2000.

14 Jean George, interview notes 2/8/2000.

15 Bruce Yunkaporter, interview tape, 28/8/2000.

16 Such a story is told by Bowie Gostelow, interview tape 9/11/2000.

17 Taylor 1984: 271-272.

18 Gladys Williams, interview notes 19/10/2000.

19 Gladys Williams, interview notes 19/10/2000.

20 Gladys Williams, interview notes 19/10/2000.

21 For example see Taylor 1984: 520.

22 Ina Hall, interview tape 12/8/2000. See also Pearson 1998: 171.

23 Ina Hall, interview tape 12/8/2000.

24 MacKenzie 1981: 190.

25 MacKenzie 1981: 49.

26 Dulcie Costello, personal communication, June 1999.

27 Gordon Pablo, interview tape 23/9/2000.

28 Gordon Pablo, interview tape 23/9/2000.

29 Gwen Molony, interview notes 16/9/2000.

30 Flo Kennedy, interview tape 21/9/2000.

31 Flo Kennedy, interview tape 21/9/2000.

32 John Coleman, interview tape 5/7/2000.

33 Gordon Pablo, interview tape 23/9/2000.

34 Royce Lee, interview tape 19/6/2000.

35 Jean George, interview tape 2/8/2000.

36 Peter Costello, personal communication, 1999.

37 MacKenzie 1981: 171; Gostelow 1988: 15.

38 Ina Hall, interview tape 12/8/2000.

39 Contemporary examples are Seaman Dan and the Mills Sisters.

40 See Read 2000: 115-120.

41 Bowie Gostelow, interview tape 9/11/2000.

42 Gostelow 1998: 3-8.

43 Gostelow 1998: 2.

44 Gostelow 1998: 10.

45 Gostelow 1998: 46-7, 65, 168.

46 Gostelow 1998: 15-17.

47 Gostelow 1998: 29.

48 Simon 1995: 84.

49 Walter Bowen, interview tape 29/6/1999.

50 See Rigsby 1994.

51 Department of Native Affairs, 'Register of Removals 1908-1936', Queensland State Archives, Brisbane.

52 Nancy Ross, interview tape 12/7/2000.

[53] Nancy Ross interview notes 13/7/2000.

[54] Wampoo Keppel, interview tape 7/10/2000.

[55] Bamboo Friday, interview notes 6/7/1999, also Royce Lee, interview tape 19/6/2000.

[56] Wampoo Keppel, interview tape 7/10/2000.

[57] Security Service, Report 2/12/49, 'Survey Cape York Peninsula (within shire of Cook)', A/9108/3 Roll 17/47, National Australian Archives, Canberra.

[58] See Henningham 2000.

[59] Such as Rose Gostelow, Therese Heinemann and Tommy Nakata's wife.

[60] Peter Costello, interview tape 25/6/2000.

[61] Peter Costello, interview tape 25/6/2000.

[62] Manguel 1999: 39.

[63] For a discussion of the colonial masculine environment and its legacy, see Moore 1998: 39.

[64] Moore 1998: 46.

[65] McConnel 1933 details the many complex parts of the story relating to women and community. For a men's version of the story, see Trezise 1969: 92-93.

[66] See Henningham 2000: 39-40.

[67] Simon 1995: 97.

[68] Waiu Whap, interview notes 4/9/2000.

[69] Dulcie Costello, interview tape 30/6/1999.

[70] George Musgrave, interview tape 30/6/2000.

[71] George Musgrave, interview tape 30/6/2000.

[72] Willie Lawrence, interview tape 5/10/2000.

[73] Silas Wolmby, interview tape 22/8/2000.

[74] Peter Costello, interview tape 25/6/1999.

[75] Peter Fischer, interview tape 26/6/2000.

[76] Peter Fischer, interview tape 26/6/2000.

[77] Foucault cited in Simon 1995: 84.

[78] Blake 1790: 61.

[79] Simon 1995: 84.

'Hanging no good for blackfellow': looking into the life of Musquito

Naomi Parry

On the morning of 25 February 1825 in the Hobart Town Gaol, two Aboriginal men were hanged, alongside six white bushrangers. The Aboriginal men were known only by the nicknames of Musquito and Black Jack. Musquito had been convicted of aiding and abetting the wilful murder of a stock-keeper at Grindstone Bay on Tasmania's east coast in 1823, and Black Jack faced the gallows for a second murder. In 1826 two more Aborigines, Jack and Dick, were convicted of murder and hanged. These four hangings took place after a surge of Aboriginal violence. The newly-arrived Lieutenant-Governor George Arthur declared they were intended to set an example.[1] All they achieved was to demonstrate the partiality of British law, for no colonist was ever tried, let alone executed, for killing an Aborigine in Tasmania. After the executions Aboriginal attacks on settlers escalated, and the four hangings have, rightly, been seen as a turning point in what was to become known as the Black War.[2]

While the lives of Jack, Dick and Black Jack are largely inaccessible to the historian, much can be known about Musquito, whose activities were recorded in New South Wales and Tasmania for 20 years before his death. Governors wrote despatches about him and the press reported his 'outrages' in the Hawkesbury River area in 1805 and in Tasmania in 1824. Between those restless times his life amongst settlers and convicts was recorded in colonial documents.[3] For historians interested in Aboriginal accommodation and adaptation in the early colonial period,[4] the life of Musquito offers many opportunities for contemplation. But historians have, thus far, focused on his violent escapades. Some twentieth-century writers have celebrated Musquito as a resistance leader, presenting him as a valiant guerilla, fighting for the freedom of the Indigenous Tasmanians.[5] Others, both antiquarian and modern, have portrayed Musquito as an outlaw against both black and white mores, a desperate leader, a criminal, an evil influence on the formerly peaceable Tasmanians.[6] Such views exaggerate his influence over the Tasmanians, and, whether by accident or design, diminish their agency. This minimises the historical importance of Musquito's life, and prevents evaluation of the choices he made as an Aboriginal man in troubled times. The depiction of Musquito as an outlaw is a trope that obscures the transgressions of the white colonists, who had dispossessed the Tasmanians then abused their own laws to make an example of Musquito.

* * *

Because most writers have been preoccupied by the violent events in Musquito's life, they have concentrated on his 'outrages'. Yet we can know much more of him, and it is necessary that we do before trying to understand the ways Musquito's life has been fashioned through history. Musquito's earliest years are lost to public record, and we cannot be sure when he was born. He was a man when we first hear of him, and died before he became old, so was probably born around 1780. In the historical record Musquito was always described as a Broken Bay man, generally considered Gu-ring-gai country, but living descendants refine this to Gai-Mariagal. Musquito's ancestral country was therefore around Middle Harbour and Manly, reaching north to Broken Bay and north-west to vital sites on the Hawkesbury River.[7]

The colonists' habit of bestowing nicknames on Aborigines presents another complication. In the early 1800s there were two men known by the name of 'Musquito' at Port Jackson. One of them was part of Bennelong and Nanbaree's circle, and fought numerous battles before crowds in Sydney.[8] A striking portrait of 'Mousquéda' (Y-Erran-Gou-La-Ga), painted by Nicolas-Martin Petit of the Baudin expedition in 1802, is also thought by many commentators to depict the subject of this paper.[9] However appealing that might be, it is equally possible the sitter was Nanbaree's friend. That man remained in Sydney for the duration of the Hawkesbury conflict, and died in February 1806, after being speared in retaliation for a drunken attack on the boy Pigeon.[10]

While that Musquito was staging mock fights in Sydney, another Musquito was readying himself for a real fight on the banks of the Hawkesbury River. The riverbanks offered fine alluvial soil, unmatched on the Cumberland Plain and irresistible to hungry colonists, at a time when Aboriginal people could no longer move out of the way of white settlement. As Alan Ward argues, the Hawkesbury River was a highway for many Aboriginal groups,[11] and its peoples depended upon it for everything. Yams grew along its banks and its waters provided fish, crustaceans, and sustenance — nurturing life and ceremony. It was inevitable that the lower Hawkesbury River would become a battleground. The area was also perfectly suited to Aboriginal styles of warfare. The western reaches of the lower Hawkesbury wind through a sandstone valley, depositing soil on the bends but also cutting cliffs that are surrounded by thick bush. These cliffs and spurs repelled European horses but provided the Aborigines with sanctuary and staging points for ambush. Profiting from the terrain, the Aborigines had repelled settlement from the lower Hawkesbury between 1796 and 1804.[12]

In 1804 settlers made another attempt to occupy the riverbanks. By April 1805 colonists at South Creek, near Windsor, were suffering a series of Aboriginal attacks on their houses and their ripening crops. Governor King at first thought the Aborigines' corn raids, firing of crops and houses and thefts of rations and clothing were responses to starvation. He encouraged settlers to offer food to the Aborigines, but after several horrifying murders of whites, became exasperated. King decided the Aborigines were treacherous, and unforgiving of 'real or imaginary Evils'.[13] He sent in the formidable NSW Corps, and issued General Orders that natives should not be suffered to approach any settler's property or person until the murderers were given up.[14]

The conflict was worrying to the residents of Sydney. In May 1805 the *Sydney Gazette* published an account of a party of settlers and constables that had gone out to 'disperse' natives in the 'Pendant [Pennant] Hills' area. They captured Tedbury, who had by 'horrible tuition and example … imbibed propensities of the most diabolical complexion' from his father, 'the assassin' Pemulwuy. The Parramatta Magistrate, Reverend Samuel Marsden, then persuaded Tedbury to take another expedition out to find stolen corn. This second party fell in with a small group of Aborigines, one of whom 'saluted [the party] in good English', and, with not a little audacity, declared 'a determination to continue their rapacities', before melting into the bush.[15] This man was named by the *Sydney Gazette* as 'Bush Muschetta'. Muschetta is an old spelling of mosquito,[16] and 'bush' differentiated him from the man already known to its Sydney readers. This was 'our' Musquito.

By the end of June, the NSW Corps had captured nine Aborigines and gaoled them at Parramatta. Some agreed to guide parties 'in quest of their infatuated kinsmen', an action the *Gazette* interpreted as gratitude for fair treatment[17] and which Governor King interpreted as voluntary surrender.[18] These explanations are improbable. The prisoners were bargaining for their freedom, and that of Tedbury. They may also have been trying to enlist the support of their captors against their enemies. Rival groups in the Hawkesbury had continued their traditional warfare and enmities, in spite of the presence of strangers. There had even been local alliances between Aborigines and settlers, such as between the Burraberongal group of the Darug and settlers at Richmond.[19] However there was no love lost between the various groups of the Darug and Musquito's people, the Gai-Mariagal.[20] As winter set in, faced with the unrelenting NSW Corps, some of the Aborigines evidently decided to trade Musquito in the name of peace. They told the British that it was he who 'still keeps the flame alive'. Marsden liberated two of the captured Aborigines to find Musquito, and they lodged him in Parramatta Gaol on July 6, 1805. The next day Governor King announced that those who had given up 'the Principal in the late Outrages' desired to come in to Parramatta, and should not be molested. He optimistically proclaimed that a 'RECONCILIATION will take place with the Natives generally' (original emphasis).[21] Tedbury was released, and the 'outrages' were thus terminated. The *Gazette* expressed relief and the hope that 'the lenity shown to them at all times when the spirit of destruction ceases to predominate' would convince the Aborigines that their safety depended not upon their own ability, but on the clemency of the Government.[22]

Musquito and his comrade 'Bull Dog' were not acquiescent. They maintained their 'spirit of destruction' in Parramatta Gaol, threatening to set it on fire and destroy every white man in it. Their attempt to loosen the mortar of the stonework and escape was only foiled when a white prisoner informed the turnkey.[23] Meanwhile, Governor King was unsure how to proceed. He felt the captives were implicated in the murders of four settlers, but was sufficiently fair-minded to consider that settlers had killed six Aborigines during the 'coercive measures' and to forego further retaliation. King believed that the fact that the Aborigines had given up Musquito showed their collective sorrow for what had passed. He decided to exile the prisoners to another settlement, revealing his inability to comprehend the local political situation when he remarked that the plan was 'much approved of by the rest'.[24]

Judge-Advocate Richard Atkins, who advised that the Aborigines were 'not bound by any moral or religious tye' and so could not give evidence or bear charging, confirmed the legality of King's decision.[25] The two Aborigines were sent to Norfolk Island, to be victualled at government expense and brought to labour if possible.[26] Isolated on a tiny island penal colony in the middle of the Pacific Ocean, Musquito and Bull Dog had no choice but to live peacefully. They worked as charcoal burners, and at some stage Bull Dog was allowed to return home.[27] After eight years, the settlement on Norfolk Island was evacuated to save costs, so Musquito travelled to Port Dalrymple (Launceston) on board the last transport, *Minstrel II*, arriving in March 1813.[28]

At Port Dalrymple, Musquito was technically free, and his brother Phillip at Port Jackson asked Governor Macquarie if Musquito could be repatriated. In August 1814 Macquarie agreed, and instructed Davey, the Tasmanian Lieutenant Governor, to comply.[29] It was not to be. Musquito, who had lived in the white world for so long, had become valuable because of his Aboriginal skills, and was sent to track convict 'freebooters' who were plaguing the colony with their bushranging. In October 1817 Lieutenant-Governor Sorell informed Macquarie that Musquito still desired to return home, after giving constant service guiding parties in search of bushrangers. He was to be sent to Sydney via *The Pilot*, with a convict named McGill, whose diligent assistance against the bushrangers had made him 'odious amongst the prisoners', and Black Mary, mistress of the feared bushranger Michael Howe.[30] Once more the promise was broken, and Musquito and McGill stayed. Musquito then began work for Edward Lord, a flamboyant and wealthy entrepreneur who intended to take Musquito to Mauritius in February 1818.[31] Again, Musquito appears to have been prevented from leaving. Lord took two other servants,[32] and McGill and Musquito resumed tracking.

They found and killed Michael Howe, in dramatic circumstances, on 4 October 1818.[33]

Despite Musquito's evident heroism, all thoughts of returning him to Sydney were forgotten. Early accounts report that Musquito was ostracised by convicts who resented his work at recapturing bushrangers, and felt keenly his betrayal by the governors. Musquito walked into the bush, heading south where he joined a 'tame gang' that was affiliated with the Oyster Bay people. 'Tame gangs' were bands of Aborigines who had become disconnected from their own people, including some who had spent their childhoods in white households. They lived on the fringes of white settlement and were considered 'inoffensive', unlike the 'wild' Aborigines in the interior. In June 1823 a visiting Wesleyan missionary, Reverend William Horton, met 'Muskitoo's tribe' at Pitt Water in Sorell, between Hobart and the Tasman Peninsula. Reverend Horton believed, erroneously, that Musquito was a convict who had been transported for the murder of a woman. Musquito conversed at length with Horton, and interpreted the customs of the Aborigines to their bewildered observer. Although Horton had a very low opinion of Tasmanian Aborigines, he could not help but be impressed by the charismatic Sydney man, and Horton's is the only account that gives us any corporeal sense of Musquito. Horton gathered that Musquito's 'superior skill and muscular strength' had raised him to his 'present station' as 'leader' of this 'tame gang'.

Keith Windschuttle has suggested that Musquito and the tame gangs were 'detribalised', an awkward word implying they were less than Aboriginal.[34] Yet Horton's account shows that Musquito's associates had adopted few white habits, apart from a liking for tobacco, liquor and roast potatoes and their willingness to accept benevolent handouts. The mob consisted of 20 or 30 men, women and children. Horton was disgusted by their diet, particularly the way they ate semi-cooked meat, and their social habits. He thought it deplorable that they never worked or settled, but wandered, subsisting on kangaroos, possums and oysters, 'lodging in all seasons around their fires in the open air'. Noting they suffered from a skin disease, Horton concluded it was a kind of scurvy exacerbated by their 'extreme filthiness' and habit of sitting too close to the fire. Horton was particularly disturbed that people who had been accustomed to clothing should choose to be completely naked and instead keep the winter cold at bay by smearing their tattooed skins with red gum and animal fat. Horrifying as it appeared to Horton, this was a visual manifestation of the strength with which the 'tame gang' held to a culture of their choosing. Even if the red gum and fat was a (re)invented tradition, the gang's preference for it over English clothes was a conscious display of Aboriginal ways.

Horton wrote that he asked Musquito 'if he was tired of his present mode of living, and if he was willing to till the ground and live as the English do'.

Musquito apparently replied that 'he should like it very well', but thought none of the rest would. Horton was appalled that these people were unwilling to advance 'one step from their original barbarism', despite having once beheld the 'superior comforts and pursuits of civilised man'.[35]

By the time of Horton's visit in 1823, the spread of settlement in Tasmania approximated that of today, and the Aborigines had been pushed out of most of their natural range.[36] Although Horton had some hopes that the 'tame gang' might be used to open an intercourse with the Aborigines of the interior, he also knew that the 'wild' Aborigines had become 'very hostile' towards Europeans. The Oyster Bay people, who favoured the eastern coast and Midlands plains, had nowhere left to go. Musquito's interlude with Horton was to be one of the last peaceful moments of his life, for within a few short months his life was entwined with the Oyster Bay people, and the events at Grindstone Bay would make him a fugitive, and lead to his execution.

The story of the Grindstone Bay attack was told by the sole white survivor, an assigned convict stock-keeper called John Radford, who testified in the Supreme Court in 1824. He said that Musquito and Black Jack had arrived at his hut with 60 'wild' Oyster Bay Aborigines in November 1823. Radford did not say so, but the hut was new and built on a secluded portion of rough pasture that was, according to James Erskine Calder, who knew Radford in the 1870s, a favoured emu and kangaroo hunting ground.[37] As the band included women and children it could not have been a war party, and they may have been surprised to see the hut. Radford told the court that at the time the Aborigines arrived there were three convict stock-keepers at the hut: Radford, an Otaheitan called Mammoa and William Hollyoak, who was an invalid traveller. The Aborigines camped near the hut for three days, playing games and hunting, while Musquito sat inside with the uneasy stock-keepers, eating heartily of their provisions and reassuring them there was no likelihood of attack. However something happened to alter this nervous coexistence. Possibly it was the manner in which the stock-keepers dealt with women that Musquito had taken to the hut, although Radford denied any impropriety when later questioned in court. At break of day on 15 November 1823 the Aborigines called the stock-keepers out of their hut. The trio were confronted with a forest of spears and realised, too late, that they had left their firearms unattended. Musquito, who carried just a waddy and spoke not a word, took their dogs away, despite the white men's protests. When the Aborigines raised their spears the men ran for their lives. Radford was speared, but managed to escape. He ran so fast he could not see who speared his hapless companions, though he heard their screams.[38]

This dramatic tale sealed Musquito's fate, but it is difficult to assess his role in the attack. His visits to the hut show nothing more sinister than a taste for English food, tea and conversation. Radford never saw who speared Hollyoak, and did not witness Mammoa's death. Musquito could not take the blame for the actual murders, and it is not clear whether he 'aided and abetted' the Aborigines. It is especially doubtful whether Musquito had any leadership role, as many scholars think. It was the 'wild' Aborigines who approached the hut with spears bristling, while Musquito was only lightly armed with a waddy, and remained silent. Nevertheless, as news of the murders spread, Musquito and Black Jack were named as protagonists.

The events at Grindstone Bay were the first of a number of violent attacks against settlers that continued into 1824, but there is little evidence of Musquito's direct involvement in later incidents. In March 1824, Aborigines burnt down a hut at Blue Hills[39] and a stock-keeper was speared the next month. Musquito and Black Jack were not present on either occasion, but the *Gazette* thought they might have been nearby 'from the circumstances of the Natives having been with one or two instances only excepted, entirely harmless until these two blacks have lately appeared among them'.[40]

A local tradition that attributed the sudden outbreak of violence to the influence of Musquito and other Aborigines who had spent time with white people was developing.[41] Musquito was well known in the colony, having lived amongst convicts and worked for the notable and notorious Edward Lord. He attracted attention, being tall, charismatic and fluent in English, and he had been present at one of the most frightening murders in Tasmanian history. It was far easier to blame him than contemplate the nightmare that the other Aborigines had themselves resorted to warfare. If Musquito had caused the violence, there was hope that his capture might restore peace, and no need to question the colonial enterprise. It was a myth that offered some consolations. Their fear was real, and not without foundation. However, we must be mindful that Musquito's reputation in Tasmania was not enhanced by any knowledge of his past in the Hawkesbury. The Tasmanian colonists were ignorant of that, for terrifying stories circulated without any talk of it. Today we know that Musquito spent his youth fighting colonists, and it seems likely that he did inspire his Tasmanian associates to fight, although it does not appear that he did so at Grindstone Bay. However there were many causes of the conflict, and he could not have been the sole leader of the Aborigines. It is inconceivable that one man could have organised disparate bands of Tasmanians across such a large front. The attacks of 1824 occurred across most of southern Tasmania, from the east coast into the Midlands, taking in the territories of the Oyster Bay people, with whom Musquito was associated, and their neighbours, the Big River people. With hindsight, it is obvious that the attacks of 1824 represented an outbreak of generalised resistance to white settlement, and that numerous Tasmanian groups were launching their own attacks.

The evidence confirms this view. In June 1824 Matthew Osborne was killed and his wife severely wounded at their property at Jericho near New Norfolk in southern Tasmania. The *Gazette* reported Widow Osborne's recovery on 16 July 1824, and she told the paper that Black Tom (Kickerterpoller) had led the raid in company with 50 Aborigines. Later writers would link Tom and Musquito, but they appear to have lived with separate bands at this time. Although Mrs Osborne did not name Musquito, the *Gazette* was unwilling to abandon the view of Musquito's involvement, and said

> The only tribe who have done any mischief, were corrupted by Musquito, who with much and perverted cunning, taught them a portion of his own villainy, and incited them time after time to join in his delinquencies.[42]

By that time a certain hysteria about Musquito was apparent. On the day the *Gazette* reported Widow Osborne's recovery, the Oatlands Magistrate, Charles Rowcroft, wrote a letter to the Governor, pleading for military assistance because Musquito's band was 'infesting' the district of Murray. Rowcroft blamed Musquito for two murders at Abyssinia and one at Big River, for maltreating assigned convicts on an Oatlands property, and torching a stock hut at Great Lakes. He also accused Musquito of Osborne's murder and declared the widow's life was 'despaired of'.[43] The information provided by Rowcroft, who was very green in the colony,[44] demands scrutiny.[45] These incidents occurred in the lower Midlands, yet this was the country of the Big River (Ouse) people. The Oyster Bay people, with whom Musquito was living, had good relationships with the Big River people, but spent winter on the east coast, and were unlikely to be so far inland in June.[46] Rowcroft was undoubtedly frightened, but clearly Musquito's band was not the only Aboriginal group raiding at the time, and the letter cannot have been taken too seriously, since no military detachment was sent.

In the Oatlands area around this time there was also a rumour that Musquito had a gun and ammunition and had taught the Tasmanians that firearms were useless after one shot,[47] although the Tasmanians learned this from a variety of means.[48] In all, there were 12 attacks between November 1823 and August 1824,[49] but we can be sure Musquito was involved in just two of these. The first was Grindstone Bay, and the second was at Pitt Water (Sorell). In that instance Musquito enticed a settler from his hut with a cooee then speared him, but as he left the settler alive there is a possibility the attack was some personal retaliation. It was certainly not the work of a rampaging murderer. The *Gazette* knew it could not blame all the attacks on Musquito, so it argued that he had made the 'formerly harmless' Tasmanians 'sensible' of the unprovoked aggressions and 'mischievous conduct' of stock-keepers.[50] The local tradition, which held Musquito responsible for the violence by deed and influence, was now firmly established. His apprehension became an 'overpowering psychological necessity'.[51]

Less than a week after the Pitt Water spearing, Musquito was captured, once more by an Aboriginal person. A boy called Tegg (or Teague) and two white servants found him unarmed with two women on the east coast, and Tegg shot and wounded Musquito as he tried to flee.[52] Remarkably, Tegg had been raised in the household of the disreputable Surgeon Edward Luttrell. The Luttrells had owned land in the Hawkesbury district during Musquito's time there, and probably remembered him well. One Luttrell son had been killed by Aborigines in Sydney in 1811.[53] Another, Edward Jr, had been charged in 1810 with shooting and wounding Tedbury in Sydney, and would later claim for himself the credit for Musquito's capture in Tasmania.[54] These parallel lives highlight the peculiar narrowness of colonial society. Not only was Musquito unfortunate enough to find the same tensions in Tasmania that he had survived in the Hawkesbury, but he saw the very same people.

After his capture, Musquito was hospitalised and may have been visited by Governor Arthur, but their conversation was not recorded.[55] Black Jack was captured soon afterwards, and together they faced trial in the new Supreme Court in December 1824.[56] Contemporary reports do not mention Musquito's Hawkesbury years, so Hobart townspeople remained ignorant of his past. Unfortunately, it also seems that Governor Arthur was ignorant of the precedent set by King's fair-minded decision of 1805. Suffice to say, the principles expressed by Judge-Advocate Atkins, that Aborigines were incapable of being brought before a criminal court, either as criminals or witnesses, were not applied. Both Aboriginal men were tried for a capital offence; yet neither was allowed to speak in his own defence, call witnesses or brief counsel. There was doubt about the reliability of the convict Radford and the evidence was entirely circumstantial, yet Musquito was convicted. Melville acidly commented that the resulting executions were 'looked upon by many as a most extraordinary precedent'.[57] In light of King's humane remedy to a similar crisis, Arthur's assent to the trial and hangings looks brutal and arbitrary.

Musquito was said to have insisted his execution was useless as an example to the Aborigines, and to have told Gaoler Bisdee, 'Hanging no good for black fellow'. Bisdee asked 'Why not as good for black fellow as for white fellow, if he kills a man?' to which Musquito replied 'Very good for white fellow, for *he* used to it'.[58] In September of the next year Jack and Dick were also hanged. Arthur issued a government notice stating that the hangings were intended to provide an example to the Aborigines, and induce in them a more conciliatory line of conduct. This cruel example seems to have had the opposite effect. 'Incidents', as NJB Plomley politely describes them, increased dramatically and continued until 1831.[59] Gilbert Robertson, who led roving parties in search of

Aborigines, thought Musquito's execution only served to cause further murders.[60] As James Erskine Calder put it, 50 years later, after the hangings the Aborigines 'sullenly withdrew to the woods, and never more entered the settled districts, except as the deadly enemies of our people'.[61] As attacks escalated in 1826 Arthur allowed settlers to apply force if they felt Aborigines showed any determination to attack, rob or murder, and to treat them as rioters if they assembled in numbers.[62] The stage had been set for the Black War.

* * *

Although dead, Musquito continued to have a role in the conflict in Tasmania, by providing a means to explain Tasmanian antagonism. Governor Arthur had to account to his masters for his failure to conciliate the Aborigines and protect the settlers. In April 1828 he reported that it would be 'in vain to trace the cause of the evil which exists; my duty is plainly to remove its effects'.[63] By January of the following year Arthur had despaired, and hoped for permission to unleash war. He now traced 'the evil'. To deflect blame from the colonists or the administration, he incriminated the lower orders of Tasmanian society — the sealers, convicts and bushrangers — and invoked the local tradition of Musquito's influence. He said that the Tasmanian Aborigines had been 'led on by a Sydney black' and by two other 'partially civilised men' (Black Tom and Black Jack). Black Tom's rejection of his adoptive white family was 'a circumstance which augurs ill for any endeavour to instruct these abject beings'.[64] This theory of outside influence served two purposes. It enabled Arthur to avoid criticism for his poor management and helped him to overcome any liberal feeling in the Colonial Office by establishing the hopelessness of the situation. The Colonial Office chided Arthur for his 'ineffectual efforts to establish a friendly intercourse' between the whites and the Aboriginal tribes, but it sanctioned his declaration of martial law in 1828.[65]

The utility of the depiction of Musquito as an outsider and bad influence has been noted by Christine Wise in her 1983 article 'Black Rebel'.[66] However, not everyone in the Colony agreed with Arthur. An 1830 Committee into the Military Operations against Aborigines in Van Diemen's Land questioned respectable settlers about the origins of Aboriginal hostility. Clearly local traditions about Musquito were fading in the light of the continuing Aboriginal attacks. Although many of the witnesses had endured stock and property losses and the murder of their servants, only the briefest mentions of Musquito were made. One remembered Musquito had behaved ill to his wife and another noted that Tom and Musquito had 'been much with Europeans'.[67] The clearest testimony was from the former roving party leader Gilbert Robertson, a man of mixed race from the West Indies who had been friendly with Musquito and Tom. He said Musquito had been driven into the bush by the 'breach of faith on the part of the Government' and that Musquito's first murders had been committed in self-defence. Robertson humanised Musquito, fondly narrating how he had helped around his property, and was so skilful that he could knock the head off a flying pigeon with a stick. Robertson also stressed the hangings had only caused further murders.[68]

When the Committee prepared its summation it did not mention Musquito or any of the other Aborigines who had lived alongside whites as causes of the violence. It did say that the hangings of the four Aborigines in 1825-1826 had contributed to a permanent estrangement between the Aborigines and white society. However the overwhelming causes were the shooting of Aborigines at Risdon Cove in 1804, general lawlessness, abuse, the loss of land and food supplies and the thefts of women and children. It was the Committee's view that the dissolute and abandoned whites had caused the 'universal and permanent excitement' of the Aborigines' spirit of 'indiscriminate vengeance'.[69] It was however too late to halt the tragic war.

By 1835, a sort of peace was descending, but not everyone rested easily. Henry Melville, a strident critic of Governor Arthur, used a spell in gaol for contempt of court to pen a history of Van Diemen's Land. He argued that the Tasmanians had been a sovereign people, 'the proper, the legitimate owners of the soil', who owned it by virtue of their ancestors' bloody conquest. The Tasmanians had become aggravated by the loss of their hunting grounds, and their ill treatment.[70] Melville saw the 'war' as just — a '"Guerilla"'[71] campaign of self-defence — and the trial as a travesty of justice, for Musquito had 'been made acquainted with English manners, but not with English laws'. In Melville's view Black Jack, as a Tasmanian, was a 'legitimate prisoner of war', and the attorney general ought not have pressed for 'the conviction of the offenders against laws brought by the invaders to the country'.[72] Melville also thought Musquito's reputation was exaggerated. As he put it, 'many deeds of terror are laid to Musquito's charge, which it is impossible for him to have committed, but doubtlessly, several lives were sacrificed by him'. Although Musquito was 'a most daring leader of a hostile tribe' of 'the worst sort of Aborigines', he did not instigate the war.[73]

In the footnotes to his history Melville also included a conversation Musquito was supposed to have had with an unnamed benefactor. Melville almost certainly drew on Robertson's 1830 deposition to put broken English into Musquito's mouth, but it is a poignant evocation of betrayal and lost country.

> I stop wit white fellow, learn to like blanket, clothes, bakky, rum, bread, all same white fellow: white fellow giv'd me. By and by Gubernor send me catch bushrangers — promise me plenty clothes, and send me back Sydney, my own country: I catch him, Gubernor tell too much lie, never send me. I knockit about camp, prisoner no liket me then, givet me nothing, call me b——y hangman nose. I knock one fellow down, give waddie, constable take me. I then walk away in bush. I get along wid

mob, go all about beg some give it bread, blanket: some tak't away my *"gin:"* that make a fight: mob rob the hut: some one tell Gubernor: all white fellow want catch me, shoot me, 'pose he see. I want all same white fellow he never give, mob make a rush, stock-keeper shoot plenty, mob spear some. Dat de way me no come all same your house. Never like see Gubernor any more. White fellow soon kill all black fellow. You good fellow, mob no kill you.[74]

After Melville, few writers were interested in Musquito's motivations. The war had ended with George Augustus Robinson's 'conciliation', in which the surviving Aborigines were coaxed into exile on Flinders Island. Robinson's diaries provide the only surviving Tasmanian Aboriginal recollections of Musquito. In October 1837, Lucy of the Big River tribe told Robinson that she had lived with 'Muskeeto the Sydney black' and that he had taken her from her people. Lucy said Musquito had taken other black women, had killed a Big River man and had shot a woman dead with a musket while she was gathering possum from a tree on Hobart's 'big hill' (Knocklofty). Another Aborigine, Frances, told Robinson that Musquito 'encouraged and excited the VDL aborigines to kill the white men, saying "kill DRYER, kill LUTERTWEIN"'. These wholly negative accounts should not be accepted without qualification. George Augustus Robinson viewed the Tasmanians as abused innocents, and worked tirelessly to persuade the Government that the Flinders Island Aborigines needed to be preserved and protected, at government expense. Musquito provided a means of excusing Tasmanian violence. As Robinson wrote:

> This evidence strongly proves that the whites have occasioned the greatest misery to these poor people the aborigines to an unknown extent, not only by importing the depraved of their own species but also that of the Sydney aborigines who has tended to annihilate them [sic]. Such did Muskeeto. He had murdered several at Sydney and was sent here to be out of the way. What a policy![75]

Lucy and Frances may have told Robinson the truth, but in their words Robinson found a way to redeem the Tasmanian Aborigines in the eyes of the colonists and the government.

* * *

Around this time the first historians endeavoured to create narratives of the foundation of the colony of Van Diemen's Land. Some time in the late 1830s, the Norwegian adventurer Jorgen Jorgenson prepared a manuscript account about the Tasmanian Aborigines. A seaman who had been present at the foundation of Risdon Cove in 1803 and Port Dalrymple in 1804, Jorgenson had returned as a convict in 1826. He became a roving party leader and policeman, but was rendered unemployable by his drunkenness, so turned instead to journalism.[76]

Like most early Tasmanian writers, Jorgenson wrote for a London market, and his accounts of Tasmanian Aboriginal customs were usually sympathetic. He explained the violence by depicting Musquito as a savage figure, a 'cunning and crafty knave', who 'stirred' the Tasmanian Aborigines 'up to all manner of mischief'. Jorgenson never knew Musquito, but unlike Melville or Robinson, was able to access colonial records. He knew the real reasons for Musquito's exile. Yet to dramatise the Aboriginal man's savagery Jorgenson embellished his biography. He introduced a curious and enduring myth that Musquito and Bull Dog's crime had been to 'cut a child out of the womb of the mother', although there is no record of any such horrific event occurring at Port Jackson. Jorgenson enhanced the imagery of Musquito's criminality by saying Musquito had been assigned as a convict stock-keeper at Antill's Ponds and had murdered his wife, Gooseberry, in the Government Paddock in Hobart. Again, there is no evidence to corroborate either of these claims, nor for Jorgenson's account that Musquito was a 'great drunkard' who would beg bread for the blacks, exchange it for tobacco and then sell the tobacco for rum.[77] These colourful tales added zest to Jorgenson's writing and increased its potential profitability, whilst underlining the depraved influence of Musquito. Jorgenson shaped Musquito into a form that later writers — both historians and hacks — would perfect.

Charles Rowcroft, who had been ruined after a disastrous affair with the wife of Musquito's old boss, Edward Lord, and had returned to London late in 1824,[78] also began writing for profit. In the 1840s he fictionalised his experiences as a Vandemonian magistrate, presenting Musquito as a child abductor, 'the cruellest savage that ever tormented a colony'.[79] The novel portrays the Tasmanians in derogatory terms:

> I have often had occasion to observe the dull, listless and almost idiotic appearance of the natives of Van Diemen's Land, when not excited by hunger or some passionate desire ... in this respect they much resemble the unthinking beasts of the field, so inanimate and log-like is their usual manner.[80]

Rowcroft's silly fiction expressed the stereotype that the Tasmanians were too stupid and sullen to engage in warfare without the influence of vigorous outsiders, such as Musquito, who was more bushranger than Aborigine.

The two notions, of Tasmanian innocence and incapacity and Musquito's evil influence, are evident in much historical material produced after the 1840s. Colonial writers carefully pondered the destruction of the Tasmanian Aborigines. It provided them with opportunities to write history that considered grand philosophical and literary themes about the progress and decay of societies. Hobart writers also worried how their island and its new people would be perceived. As Rebe Taylor has noted, they looked across 'a geography that maps morality and confines it to the colonised spaces'.[81] The history of the Aboriginal

Tasmanians enabled writers to explore and define the gulf between 'savagery' and 'civilisation'. While Musquito necessarily had a small part in the history of Tasmania, the manner of his depiction is significant. He proved that Aborigines could not discard their 'savagery', and confirmed the 'civilisation' of the colonists.

The great early historian of Tasmania, John West, felt the civilisation of 'a barbarous people' was impossible in the presence of white men. 'The contrast is too great, and the points of contact too numerous and irritating ... the white man's shadow is, to men of every other hue, by law of Heaven, the shadow of death'.[82] Nevertheless, he was still interested to trace the process of destruction. He began his account of the Tasmanian Aborigines with the 1804 massacre at Risdon Cove, reporting that 50 Aborigines had died there and musing how

> The sorrows of a savage are transient: not so, his resentment. Every wrong is new, until it is revenged: and there is no reason to suppose these terrible sacrifices were ever forgotten.[83]

While West documented settler abuses of Aborigines, he perceived the Aboriginal violence as a childlike response to white provocation. Musquito was placed first on West's list of the causes of 'that long and disastrous conflict', in which 'a people, all but a fading fragment, became extinct'.[84] West's Musquito is a statesmanlike figure, who would enter settlers' huts and sit down 'with great dignity' whilst mobs of one or two hundred Aborigines would patiently await his signal to approach. No contemporary record verifies such an extraordinary occurrence, although there are obvious resonances with Radford's account. West also depicts Musquito directing deeds of 'great enormity' as he 'propagated his spirit', commanding large bodies under a 'common impulse', with 'military unity and skill'.[85] But this leadership was not valorous, but self-aggrandising. West also claimed that Musquito had, before joining them, pursued the Tasmanian blacks and stormed their huts.[86] Like Jorgenson, West wrote that Musquito was transported for murdering a woman. The destruction of a woman, a symbol of innocence and vulnerability, is further evidence of Musquito's violation of the laws of man. West's Musquito is a threat to both black and white, truly an outsider.

Though West acknowledges contemporary concerns about the trial, he declares he will not extenuate the Aboriginal men's 'treachery' by questioning it. For West the tragedy of Musquito's story is not in his own life or death, but that his deeds 'justified hatred to the race, and finally systematic massacre'.[87] Under Musquito's 'pernicious' influence the Tasmanian Aborigine 'appeared to be a fiend full of mischief and spite, marked out by his crimes for utter extinction'.[88] West does write about the crimes of the colonists, but Musquito expiates those crimes by representing an evil so profound and so enduring that the only solution was to conquer the Tasmanians, and thus eradicate it.

Twenty years after West, James Bonwick also pondered the destruction of Tasmanian Aboriginal society. A great archivist, Bonwick spent years gathering colonial documentary sources, creating the Bonwick Transcripts, which are now housed in the Mitchell Library. He wrote two books on the subject of the Tasmanian Aborigines and their destruction, using colonial source material. His work is considered definitive, yet the archivist's selection of sources about Musquito raises questions about Bonwick's history. His Musquito was an amplified version of Jorgenson's[89] with some source material, along with spurious quotations from 'old hands' to put flesh on the bones of the story when needed. In his books Musquito is a degraded individual, whose experiences on the frontier had filled him with the vices of both Aboriginal and white society — a hyperbole of savagery. As Bonwick told it, Musquito was 'indebted to his acquirements in civilisation for his extra ability in working mischief', and 'an English scholar in our national vices of drinking and swearing, as well as in the employment of our tongue'. Bonwick made no mention of Governor King's exile, but uses Jorgenson's story that Musquito had murdered a pregnant woman. He makes it even more lurid, telling his readers that Musquito and Bull Dog, after 'gratifying their horrible propensities', ripped the woman open and destroyed the body of her child. Bonwick's Musquito murdered both Gooseberry and a new character, 'Black Hannah' and severed the breast of his 'gin' because she persisted in suckling her child, against his orders.[90] He is a bizarre hybrid who ruins the Tasmanian Aborigines. The members of the 'tame mob' too were cultural exiles, who had 'transgressed tribal laws in their own districts'. Later, Musquito governed the 'equality-loving' Tasmanians after 'the approved European model' — presumably, despotism. Although Bonwick acknowledged that Musquito was frequently absent from the conflict, he argued he 'kept the tethers', orchestrating attacks from afar and using his 'demoniacal arts' to spur further violence. Bonwick did believe that the atrocities of convicts and bushrangers contributed to the conflict, but his view of Musquito's malevolent influence is uncompromising. In Bonwick's Tasmania the 'Darkies were quiet as dogs before Musquito came'.[91] As did West, Bonwick draws Musquito in such a way that the actions of the colonists are rendered natural. Musquito underpins West's and Bonwick's ideology that the destruction of the Tasmanian race was inevitable.

Not all early historians felt the same way. James Erskine Calder was a contemporary of Bonwick, with a similar command of colonial source material. A surveyor of long residence in Tasmania, he avidly collected information about Aboriginal languages and culture from black and white informants. Calder felt — though Tasmanians may not agree with him — 'the most interesting event in the history of Tasmania, after its discovery, seems to be the extinction of its ancient inhabitants'. Although Calder argued that respiratory disease was a major factor in the decline of the Aborigines, he did not see their destruction as either inevitable or necessary.

In *Some Account of the Wars, Extirpation, Habits etc. of the Native Tribes of Tasmania,* Calder condemned the hangings for severing relationships between black and white. He endorsed many of Melville's views, including his point that the Aborigines were prisoners of war who ought not to have suffered for 'acts justified in war time by the usages of all nations'.[92] Calder said that Musquito was a *'civilised black'* who had been betrayed by the Governor, and while he did not shy from portraying him as a 'most desperate fellow', Calder felt there was not enough evidence to convict Musquito 'beyond presence at the hut with sixty or seventy or more', and that his atrocities were very much exaggerated.[93] Calder saw Musquito's hanging as a sacrifice 'to intimidate his surviving brethren into submission to the superior race', concluding that 'I don't believe justice, or anything like it, was always done here fifty years ago'.[94]

The key to Calder's sympathetic depiction of Musquito was his high estimation of Aboriginal people. He repudiated Horton's assessment of the Tasmanians, on the basis that they were 'naturally very intellectual and highly susceptible of culture'. He appreciated their religious complexity and wrote elegantly of their skilful exploitation of the bounty of the Tasmanian environment.[95] Calder acknowledges that the Tasmanians learned something of European habits from Musquito and other 'half civilised' Aborigines, but once this brief association concluded, the Tasmanians 'cleverly' planned all their attacks 'in which they seldom failed of success'.[96] For Calder the Tasmanians were 'a most mischievous, determined, and deadly foe', who devastated property and 'took life about five times as often as it was inflicted upon themselves'.[97]

Calder's work is frequently overlooked in favour of Bonwick, particularly today, when Calder's book is held by few libraries, whilst Bonwick's and West's have been frequently reprinted, in Australia and elsewhere. While Clive Turnbull used Calder and Melville to write *Black War,*[98] the West/Bonwick narrative of Musquito's transgressive influence percolated through historiography and literature until well into the twentieth century. An example is George Mackaness's 1944 *Lags and Legirons,* a series of tales of colonial bounders fictionalised to the point of fancy. In Mackaness Musquito was active in Governor Sorell's time, was defended in court by Gilbert Robertson, and declared on the gallows 'hanging no blurry good for blackfellow'.[99] Yet Mackaness was a serious antiquarian who edited Melville. To write such an account even in fiction was an abuse of history. These views were repeated in bestselling works such as A Grove Day's *Adventurers of the Pacific,* with a chapter called 'Demons of Van Diemen's Land' that began with the immortal line 'There were monsters in those days. One was named Musquito.'[100]

In the 1970s authors who sought to recover a sense of Aboriginal agency in colonisation gave Musquito new prominence as a resistance leader. At this time the late Lin Onus painted his haunting images of Musquito's movements between black and white worlds (*Quiet as Dogs, White Man's Burden*), drowning in white documents (*Wanted, One Rope Thrower*).[101] While most modern writers explored the symmetry between Musquito's life in the Hawkesbury and in Tasmania, they frequently relied on Bonwick as a source. Willey paraphrased Bonwick by writing that Musquito 'directed' the Tasmanian Aborigines and organised 'large numbers of warriors with tactics aimed at emulating the military discipline and skills of the Europeans'. Knowing that Hawkesbury Aborigines had turned Musquito in, Willey decided that Musquito and Bulldog had been betrayed because the confected story of the rape and murder of women 'demanded vengeance under the tribe's own laws'.[102] The late Al Grassby with co-author Marj Hill wrote that Musquito 'welded [the Tasmanians] into a fighting force and began a guerilla war such as he had pursued with considerable success in his native land', which he continued for 'several years'.[103] David Lowe also drew on Bonwick and presented Musquito as the leader of the resistance in Tasmania — the 'civilised native' who taught the Aborigines guerilla tactics.[104] These authors, whilst intending to promote the idea of Aboriginal resistance, overstated the level of organisation of the war in Tasmania, and Musquito's role in it. They inadvertently diminish the Tasmanians by denying their agency in the conflict. The narrative of the gentle Tasmanian infected with the wrath of a more vigorous Sydney Aborigine was continued.

A deliberate attempt to remove the historical agency of the Tasmanians is Keith Windschuttle's *The Fabrication of Aboriginal History*. Windschuttle lays the blame for almost all Tasmanian Aboriginal violence at Musquito's feet, who, he claims, was not even an authentic Aborigine, but an interloper, a bushranger leading a violent crime spree in a foreign country. Having rebutted Windschuttle's views in other forums, I reiterate that it contains many factual and interpretive errors, including ignorance of Musquito's career in Sydney.[105] Windschuttle exaggerates Musquito's involvement in the attacks of 1823-1824 and ignores the questions around the legality of the convictions and executions. Without any apparent awareness of the ideologies of Bonwick and West, Windschuttle propagates the belief that Musquito inculcated violence in the Tasmanians, and took them down the path to destruction. This inflated view of Musquito's involvement in the Tasmanian campaign is the cornerstone of Windschuttle's arguments against the 'guerilla war thesis'. He sees Musquito's 'criminal' behaviour as inimical to resistance, and argues there was no genuine Tasmanian campaign. The assertion that the Tasmanians had no political or historical agency is central to Windschuttle's view of the benign nature of Tasmanian colonisation, and his challenge to the legitimacy of modern Tasmanian Aboriginal claims.

Windschuttle's 'discovery' of Musquito is a device to counter the views of Lyndall Ryan, amongst others. In telling the story of Tasmanian cultural survival,

Ryan (as did Christine Wise) placed Musquito alongside the Tasmanian Aborigines — the leader of one band, but not of a movement.[106] Ryan did not present a complete account of Musquito, and did not consider his motivations in depth. Neither did she cover his past in New South Wales. However Ryan's was a book about Tasmania, and while Musquito's life is worthy of detailed attention, it does not encapsulate the Tasmanian Aboriginal story, because Tasmanians were engaged in violent conflict independently of Musquito. Musquito's rage, if that is what it was, lasted but a few short months, and he was dead before the Black War really began. Though many historians have argued otherwise, in the theatre of the Black War the Tasmanians were the major actors, and Musquito had only a walk-on part.

* * *

Now that we have some understanding of what historians have made of Musquito's life, it is time to look again. Historians have fitted his life to their narratives. The focus on his 'outrages' has meant that we have missed much that was extraordinary about him and his times. Perhaps if we return to that moment at Pittwater, when Reverend Horton observed the 'tame gang' remaking themselves in the firelight with red gum and animal grease, we can look again at the ways both Musquito and the Tasmanians tried to navigate the tumultuous world of early colonial society.

References

Primary sources

Archives Office of Tasmania

Colonial Secretary's Office Papers, CSO 1/316/7578/1 and CSO 1/177/4306.

Crowther *Port Certificates,* Book L: 33.

Departures Index, Lord 17 March 1818.

Kemp, Susan M 1969, 'John Leake 1780-1865: Early settler in Tasmania', MA thesis, St John's College, York, NS 242.

Minutes of Committee for Care etc of Aborigines 1830, CBE1/1.

Sorell Despatches, CY 1096.

Mitchell Library, State Library of NSW

Wesleyan Mission Papers, Bonwick Transcripts BT 52, Volume 4.

Newspapers

Sydney Gazette

The Hobart Town and Van Diemen's Land Gazette

NSW State Records

Colonial Secretary's Correspondence 1788-1825, Reel 6004, 4/3493 and Reel 6040, ML Safe 1/51.

Reference Works

'Edward Lord', *Australian Dictionary of Biography,* Vol II (L-Z), 1788-1825: 127-128.

'Edward Luttrell', *Australian Dictionary of Biography,* Vol II (L-Z), 1788-1825: 139-140.

'Charles Rowcroft', *Australian Dictionary of Biography,* Vol II (L-Z), 1788-1825: 402.

Baxter, Carole J 1987, General Musters of NSW, Norfolk Island and Van Diemen's Land 1811, Sydney.

British Parliamentary Papers, Colonies, Australia, 4, Correspondence and Papers relating to the Government and Affairs of the Australian Colonies 1830-1836, 1970, Irish University Press, Shannon.

Historical Records of Australia, 1915, Series I, Volume 5, July 1804-August 1806, Commonwealth Parliamentary Library Committee, Canberra.

Historical Records of Australia, 1921, Series III, Volume 2, July 1812-December 1819, Commonwealth Parliamentary Library Committee, Canberra.

Other Primary Sources

Foley, Dennis 2003-2004, personal communication.

Martin-Petit, Nicolas 1802, *Mousquéda, Portrait of an Aborigine from New Holland,* Muséum d'Histoire Naturelle, Le Havre.

Tasmanian Legislative Council 1867. Mrs Luttrell's Case. Report of Select Committee. *Tasmanian Journals & Parliamentary Papers.*

Secondary sources

Bonwick, James 1872, *The Last of the Tasmanians: or, the Black War of Van Diemen's Land*, Johnson Reprint Corporation, Baltimore, 1970.

—— 1884, *The Lost Tasmanian Race*, Samson Low et al, London.

Boyce, James 2003, 'Fantasy Island', in R Manne (ed.), *Whitewash*, Black Inc, Melbourne: 17-80.

Calder, James Erskine 1874, 'Some Account of the Wars of Extirpation, and Habits of the Native Tribes of Tasmania', *Journal of the Anthropological Institute of Great Britain and Ireland* 3: 7-28.

—— 1875, *Some Account of the Wars, Extirpation, Habits &c of the Native Tribes of Tasmania*, Henn & Co, Hobart.

Carment, David 1980, 'The Wills Massacre of 1861: Aboriginal-European Conflict on the Colonial Australian Frontier', *Journal of Australian Studies* 6: 49-55.

Connor, John 2002, *The Australian Frontier Wars, 1788-1838*, UNSW Press, Sydney.

Fels, Marie 1982, 'Culture Contact in the County of Buckinghamshire, Van Diemens Land 1803-1811', *Tasmanian Historical Research Association Papers and Proceedings* 29(2): 47-79.

—— 1988, *Good Men and True: The Aboriginal Police of the Port Phillip District*, Melbourne University Press, Melbourne.

Foley, Dennis 2001, *Repossession of Our Spirit*, Aboriginal History Inc, Canberra.

Grassby, Al and Hill, Marji 1988, *Six Australian Battlefields: Black resistance to white invasion and the struggle against colonial oppression*, Angus and Robertson, Sydney.

Grey, Jeffrey 1999, *A Military History of Australia*, Cambridge University Press, Melbourne.

Grove Day, Andrew 1969, *Adventurers of the Pacific*, Meredith Press, New York.

Lowe, David 1994, *Forgotten Rebels: Black Australians who fought back*, Permanent Press, Melbourne.

Mackaness, George 1944, *Lags and Legirons*, Angus & Robertson, Sydney.

Melville, Henry 1836, *The History of Van Diemen's Land from the year 1824-1835*, (ed. George Mackaness), Horwitz-Grahame, Sydney, 1965.

National Museum of Australia, 'Musquito: Criminal or resistance fighter?', in *Outlawed! Rebels, revolutionaries and bushrangers*, [Exhibition Catalogue], National Museum of Australia, Canberra, 2003: 34-37.

Parry, Naomi 2003a, 'More on Windschuttle', *Overland* 171 (Winter): 69-70.

—— 2003b, '"Many Deeds of Terror": Windschuttle and Musquito', *Labour History* 85 (November): 207-212.

—— 2004, '"Many Deeds of Error": Response to Windschuttle's Defence of his View of Musquito', *Labour History* 87 (November): 236-238.

—— 2005, 'Musquito', in C Cunneen, J Roe, B Kingston and S Garton (eds), *Australian Dictionary of Biography Supplement 1580-1980*, Melbourne University Press, Melbourne: 299.

Pederson, Howard 1984, '"Pigeon": An Australian Aboriginal Rebel', *European-Aboriginal Relations in Western Australia*, (December): 7-15.

Plomley, NJB 1987, *Weep In Silence: a history of the Flinders Island Aboriginal Settlement and the Flinders Island Journals of George Augustus Robinson 1835-1839*, Blubber Head Press, Hobart.

—— 1990-1991, 'Aborigines and Governors', *Bulletin of the Centre for Tasmanian Historical Studies* 3(1): 1-18.

—— (ed.) 1991, *Jorgen Jorgenson and the Aborigines of Van Diemen's Land*, Blubber Head Press, Hobart.

Reynolds, Henry 1995, *Fate of a Free People*, Penguin, Melbourne.

Roberts, David 1995, 'The Bells Falls Massacre and Bathurst's history of violence: local tradition and Australian historiography', *Australian Historical Studies* 26(105): 615-633.

Rowcroft, Charles 1846, *The Perils and Adventures of Mr William Thornley*, J Walch & Sons, Hobart, reprinted, n.d.

Ryan, Lyndall 1981, *The Aboriginal Tasmanians*, Allen & Unwin, Sydney, 2nd edition 1996.

—— 1997, 'The Struggle for Trukanini 1830-1997: PR Eldershaw Memorial Lecture', *Tasmanian Historical Research Association Papers and Proceedings* 44(3): 153-173.

Taylor, Rebe 2002, *Unearthed: the Aboriginal Tasmanians of Kangaroo Island*, Wakefield Press, Adelaide.

Turnbull, Clive 1948, *Black War: the extermination of the Tasmanian Aborigines*, Cheshire-Landsdowne, Melbourne, 2nd edition 1965.

Ward, Alan 2004, 'They did not "disappear": Aboriginal communities on the Cumberland Plain, c. 1840-1940'. Unpublished paper given to Australian Historical Association Conference, University of Newcastle, 7 July 2004.

West, John 1852, *The History of Tasmania*, (edited AGL Shaw) Angus & Robertson, Sydney, 1971.

Willey, Keith 1979, *When the Sky Fell Down: The Destruction of the Tribes of the Sydney Region, 1788-1825*, Collins, Sydney.

Windschuttle, Keith 2002, *The Fabrication of Aboriginal History: Volume 1, Van Diemen's Land 1803-1847*, Macleay Press, Sydney.

—— 2004 'Guerilla Warrior and Resistance Fighter? The Career of Musquito', *Labour History*, 87 (November): 221-235.

Wise, Christine 1983, 'Black Rebel: Musquito', in E Fry (ed.), *Rebels and Radicals*, George Allen & Unwin, Sydney: 1-7.

Wright, Reginald 1986, *The Forgotten Generation of Norfolk Island and Van Diemens Land*, Library of Australian History, Sydney.

ENDNOTES

[1] Government Notice 13 September 1826, Correspondence Relative to Military Operations against Aborigines in Van Diemen's Land 1831, *British Parliamentary Papers, Colonies, Australia, 4*, Volume XIX: 191-192.

[2] Bonwick 1872: 104; Bonwick 1884: 84; Calder 1875: 45.

[3] Parry 2005.

[4] See for example Reynolds 1995; Fels 1988; Carment 1980; Pederson 1984.

[5] Grassby and Hill 1988: 53-55; Willey 1979: 167, 181-182; Lowe 1994: 9-14.

[6] Plomley 1991: 74; West 1852: 267-269; Bonwick 1872: 92-104; Bonwick 1884: 74-84; Windschuttle 2002: 65-75, 130, 377-386, 399.

[7] Personal communication, Dennis Foley, 2003 and 2004.

[8] *Sydney Gazette,* 23 December 1804; 13 January 1805; 12 January 1806.

[9] Petit 1802: 10n; Lowe 1994: 9-10.

[10] *Sydney Gazette,* 12 January 1806; 19 January 1806; 2 February 1806.

[11] Ward 2004.

[12] Grey 1999: 35; Connor 2002: 43.

[13] Gov King to Earl Camden, 30 April 1805, *Historical Records of Australia*, Series I, Volume 5, 1915: 306-307.

[14] *Sydney Gazette,* 28 April 1805.

[15] *Sydney Gazette,* 19 May 1805.

[16] Oxford English Dictionary.

[17] *Sydney Gazette,* 30 June 1805.

[18] King to Camden, 20 July 1805, *Historical Records of Australia*, Series I, Volume 5, 1915: 497.

[19] Connor 2002: 44-45.

[20] Foley 2001: 7.

[21] *Sydney Gazette,* 30 June 1805; 7 July 1805.

[22] *Sydney Gazette,* 4 August 1805.

[23] *Sydney Gazette,* 11 August 1805.

[24] King to Camden, 20 July 1805, *Historical Records of Australia*, 1915: 497.

[25] King to Camden, 20 July 1805, *Historical Records of Australia*, 1915: 502-504.

[26] King to Piper, 18 August 1805, Colonial Secretary's Correspondence, NSW State Records, Reel 6040, ML Safe 1/51, p. 41; The absence of charges is confirmed in Baxter 1987: 94, 152.

[27] Wright 1986: 30-31.

[28] Colonial Secretary's Office, CSO 1/177/4306, Archives Office of Tasmania.

[29] NSW Colonial Secretary to Lt Gov Davey, 17 August 1814, Colonial Secretary's Correspondence 1788-1825, NSW State Records, Reel 6004, 4/3493: 251.

[30] Lt Gov Sorell to Gov Macquarie, 13 October 1817, *Historical Records of Australia*, Series III, Volume 2, 1921: 282-284.

[31] *Hobart Town and Van Diemen's Land Gazette*, 14 February 1818.

[32] Archives Office Tasmania Departures Index, Lord 17 March 1818, Crowther *Port Certificates,* Book L: 33.

[33] Lt Gov Sorell to Gov Macquarie, 20.10.1818, Sorell Despatches, Archives Office of Tasmania, CY 1096: 91.

[34] Windschuttle 2002: 67.

[35] Rev W Horton to Secretaries of Wesleyan Mission Society, 3 June 1823, Wesleyan Mission Papers, Mitchell Library, Bonwick Transcripts, BT52, Volume 4.

[36] Fels 1982; Boyce 2003: 47-59.

[37] Calder 1875: 48.

[38] *Hobart Town and Van Diemen's Land Gazette*, 3 December 1824.

[39] *Hobart Town and Van Diemen's Land Gazette*, 26 March 1824.

[40] *Hobart Town and Van Diemen's Land Gazette*, 2 April 1824.

[41] Roberts 1995.

[42] *Hobart Town and Van Diemen's Land Gazette*, 16 July 1824.

[43] Charles Rowcroft to Lt Gov Arthur, 16 June 1824, Archives Office of Tasmania, CSO 1/316/7578/1: 6-7.

[44] 'Charles Rowcroft', *Australian Dictionary of Biography*, Vol II (L-Z), 1788-1825: 402; 'Edward Lord', *Australian Dictionary of Biography*, Vol II (L-Z), 1788-1825: 127-128.

[45] Windschuttle takes it at face value. Windschuttle 2002: 69.

[46] Ryan 1981: 14-27.

[47] Kemp 1969: 17; O'Connor to Parramore, 11 December 1827, Archives Office of Tasmania, CSO/323/7578.

[48] Connor 2002: 88-89.

[49] Plomley 1990-1991: 15.

[50] *Hobart Town and Van Diemen's Land Gazette*, 6 August 1824.

[51] Wise 1983: 4.

[52] *Hobart Town and Van Diemen's Land Gazette*, 20 August 1824.

[53] 'Edward Luttrell', *Australian Dictionary of Biography*, Vol II (L-Z), 1788-1825: 139-140.

[54] *Sydney Gazette*, 24 February 1810, Tasmanian Legislative Council 1867, Mrs Luttrell's Case, Report of Select Committee.

[55] *Hobart Town and Van Diemen's Land Gazette*, 20 August 1824.

[56] *Hobart Town and Van Diemen's Land Gazette*, 3 December 1824.

[57] Melville 1836: 37-39.

[58] Melville 1836: 39-40n.

[59] Plomley 1990-1991: 14-15.

[60] Minutes of Committee for Care etc of Aborigines 1830, Gilbert Robertson, Archives Office of Tasmania, CBE1/1: 17.

[61] Calder 1875: 46.

[62] Government Notices 13 September 1826, Colonial Secretary's Office, Correspondence Relative to Military Operations against Aborigines in Van Diemen's Land 1831, *British Parliamentary Papers, Colonies, Australia, 4,* Volume XIX: 191-192.

[63] Lt Gov Arthur to Secretary Huskisson 17 April 1828, Correspondence Relative to Military Operations against Aborigines in Van Diemen's Land 1831, *British Parliamentary Papers, Colonies, Australia, 4,* Volume XIX: 177.

[64] Lt Gov Arthur to Viscount Goderich 10 January 1828, Correspondence Relative to Military Operations against Aborigines in Van Diemen's Land 1831, *British Parliamentary Papers, Colonies, Australia, 4,* Volume XIX: 175.

[65] Secretary Sir George Murray to Lt Gov Arthur, 25 August 1829, Correspondence Relative to Military Operations against Aborigines in Van Diemen's Land 1831, *British Parliamentary Papers, Colonies, Australia, 4,* Volume XIX: 186.

[66] Wise 1983: 6-7.

[67] Minutes of Evidence, Committee for the Affairs of Aborigines, Correspondence Relative to Military Operations against Aborigines in Van Diemen's Land 1831, *British Parliamentary Papers, Colonies, Australia, 4,* Volume XIX: 221, 226.

[68] Minutes of Committee for Care etc of Aborigines 1830, Gilbert Robertson, Archives Office of Tasmania, CBE1/1: 16-17; Minutes of Evidence, Committee for the Affairs of Aborigines, Correspondence Relative to Military Operations against Aborigines in Van Diemen's Land 1831, *British Parliamentary Papers, Colonies, Australia, 4,* XIX: 220.

[69] Report of the Aborigines Committee 19 March 1830, Correspondence Relative to Military Operations against Aborigines in Van Diemen's Land 1831, *British Parliamentary Papers, Colonies, Australia, 4,* XIX: 210-211.

[70] Melville 1836: 30-31.

[71] Melville 1836: 33.

[72] Melville 1836: 37-38.

[73] Melville 1836: 32-33.

[74] Melville 1836: 39-40nn.

[75] Plomley 1987: 481-482.

[76] Plomley 1990-1991: 4-6.

[77] Plomley 1991: 75.

[78] 'Charles Rowcroft', *Australian Dictionary of Biography,* Vol II (L-Z), 1788-1825: 402; 'Edward Lord', *Australian Dictionary of Biography,* Vol II (L-Z), 1788-1825: 127-128.

[79] Rowcroft 1846: 67-68, 155-173.

[80] Rowcroft 1846: 167.

[81] Taylor 2002: 42-43.

[82] West 1852: 268-270.

[83] West 1852: 262-263.

[84] West 1852: 267.

[85] West 1852: 268.

[86] West 1852: 267.

[87] West 1852: 268-270.

[88] West 1852: 277.

[89] Plomley 1990-1991: 39.

[90] Bonwick 1884: 93-94.

[91] Bonwick 1884: 78.

[92] Calder 1875: 45.

[93] Calder 1875: 47.

[94] Calder 1875: 54.

[95] Calder 1874.

[96] Calder 1875: 55.

[97] Calder 1875: 55.

[98] Turnbull 1948.

[99] Mackaness 1944: 112-117.

[100] Grove Day 1969: 235.

[101] Onus' Musquito series was included in *Outlawed!,* a National Museum of Australia exhibition that toured to Melbourne and Queensland in 2003-2005. National Museum of Australia 2003.

[102] Willey 1979: 180-182.

[103] Grassby and Hill 1988: 54.

[104] Lowe 1994: 9-14.

[105] Parry 2003a, b; Windschuttle 2004; Parry 2004.

[106] Ryan 1997: 87-88. Wise 1983.

Leadership: the quandary of Aboriginal societies in crises, 1788 – 1830, and 1966

Dennis Foley

Introduction

The sound of a British officer's leather-soled boot crunching on Hawkesbury sandstone in January 1788 resonated with change in Indigenous Australian epistemologies forever. The British invasion brought a new form of 'science' to the Australian landscape. Western knowledge systems were to be the 'truth' without peer.[1] The imposition of the British system resulted in a progressive elimination and near extermination of Indigenous Australian social systems, knowledge, governance, economy and education.[2] Perhaps the most devastating aspect of this conquest was the social construction of race that placed Indigenous Australians in a scientifically inferior space. Indigenous people were seen as sub-human with no societal or scientific systems in place.[3] Indigenous knowledge was reinterpreted through Western ethnocentric scientific discourse based on a language and an audience that was non-Indigenous.[4] This resulted in many misunderstandings of Indigenous knowledge, including its links to power and leadership.

Leadership as understood by the British post-1788, particularly in the early years of the colony, are examined in this paper. The factors that resulted in some Indigenous leaders' emergence from societal chaos and the need for military reaction are also examined. This includes discussion of the leaders Pemulwuy, Mosquito and Windradyne. The illegitimate imposition of leadership by the British on Bungaree will then be examined, to show that chiefdom status was often a term of convenience imposed by the coloniser. This is followed by discussion of Mr Vincent Lingiari, reviewing the circumstances that resulted in his emergence as an internationally recognised Indigenous Australian leader.

The construction of knowledge in the late eighteenth century

It is important to understand that several of the British officers in the First Fleet and subsequent garrison reinforcements had seen active service in the French-American War and the American War of Independence. For example, the background military service of some of the early British invading forces included:

- Captain John Hunter was at the siege of Quebec;
- Captain Watkin Tench spent three months as a prisoner in Maryland;
- Lieutenant William Dawes was wounded in action against the French at Chesapeake Bay;
- Judge Advocate David Collins served in Nova Scotia and was at the Battle of Bunker Hill;
- Lieutenant Gidley King and Major Robert Ross were at Quebec and later captured by the French;[5] and
- Governor Lachlan Macquarie, who assumed office as the fifth Governor of the colony on 28 December 1809, had seen active service as a lieutenant in the American War of Independence.[6]

This frontier experience on the eastern seaboard of North America provided these officers with a simplistic model of First Nations people. Having seen Native Americans and their tribal system of chiefs, they assumed that the Port Jackson clans were similar. They often referred to the Indigenous Australians as Indians.[7]

The subsequent appointment of Aboriginal 'chiefs' by Governor Macquarie altered the dynamics of an already fragile and fractured Indigenous society within the Sydney environs in 1815-16.[8] The Eora society had already been decimated by smallpox, venereal disease and a protracted guerrilla war of attrition as the colony spread into Aboriginal pastures and fisheries, depriving them of food and disrupting what had been a stable co-existence within the landscape.[9] The misinterpretation of the concept of a chief, or kingship, blinded the invaders to an understanding of the pluralistic societies of Indigenous Australia. A possible exception was Lieutenant William Dawes whose relationship with a young Indigenous woman, Patyegarang, enabled him not only to grasp the Eora languages, but it seems from his journals that he may also have obtained an insight into the Eora societal structure.[10] Apart from Dawes, within the Western scientific knowledge system there was little debate over the preconceived idea of the supremacy of normal science in the identification and determination of legitimate knowledge. Indigenous Australia was not granted any legitimacy.[11]

The pluralistic style of society of Aboriginal Australia was an unknown concept to the invader. In their ignorance, the British could only determine chiefdoms. Subconsciously or consciously this system imposed a male-dominated class system over the once peaceful, homologous matrilineal Eora, which includes (but is not limited to) Wangle, Cadigal, Gai-mariagal, Gur-ing-gah, Bidgingal, Wallumattagal, Burramattagal and Darug clans.[12] The acceptance of a male-dominated class system is based on an incorrect assumption that has been retained by several generations of Australian-born descendants of the British invaders.

Accustomed to Native America, the British also incorrectly assumed that the major social divisions were tribes,[13] with a tribe considered to be a group of people under a recognised chief. Anthropologist Ronald Berndt has said 'most of us have become so used to speaking of Australian aboriginal tribes that we have rarely paused to examine their composition or the appropriateness of such a term'.[14]

The Eora pre-1788 was a society devoid of individuals seeking status, revenge or capital gains, as these were negative personal attributes not tolerated in the Elders circle.[15] It was a pluralist society that did not experience dominance and leadership in the Western sense. While I accept that some group members had greater powers and rights than others, these differences were due to seniority of age and knowledge such as that gained though initiation, for example.[16]

An Indigenous academic, I am not a member of a tribe, I belong to a clan. Through my mother, I am a member of a matrilineal clan, the Gai-mariagal people of the Guringah language group. My matrilineal land is that country which is now called the northern suburbs of Sydney. I will use several oral history references from them. My father is of Wiradjuri, Capertee/Turon River clan descent, which is also a rich oral history resource that I use in this paper. Critics of this paper in its draft form stated that oral histories and family viewpoints do not add to overall knowledge. The denial of oral history when compared to history from the pen of an English military person, or the primary records of a missionary, a police officer or public servant reinforces the Eurocentric concept that 'knowledge is power, or power is knowledge'[17] — as long as you are white, protestant and a male, especially in the early days of the colony. It is widely accepted that oral history is fragmented, and that the knowledge that has been retained is subject to societal destruction. This means that Indigenous scholars are forced to confirm their history only from within modernity's biased written record. This is a transgressive step away from acknowledging the implications of oral history and the substantiation of Indigenous epistemologies. The role of Indigenous Australian narrative discourse 'plays a decisive role … [in] personal and social identity as well as in the transmission of cultural knowledge'.[18] Indigenous oral history is a legitimate reference for the recipients of such knowledge within their own clan.

From this inheritance, I am asserting that Australia has an Aboriginal history, a history that allows Indigenous epistemological practices.

Aboriginal society pre-contact

What were the social constructs of power like in the Eora clans pre-contact? Aboriginal society in the late eighteenth and early nineteenth century within the Eora and Gai-mariagal people are discussed in the following section.

The English described the Eora as a stubborn and proud people that were unwilling to conform to habits that the Europeans wished to enforce, such as the wearing of clothes and adopting a settled life.[19] We were proud and stubborn, we still are. What was considered a 'settled life' pre-1788 and how did this relate to Indigenous social construction? In British eyes a 'settled life' was a rural economy with surplus production. They had no understanding of the already existing structured 'settled life' of the Eora pre-1788. They failed to see the existing demographic patterns or land-use management practices and social constructs. Geoffrey Blainey reminds us of the contrasts that could be made regarding British concepts of civility:

> If an Aborigine in the seventeenth century had been captured as a curiosity and taken in a Dutch ship to Europe, and if he had traveled all the way from Scotland to the Caucasus and had seen how the average European struggled to make a living, he might have said to himself that he had seen the third world and all its poverty and hardship.[20]

Blainey shows Europe interpreted as a possible land of 'savages'. In contrast, prior to European invasion, the Eora lifestyle was complex, based within a matrilineal society.[21] Senior men sat in ceremony (both within Gai-mariagal Guringah and other east coast clans) to decide important issues. Due to their age and status they enjoyed a level of power and prestige.[22] Not all men were in this body that is generally called 'Elders'. Admittance was restricted to the most intelligent, diligent and, some would suggest, conformist over the long period of learning the ceremony and sacred knowledge of the clan. Kinship and tradition were the strengths that bound senior men who enforced a strict system of law. Likewise women also gained power, knowledge and prestige. Those of strong character were never outmatched by their gender equivalents as women also had a key role in the application of Indigenous law and resultant leadership functions within the clan.[23]

In contrast to the invading settler society, the Eora had an intimate relationship with nature and a non-materialistic philosophy. This is reinforced in oral history, through which we were instructed on the management of the wetlands, the abundance of foodstuffs in seasonal periods at what is now Queenscliff, Curl Curl and the Dee Why lagoons. We learnt how the oyster was harvested, the mullet caught in nets, the fat fish taken on line, the larger fish taken on burley and speared off the rocks, how the turtle was a feast in late summer, and similar stories of winter of the fat possum, the echidna, the fruit bat, the wallaby and kangaroo. Our calendar was based on the development of the family, when a child could be born, when food was available, when it was time to live on the coast, to eat shellfish, or when it was cooler and time to move inland. Pre-1788 this was a civil, settled culture that was 'admirable'.[24]

Leadership

Koori concepts of consciousness and responsibility demand that the responsibility for managing relationships is taken by all parts of the kinship system, to differing degrees, because all of the parts regulate each other. Deborah Rose reached a similar understanding in the Victoria River District of the Northern Territory.[25] Leadership in the singular did not exist; it was actually stratified through various senior clan members. The concept of 'a leader' within Koori society is misunderstood in some oral histories, in much anthropology and within colonial and later history.

Aboriginal leaders

One individual, Pemulwuy (Pim-el-wi)[26] has been recorded as a leader of the Bidjigal[27] people of Botany Bay and the Georges River, and a leader the Eora wars of 1790 to 1802. Another felon wanted by the British during this same period was Musquito of the Hawkesbury clans who was captured and exiled to Norfolk Island in July 1805 for raids on settlers' properties in the Hawkesbury and Georges River districts. Later he gained notoriety for his alleged leadership of the wild Oyster Bay tribe in Tasmania.[28]

Both Pemulwuy and Musquito were seen by the colonialists to be Aboriginal leaders. It is debatable whether their leadership in guerrilla warfare legitimately arose from a clan Elder consultative process. Rather their leadership may have been the result of their personal aspirations. Or perhaps they became military leaders out of the desperate necessity to survive following the destruction of Eora society after the 1789 smallpox epidemic? Were these men forced to take on a transgressive role and become leaders in a manner which went against their societal values, bearing in mind that their constructs of law and land management were also destroyed through the colony's greed for land? Perhaps an answer is to be found in the rise in 1824 of another Indigenous guerrilla fighter, Windradyne, discussed below.[29] First I will look at a contrast to Pemulwuy and Musquito, a non-military leader, Bungaree, who was the first proclaimed Aboriginal 'chief'.

Bungaree, chief of the Sydney Blacks

If some of my comments that follow appear insolent towards Bungaree, I apologise, out of respect to his descendants, members of the Guringah Tribal Link, an incorporated Aboriginal group. They, like my mother's family, have connection to the 'Broken Bay' clans of which Bungaree is a member. Bungaree was a victim of colonisation. No blame should be attached for what he did, however we as Indigenous people should learn from illegitimate leadership, for when it is imposed on us, it can, as in Bungaree's situation, have negative outcomes for Indigenous Australians in general.

Bungaree gained notoriety for many reasons, but it is his attainment of a gorget as a mark of status that is of concern to me here. Governor Macquarie, in a naïve attempt to break Indigenous Australians of their nomadic ways, proclaimed

Bungaree as the Chief of the Broken Bay tribes on 31 January 1815 in a rather flamboyant ceremony. He further proposed that 16 adults would settle on a farm with huts, a boat, supplies and convict labourers.[30] Bungaree was issued with a king plate or gorget. This has its origin as a part of armour worn by a medieval knight. It protected the neck.[31] In Australia at that time officers of the marine infantry wore them as a part of their uniform.[32] Both the French and the English had used gorgets as gifts to Native American chiefs and warriors since the American war of 1755-62. The British and the Americans often recognised chiefs by the gorgets or they were seen as a gift to an ally.[33]

Early Russian explorers to Australia observed that the British colonial government manipulated Indigenous people into positions of dominance assisted by the use of gorgets, bypassing leadership choices made by the Indigenous community. For example, Novosil'sky noted that 'the English Government itself selects the elders'.[34] By conferring the distinction of chief as in Bungaree's case, Governor Macquarie made official a status that was usually based on an Aboriginal person's individual loyalty and how useful they could be to the colonialist.[35] From the Indigenous perspective, some say that Bungaree was nothing more than a puppet for Macquarie even though he had previously been described as a 'worthy and brave fellow' by Matthew Flinders. He was also was given a glowing character reference by Lieutenant Menzies in a letter to Governor King in July 1804 with respect to Bungaree's skill 'as an intermediary between blacks and whites'.[36]

For Bungaree, kingship allowed him to establish himself as an important identity on his own terms, using Macquarie's gifts. These suited his lifestyle, now a mix of Indigenous and Western.[37] He attempted to transgress both of these. His entrepreneurial skills were exhibited when he realised that the British had degraded the land prohibiting traditional land-use practices, so he utilised the convict help. For several years the peaches that he produced from his farm provided him with a steady income.[38] Sadly this income appears to have been squandered mostly on alcohol, as were the proceeds of the sale of most of the Governor's gifts, including a much-treasured fishing boat.

Bungaree was the first chief appointed in Australia, issued with a gorget. This became a practice implemented across the frontier. Evidence suggests that pastoralists even encouraged the inheritance of titles from father to son to maintain control and respect for the title amongst the Indigenous group.[39] Aboriginal groups would later spurn this tacky chestplate regalia that was associated with the British system.[40] By the end of the nineteenth century, following the widespread collapse of Indigenous economic and cultural bases in southern and eastern Australia, 'king plates' had no meaning and became museum pieces.[41] Bungaree's influence as an illegitimate leader dissipated, as did his assets; in time even his gorget disappeared. In 1824 a new Indigenous leader appeared on the western plains west of Sydney town. However this leader did not grace the Governor's pleasure.

Windradyne of the Wiradjuri

Following the 'discovery' of the established Indigenous trading route over the Blue Mountains by Blaxland, Wentworth and Lawson in 1813, after they were shown the way by their two Darug guides,[42] the lands of the western plains were soon invaded by graziers looking for pastures for their sheep. By 1824 the white population had increased to 1267 people with 91,636 acres cleared and fenced, and 113,973 sheep and cattle by 1825.[43] The traditional lands of the Wiradjuri were being consumed by aggressive landowners, including John Oxley and John Macarthur, 'who were devouring land with the obsessiveness of obese gluttons'.[44]

Frustrated at the destruction of sacred areas, the removal of possum and kangaroo habitat which formed a staple of their diets, the Wiradjuri were forced to kill settler livestock for food. The retaliation was swift; Windradyne was captured by Major Morisset and kept in leg irons for a month, to teach him a lesson. It had the opposite effect. Within a short period after his release he witnessed members of his family murdered by whites and within days he formed an efficient group of warriors using guerrilla tactics. He attacked isolated farming huts, beginning with a hut that when built had desecrated a sacred site used in male initiation, according to local oral tradition.[45] The pastoral industry had destroyed a site vital to sustaining Indigenous knowledge systems.

Windradyne's actions seem justified to an extent. But the declaration of martial law that followed was used to justify atrocities and massacre of the Wiradjuri people. It was an extreme over-reaction encouraged by absentee landowners who lived in Sydney and could not keep farm staff employed due to fear of the Wiradjuri.[46] Brigadier General Sir Thomas Brisbane (Governor Macquarie's replacement) is still held accountable by the Wiradjuri for the slaughter of their people[47] in an all-out war from October 1823 to 11 December 1824 which reached a peak of destruction following Brisbane's proclamation of martial law on 14 August 1824.[48]

Irish-Aboriginal oral history

A discussion of the link between oral history and written history with respect to my own background is relevant here.

Two of the sons of the former convict Samuel Foley were working as farm hands and shepherds in the Turon River district north of Bathurst at the height of the Wiradjuri wars. As the sons of Irish Catholics they had a sympathetic association with wanton destruction and indiscriminate murder of innocent souls, as their forefathers had suffered similar fates as the result of persecution, greed and murder at the hands of the British nobility and military in the conquest of Ireland. It is said that they showed respect and compassion to the Wiradjuri and were recorded by some as being kind to the Indigenous groups. For this they were spared and were treated with respect by the Wiradjuri, in a manner similar to the treatment of the settler Suttor.[49] They witnessed either directly or indirectly the possible massacres at Billiwillinga and Bells Falls Gorge[50] (or incidents nearby). In the chaos that followed they provided shelter for two young women and a small child. Several other children that they tried to defend and hide were 'sliced to pieces' by the mounted soldiers.[51]

As mentioned previously, a shared 'hatred' of the English existed between the sons of Irish Catholics and the Wiradjuri. One of these men was Thomas Foley, who was the author's grandfather's great-grandfather. At the end of the Wiradjuri wars he married one of the young women that he protected, who was later baptised as Mary. Their union was officiated in the fledgling Catholic Church at Parramatta. Their great-grandson was born at Tingha and was baptised as Johannes Foley, known to the Koori families in Glebe in the 1920s and 1930s as 'Jack', or 'John'. He spent a short period on the Tingha Mission as a child whereupon he joined up with his father and travelled on his dray and wagon, supplying the highland traders and the burgeoning towns of Inverell and Glenn Innes with freight from the steamer ports on the coast.

This oral history and knowledge was passed down through my family, from my grandfather to my father and my father's brothers.[52] The wanton slaughter of the Wiradjuri became 'real' in the family history and in some ways mirrored the Irish oral history. They were both indigenous to their sovereign states; from island nations; they were both brutally colonised by the British and they both had their leaders. In my family's oral histories, the details of the Irish atrocities have been forgotten with time, it is the Wiradjuri accomplishments on the battlefield and Windradyne's leadership that has been remembered and retold generation after generation.[53]

After two months of massacres the Wiradjuri were a spent force with no reserves to continue the military struggle. Windradyne and what was left of his family, together with other survivors of the massacres, travelled over the mountains to Parramatta and surrendered to Governor Brisbane. He lived for another decade in peace and was widely referred to as a 'chief', 'a great leader of his people'.[54] Born into a pluralist society he witnessed the destruction and extermination of his Elder system. The loss of male Elders in a patrilineal society broke down any consultative and communally acceptable decision-making process. Windradyne, in a most uncharacteristic Indigenous mode, initially took control of a fighting force out of anger, hate or reprisal for the murder of family and loss of traditional lands.[55] The precise trigger for his actions is unknown.

Windradyne exhibited those leadership qualities that Larson has defined in contemporary management literature as including creativity, inspiration, entrepreneurship and achieving a shared sense of commitment from his followers.[56] Windradyne was described on his surrender as one of the finest looking natives ever seen, as 'noble'.[57] No doubt he was a charismatic leader who came to fame as a result of the chaos of colonisation, in a similar way perhaps to Pemulwuy and later Musquito.

After Windradyne's surrender he was allowed to live in peace and was subsequently used by the colonial powers to assist them in the pastoral settlement of the western plains of New South Wales. He then became a leader whose power was illegitimate within his social order, categorised as a chief by the colonial government. He lived out his days as a token of what he had once been. He is a warrior without Elders, a clan leader without a clan, a 'chief' without land or a people. The Bathurst District Historical Society erected a plaque on his grave in 1954 that calls him the last Chief of the Aboriginals, a friend to the settlers, a true patriot.[58] Perhaps this is how history wishes to recall him in his last years, but is it as a true patriot to the colonial conquest of settlement and subsequent stealing of land, or a patriot to the Aboriginal cause? Either way he died of injuries suffered following a fight with another Indigenous person.[59] It appears his chiefly status was not universally recognised as superiority by all people.

With Windradyne's surrender it seems he became a chief in name only. Pemulwuy and Mosquito's military-like leadership status ended with their executions. In comparison, was Bungaree ever a leader or a 'chief' of his people? Western constructs of leadership resulted in the demise of all four of these individual examples of Indigenous leadership. These men would most certainly been cut off from their spiritual realms of knowledge within the circles of Elder knowledge. This would have occurred following population attrition by musket, smallpox and colonial-derived diseases. The leadership actions in military pursuits by Pemulwuy, Musquito and Windradyne took them away from family groups. This ensured that they were also unable to pass on their knowledge to their youth, as those that they associated with were inevitably killed. Leadership born from military chaos proved to be a negative attribute in the circles of their Indigenous society. The structure of Indigenous society in general made the formation of significant fighting forces almost impossible, as most groups remained small and semi-autonomous, except for periods such as the Eora mullet feast,[60] or other important non-aggressive ceremonies.[61] Clans rarely exceeded 60 people and, for the most part, Indigenous Australian gatherings pre-contact were peaceful. The dimensions of social behaviour that would provoke aggressive responses involving arguments over territory, ideology and rule by minorities were not issues normally tolerated within Aboriginal society.[62] Within our oral history we talk of the warriors Barnoo and the man who became the water dragon. Both of these individuals were soldiers in unknown battles, which is contradictory to a peaceful society. Like them, Pemulwuy, Mosquito and Windradyne appear as aggressors within their social construct. Bungaree was a political appointment with limited leadership influence.

By the end of the nineteenth century, the concept of leadership had gone full circle. Aboriginal people knew whether a person was a good choice for a chief or a king. Individuals were bestowed with a title or obtained one through coercive tactics, even when sanctions by non-Aboriginal authority figures no longer had any influence.[63] The demise of the gorget saw the rise of contemporary Indigenous leaders beginning in the early years of the twentieth century.

Contemporary leadership

The social turmoil of government-driven assimilation policies of the twentieth century, together with the stifling negative racial attitudes of over 200 years of colonial and post-colonial domination has had a major effect on Indigenous social structure. Indigenous Australians, however, have continued to learn and develop, within an oppressive struggle for the right to control their identity as a people, to determine political status, and pursue economic, social and cultural development.[64] The struggles of Pemulwuy, Musquito and Windradyne were no different, except that they used spears in addition to the tools of the modern leader, including diplomacy, tact and utilisation of the media to influence public opinion.

Numerous leaders have arisen; many have faded into obscurity. For many, if not most, gone are the traditional circles of Elder knowledge, men of high esteem.[65] In their place are contemporary people whose values are, arguably, still governed by Indigenous kinship and respect. However some of the new leaders are different. One outstanding contemporary leader never relinquished or compromised his 'high degree' status, recognised under Indigenous law.[66] He maintained his 'traditional beliefs' yet was able to transgress with his leadership qualities into the settler society of contemporary Australia. That outstanding leader is Mr Vincent Lingiari who, in the words of Sir William Deane, is without a doubt 'one of the greatest Aboriginal leaders'.[67] He has a dual role in modern leadership terminology, as a *Kadijeri*, a man in charge of secret and male ceremony,[68] that some would call a traditional law man, yet he is no less a leader of his people within the modern definition.[69]

Lingiari was illiterate in the European context in that he could neither read nor write and his English vocabulary was limited, yet 'he possessed great eloquence even in English'.[70] Softly spoken, he displayed an unwavering will to obtain his people's rights to their traditional lands.[71] Lingiari fought against assimilation and cultural extirpation. He had the knowledge of his people's creation at Seale

Gorge, near Wattie Creek, Northern Territory. He led a seven year long struggle, initially against a large British-owned pastoral company and then the Australian government. This had two significant outcomes. Firstly, he achieved the support of the North Australian Workers Union, which subsequently successfully filed an application with the Conciliation and Arbitration Commission seeking equal pay for Aboriginal workers.[72] Secondly, in 1986, the Gurindji people, with professional support, obtained inalienable freehold title to Daruragu, a part of their traditional lands. In an emotional ceremony in 1975, the Prime Minister Gough Whitlam poured sand into the outstretched hand of Vincent Lingiari. This remains an iconic image of the potential of reconciliation in Australia.[73]

When you reflect on Lingiari's life, his courage, charisma, strong leadership, vision, moral fortitude and ability to maintain solidarity amongst his people, these are personal qualities that all Australians can aspire to. A leader not just for his kin relations, Mr Lingiari is a leader for all Aboriginal people. In fact, his attributes are such that he is a role model for all Australians to aspire to; his is legitimate leadership.

Conclusion

Self-endowed leadership or a title such as king or chief has achieved little within Indigenous Australian society. I have argued that 'kingplates' were normally sanctioned where the coloniser could obtain profit from interaction with the imposed title. On the other hand the warrior leaders, driven by revenge or need for survival, were victims of technological superiority of the British fighting forces. The spear and boomerang were no match for the rifle.[74]

Aboriginal Australia has changed irreversibly since that leather boot of a British officer first crunched on Hawkesbury sandstone so many years ago. In this paper, case studies from the writer's kin connections, and a notable leader from Central Australia provide a personal approach to history and to the concepts of knowledge that are linked to Aboriginal leadership. Historically, the interactions involved violence. In contemporary times, leaders who walk within the worlds of black and white and preserve their Aboriginality are strong role models, as shown by Mr Lingiari. The ability to transgress between the two worlds ensures that Indigenous Australians do not remain frozen within a single past timeframe.

This paper has given the reader an insight into the division that Indigenous leaders experience in the struggle to retain, respect and maintain Indigenous knowledge systems and overcome prejudice within an oppressive political environment, be it in 1788 or 1966. Mosquito, Pemulwuy and Windradyne tried to do so with guerrilla military tactics. Bungaree was the symbolic leader with kingship bestowed on him by a Governor who did not understand the structures of Indigenous cultures. His was a title of convenience. Mr Lingiari, with his noble yet modest defiance and charisma, captured the hearts and minds of unionists, politicians, the legal and medical professions and large groups of the Australian public. All things being equal, and not discounting the strong support mechanisms that were vital to the 1967 referendum campaign, if Mr Lingiari had not shown such strong leadership and captured the imagination of the Australian press and public, would the pro-Indigenous questions have won the referendum so convincingly in 1967? History has shown effective legitimate leadership can produce positive outcomes for Australian society. Such is the transgressive potential of the Indigenous leader.

References

Primary sources

Budby, John 2004, Personal Interview, Brisbane, 8 March 2004.

Hobart Town and Van Dieman's Land Gazette, Hobart.

Secondary sources

Altman, JC and Hunter, BH 2003, *Monitoring 'practical' reconciliation: evidence from the reconciliation decade, 1991-2001,* Discussion Paper No. 254/2003, Centre for Aboriginal Economic Policy Research, The Australian National University, Canberra.

Attenbrow, Val 2002, *Sydney's Aboriginal past,* University of New South Wales Press, Sydney.

Barratt, Glynn 1981, *The Russians at Port Jackson: 1814-1822,* Australian Institute of Aboriginal Studies, Canberra.

Bell, D 1987, 'Aboriginal women and the religious experience', in WH Edwards (ed.), *Traditional Aboriginal society,* Macmillan Education Australia Pty Ltd, Melbourne.

Bern, J 1979, 'Politics in the conduct of a secret male ceremony', *Journal of Anthropological Research* 35(1).

Berndt, C 1950, *Women's changing ceremonies in Northern Australia,* Hermann, Paris.

Berndt, RM 1959, The Concept of 'The Tribe' in the Western Desert of Australia, *Oceania,* 30(2): 81-107.

Blainey, G 1982, *Triumph of the Nomads: a history of ancient Australia,* Macmillan, South Melbourne.

Broome, Richard 1994, *Aboriginal Australians,* 2nd edn, Allen and Unwin, St Leonards.

Budby, John 2001, 'The academic quandary — an Aboriginal experience', *Postgraduate Research Supervision: Transforming (R)Elations,* in the series Eruptions: New Feminism Across the Disciplines, Alison Bartlett and Gina Mercer (eds), Peter Lang Publishing, New York.

Coe, Mary 1989, *Windradyne: a Wiradjuri Koorie,* Blackbooks, Glebe.

Concise Oxford Dictionary 1976, *'tribe',* Claredon Press, Oxford.

Deane, William 1996, 'Some signposts from Daguragu', *The Inaugural Vincent Lingiari Memorial Lecture,* Northern Territory University, August, Council for Aboriginal Reconciliation, Kingston, ACT.

Dodson, Michael 2003, 'The end in the beginning: re(de)finding Aboriginality', in Michele Grossman (coordinating editor), *Blacklines. Contemporary Critical Writing by Indigenous Australians,* Melbourne University Press, Melbourne.

Elder, Bruce 1992, *Blood on the wattle*: *massacres and maltreatment of Australian Aborigines since 1788,* National Book Publishers, Brookvale.

Elkin, AP 1977, *Aboriginal men of high degree. Initiation and sorcery in the world's oldest tradition,* Inner Traditions, Rochester, Vermont.

Flannery, Tim (ed.) 1999, *The birth of Sydney*, Text Publishing, Melbourne.

Foley, Dennis 2001, *Repossession of our spirit: the traditional owners of northern Sydney*, Aboriginal History Inc, Canberra.

—— 2002, 'An Indigenous standpoint theory', *Journal of Australian Indigenous Issues* 5(3): 3-13.

Grossman, M (coordinating editor) 2003, *Blacklines: contemporary critical writing by Indigenous Australians,* Melbourne University Press, Melbourne.

Hills, Matt 2005, *How To Do Things With Cultural Theory.* Hodder Education, London.

Klapproth, Danièle 2004, *Narrative as social practice: Anglo-Western and Australian Aboriginal Oral Traditions*, Mouton de Gruyter, Berlin and New York.

Lambert, John 2000, *Brokers of cultural change,* John Terence Lambert, Brisbane.

Larson, Paul 1999, 'A look at leadership', *Montana Business Quarterly* 37(2): 18-21.

Marshall, PD 2004, *Celebrity and Power: Fame in Contemporary Culture*, University of Minnesota Press, Minneapolis and London.

Miller, James 1985, *Koori - a will to win: the heroic resistance, survival and triumph of Black Australia*, Angus & Robertson, Sydney.

Mulvaney, John and Kamminga, Johan 1999, *Prehistory of Australia,* Smithsonian Institution Press, Washington.

Neal, David 1987, 'Free society, penal colony, slave society, prison?' *Historical Studies* 22(89): 497-518.

Neill, Rosemary 2002, *White out: how politics is killing Black Australia,* Allen and Unwin, St Leonards.

Rigney, Lester-Irabinna 1997, 'Internalisation of an Indigenous Anti-Colonial cultural critique of research methodologies: A Guide to Indigenous Research Methodologies and its principles', *Journal of American Studies* 14(2): 109-122.

—— 1999, 'The first perspective: culturally safe research practices on or with Indigenous Peoples', in *1999 Chacmool Conference Proceedings,* University of Calgary, Alberta, Canada, 'Internationalisation of an Indigenous anti-colonial cultural critique of research methodologies: A Guide to Indigenist research methodology and its principles', *Higher Education Research and Development in Higher Education* 20: 629-636.

—— 2000, 'A first perspective of Indigenous Australian participation in science: framing Indigenous research towards Indigenous Australian intellectual sovereignty', A keynote address, *Second National Indigenous Researches Forum,* Aboriginal Research Institute University of South Australia, Adelaide.

—— 2001, 'A first perspective of Indigenous Australian participation in science: framing Indigenous research towards Indigenous Australian intellectual sovereignty', *Kaurna Higher Education Journal* 7: 1-13.

Rose, Deborah 1987, 'Consciousness and responsibility in an Australian Aboriginal religion', in WH Edwards (ed.), *Traditional Aboriginal society,* Macmillan Education Australia Pty Ltd, Melbourne.

Salisbury, T and Gresser, PJ 1971, *Windradyne of the Wiradjuri: martial law at Bathurst in 1824,* Wentworth Books, Sydney.

Sharp, Ian and Tatz, Colin 1966, *Aborigines in the economy,* Jacaranda Press, Brisbane.

Smith, Keith Vincent 1992, *King Bungaree,* Kangaroo Press, Kenthurst.

Stanner, W 1979, *White man got no Dreaming,* ANU Press, Canberra.

Tench, Watkin 1979, *Sydney's first four years,* Library of Australian History, Sydney.

Turbet, Peter 1989, *The Aborigines of the Sydney District before 1788,* Kangaroo Press, Kenthurst, NSW.

Troy, Jakelin 1993, *King plates: a history of Aboriginal gorgets,* Aboriginal Studies Press, Canberra.

Vibe 2004, *Celebrity Vibe: Vincent Lingiari*, accessed 15 November 2006, <http://www.vibe.com.au/vibe/corporate/celebrity_vibe/show-celeb.asp?id=372> Issue 90, August.

Weinstein, Jay and Stehr, Nico 1999, 'The power of knowledge: race science, race policy, and the Holocaust', *Social Epistemology,* 13(1): 3-35.

Willey, Keith 1979, *When the sky fell down: the destruction of the tribes of the Sydney Region 1788-1850s*, William Collins Pty Ltd, Sydney.

ENDNOTES

1   Rigney 2001: 3.

2   Rigney 2001: 4.

3   Rigney 1999: 636.

4   Rigney 2000: 1.

5   Smith 1992: 20.

6   Smith 1992: 73.

7   Tench 1979: 50.

8   Tench 1979: 77, 85.

9   Flannery 1999: 31; Willey 1979: 56-78.

10   Flannery 1999: 26-27, 111-115; Turbet 1989: 75-76.

11   Rigney 2000: 1-2.

12   Foley 2001: 7.

13   Mulvaney and Kamminga 1999: 75.

14   Berndt 1959: 26-29.

15   Lougher, C circa 1964. Clarice Lougher is my mother's mother, a woman of Koradji training and skill, a matriarch of the northern Eora, my mentor at birth and childhood.

16   Attenbrow 2002: 60.

17   Weinstein and Stehr 1999: 4.

18   Klapproth 2004: 47-48.

19   Flannery 1999: 22.

20   Blainey 1982: v-vi.

21   Foley 2001: 12.

22   Broome 1994: 20.

23   Broome 1994: 20.

24   Broome 1994: 26.

25   Rose 1987: 259.

26   Elder 1992: 19-20; Tench 1979: 206.

27   Turbet 1989: 22.

28   *Hobart Town and Van Dieman's Land Gazette*, 26 March 1824: 2. See also Chapter 7 this volume.

29   Elder 1992: 47.

30   Smith 1992: 77.

31   Troy 1993: 2.

32   Troy 1993: 2.

33   Troy 1993: 5.

34   Navosil'sky 1820 cited in Barratt 1981: 29.

35   Troy 1993: 6-7.

36   Smith 1992: 68-71.

37   Troy 1993: 13.

[38] Troy 1993: 13.

[39] Troy 1993: 41.

[40] Troy 1993: 13.

[41] Troy 1993: 40.

[42] Troy 1993: 42.

[43] Troy 1993: 45.

[44] Elder 1992: 45.

[45] Elder 1992: 48.

[46] Elder 1992: 51.

[47] Coe 1989: 52-53.

[48] Elder 1992: 51.

[49] Salisbury and Gresser 1971: 12.

[50] Elder 1992: 51.

[51] Jack Gordon and Leo Foley (brothers), family communication 1964-1970.

[52] Foley family communication 1964-1970.

[53] Foley, Gordon, personal communication 1964-1974. The rise of the 'Kelly Gang' (which included the Foley siblings and other Koori adolescents) in the back lanes of Glebe during the Great Depression of 1929-32 no doubt helped to ensure that the defence of their 'turf' contained a mixture of Irish and Wiradjuri folklore. The Catholic Kooris maintained a struggle against Protestant whites of the surrounding estates in Sydney's working class areas (Gordon, Jack and Leo Foley, family communication 1964-1970).

[54] Elder 1992: 49-53.

[55] Coe 1989: 37.

[56] Larson 1999: 18-21.

[57] Sydney Gazette 30 December 1824, cited in Coe 1989: 37.

[58] Coe 1989: 83.

[59] Coe 1989: 64.

[60] Foley 2001: 106-6.

[61] Turbet 1989: 24-27.

[62] Elder 1992: 198.

[63] Troy 1993: 41.

[64] Dodson 2003: 31.

[65] Troy 1993: 14.

[66] Elkin 1977: 3-15.

[67] Deane 1996: 7.

[68] Deane 1996: 7.

[69] Smith 1992: 20.

[70] Smith 1992: 7.

[71] Vibe 2004: 1.

[72] Deane 1996: 4.

[73] Mr Lingiari showed respect to Anglo-Australia by subsequently pouring the sand through the Prime Minister's hand.

[74] Broome 1994.

Sedentary topography: the impact of the Christian Mission Society's 'civilising' agenda on the spatial structure of life in the Roper Region of northern Australia

Angelique Edmonds

Near the Hodgson River in Australia's Northern Territory stands a series of buildings, established initially during cattle station development and now constituting the Aboriginal settlement of Minyerri. In July 2003 the population had swollen considerably for a funeral ceremony. We waited by the women's camp a few kilometres from town, the crowds forgotten in the gravity of our anticipation. A breeze caught the edge of a hanging tarpaulin and the makeshift wall screening the women from view billowed momentarily, exposing their white faces and their application of more white body paint to cover themselves. They had been living under this makeshift shelter for some weeks now and would shortly participate in a ceremony that marked their return to town for the first time since the death of their kinsman.

Hours later, as the ceremony for their return began, the group of women emerged from beside a pink colourbond-clad house at the edge of the settlement. Their faces and bodies remained hidden from public view under an assortment of bed sheets. Other women acted as their guides leading them down the driveway, across a yard and through an opening in the wire fence marking the boundary of that block and the threshold to the more public 'street'. This was accompanied by the singing and clapsticks of men moving in a group just ahead of them. As they proceeded to a piece of ground marked by a group waiting for them, onlookers gathered in the front yards of neighbouring houses, resting against fences, sitting on or beside abandoned rusted out vehicles and crammed into any shade that was available.

***

I evoke this episode as a situated example of the continuing negotiation and inventive adaptation by groups of Aboriginal people living in remote settlements. In these places surrounded by vast expanses of country, the spatial structures imposed by the boundaries and thresholds of an essentially static built environment appear to be at odds with the versatility and adaptive mobility of traditional windbreaks and less permanent shelters readily adjusted to meet seasonal, familial and contextual changes. Yet, while the built environment appears static, mute and unresponsive to changes in context by comparison with mobile dwellings, in the greater temporal span that is drawn into focus by the death of a kinsman, the built environment begins to be revealed as a relatively transparent and temporary intervention upon an infinitely more enduring ground; that of the Land itself. As this paper will discuss, Land is the deepest temporal background for Aboriginal people in the Roper Region, determining institutions of behaviour and thus constituting the order of life. As this paper's example of ceremony surrounding the death of a kinsman will illustrate, maintaining the ontological primacy of the Land is imperative to the sustenance of life.[1]

The staging of a ceremony ensuring the safe re-entry into public life for the kin of a recently deceased member of the community is a phenomenon that goes to the heart of a community's beliefs regarding the structure of their orientation to the world and their collective response to dealing with the drama of human finitude. This ceremony, enacted as it was amongst the colourbond-clad houses, front yards, driveways, wire fences and abandoned vehicles of the settlement, in fact represents a moment within a deeper conflict confronting the heart of an Indigenous way of being and orientation to the world in contemporary Australia. It offers a moment of cross-cultural significance whereby an indigenous practice that concerns the preservation of the ontological primacy of Land (which continues to structure orientation to the world for many Alawa[2] people in the region), occurs within the imposed colonial topographical order of sedentary life. The ceremonies enacted that day ensured the maintenance of order and balance and the enduring efficacy of the Land in continuing to sustain life. This is not understood as an abstract concept but in terms of the specific country of the deceased and the relational structure between his kin and their responsibilities to him and his country. Before exploring further the significance and practice of the ceremonies that day, it is necessary to discuss the context in which static, built living environments, that clearly advocate a bias in favour of sedentary life, were introduced to this region.

Colonial exploration in the Roper River region, where the Hodgson is located, began in 1841 and expanded considerably in 1870 with the establishment of the Overland Telegraph line.[3] The Land on which Minyerri is situated was set aside as a cattle station in 1884 and named Hodgson Downs, an alternative name still used interchangeably for both the contemporary settlement and station.[4] After a series of individuals' difficulties in establishing various pastoral enterprises in the region, a single company, the Eastern and African Cold Storage Company Ltd, acquired Hodgson Downs in 1903 along with all unleased and previously abandoned pastoral leases in the region. 'Having no intention of allowing Aboriginal resistance to prevent them from carving out their huge pastoral empire, the company determined to exterminate all Aboriginal people of the region'.[5] Merlan writes that 'the Eastern and African' engaged in what was apparently the most systematic extermination of Aborigines ever carried out on the Roper.[6] Quoting Bauer, she continues, 'this was probably one of the few authenticated instances in which Aborigines were systematically hunted. For a time, the company employed two gangs of 10 to 14 blacks headed by a white man or half caste to shoot the wild blacks on sight'.[7] For the Aboriginal people of the region, during this period the only way to escape death at the hands of hunting parties despatched by the primary pastoral company, was either to live under the patronage of station owners, or retreat into the safety of the rugged and impenetrable rocky hill country of southern Arnhem Land. Yet not every group had such choices; people along the valley of the Roper River in particular did not have the option of falling back to mountain strongholds.[8]

In 1908, the Church of England established the Roper River Mission through the administration of the Christian Mission Society. The 'Eastern and African' ceased operation in the same year and both events are remembered by Aboriginal people of the region as marking the beginning of peaceful relations.[9] The charge (instructions) delivered to the missionaries in Melbourne in 1908 shortly before their departure, made it clear that the objectives of the mission were to be both spiritual and practical. The missionaries were bringing both 'Christianity and civilisation'.[10] Yet the mission was perceived by the local people as a sanctuary, within the protection of which they believed they were safe from European violence. By 1909, over 200 people had gathered at the mission, the remnants of the Mara, Wandarang, Alawa, Ngalakan and Ngandi tribes, as well as the southernmost members of Rembarrnga and Nunggubuyu tribes.[11]

The first missionaries at Roper led by Rev. Huthnance faced the same problem that missionaries all over Australia faced: how to maintain the mission program when the resident population varied in its make-up and fluctuated in numbers. Hunting and gathering people must hunt and gather to survive, and so the basic requirement to induce Aboriginal people to reside at their mission was food. While the longer-term strategy was to create a community self-sufficient in its own agriculture and livestock, in the shorter term, the mission could only retain people by providing food, thus the mission rapidly followed missions all over Australia in providing food for school children to keep them in school.[12] The mission very rapidly became an organized institution in which a daily routine including a daily service was strictly regimented.[13] The emphasis on the discipline of the daily service was not a universal mission strategy even within CMS worldwide. It was a feature of 'industrial missions', the name given to the work-oriented missions to supposedly 'primitive' or 'uncivilised' people, particularly nomadic, tribal people. It was presumed that such people had to be civilized, so missions tended to emphasise the training of people to adopt a settled agricultural lifestyle.[14] By the end of 1908, three substantial buildings had been erected for the staff, stores and school.[15] The physical facilities were little more than basic shelters for the first 40 years of CMS missions, since construction was with local materials and at first only a few buildings had corrugated iron or a floor.[16] Earthen floors created through a technique using rammed ant bed were common. Despite the simple structures, the spatial demarcation employed was an element of great significance in the conversion project. As the Mission station developed, the mission area was distinguished by a boundary fence surrounding about seven buildings that accommodated the missionaries, the school, church, workshop, ablutions blocks, a boy's dormitory and a girl's dormitory.[17] In the early years of the Mission, parents were not permitted to stay inside the mission boundary.[18] Such practices were common in many Aboriginal missions throughout Australia where missionaries anticipated greater success at conversion by segregating families and concentrating (initially at least) on conversion of the children to Christianity.[19]

Outside the Roper River mission were the huts of the Aboriginal people who worked on the mission, and beyond those, on the banks of the river, was the 'camp' where the visiting 'bush' Aboriginal people stayed.[20] In most missions there was an agreed boundary of some kind, distinguishing the 'camp people' or the 'bush blacks', sometimes referred to simply as 'myalls', as distinct from 'mission people'. The 'camp people' were treated quite differently from the 'mission people', undoubtedly as part of the 'civilising' goal. As one of the Roper missionaries recalled, one of the more severe punishments for girls in the Roper dormitory was to be treated like a 'camp person'.[21] Thus, the conversion project employed, promoted and cultivated values that favoured specific dwelling styles rather than others. It structured Aboriginal people's living environment by overlaying the Land with boundaries distinguishing areas marked by differences in expected conduct and use: a new spatial ordering for the Land. This concurs with Trigger's descriptions of the influence of Christianity in Domadgee, where he states 'people understood the spatial order of the mission in terms of places where thought and behaviour were either expressed or sheltered, from non-indigenous scrutiny and correction'.[22]

***

Figure 9.1: Children lined up for breakfast at Roper River Mission, no date.

Courtesy of the CMS Hart collection, Darwin.

Figure 9.2: The new School at Roper Mission 1937.

Courtesy of the CMS Hart collection, Darwin.

Figure 9.3: School children with work outside the school, no date.

Courtesy of the CMS Hart collection, Darwin.

The deceased man at the focus of the funeral ceremony described at the start of this paper grew up at Roper Mission, as did many of his contemporaries and their families. Many of those in attendance at the funeral also either grew up, or are descended from relatives who grew up at the Roper Mission. There are three reasons why this is important in the context of this paper.

Firstly it is important as the context for understanding the continuing influence that mission life has had on structuring the lives of those at Minyerri. It is only recently that many Alawa people returned from the settlement of Ngukurr, the contemporary settlement at the site of the former Roper mission, to live on their country, so the Mission influence remains a significant element in the structure of their lives. It was not until 1990, when (the former) Aboriginal Torres Strait Islander Commision (ATSIC) purchased Hodgson Downs station (where the settlement of Minyerri lies) for the Hodgson Downs Community Incorporated, made up of the traditional owners, the Alawa people, that the majority of current residents returned to Minyerri. At the time the sale was negotiated there were 170 people in residence. The previous owners of the station had a white manager in residence who padlocked all the access gates on the property to limit the movements of the Aboriginal people and to keep them under control. When the sale was being negotiated, the people were insistent that they never again wanted to be subjected to white management.[23] In 1992 there were 210 people living at Hodgson Downs, with numbers increasing as people returned from Ngukurr and other nearby settlements. By November 2003, a few months after the ceremony described in the opening of this paper, Minyerri's population was recorded as 450.

The second reason the Roper mission's influence is important in the funeral ceremony at Minyerri, lies in the evident commitment by people in the region to the maintenance of highly mobile lifestyles, linking kin between Minyerri and Ngukurr. More than 100 people were in attendance at the funeral business at Minyerri that day. Many of them had travelled from Ngukurr and other surrounding settlements specifically to be present for the funeral and associated business, affirming the vast webs of kin relatedness and individual roles and responsibilities within that web. Inter-community mobility in the Roper River region is frequent and important. Movement related to funeral business (often several weeks in duration) is but one of many reasons for this mobility. This has been maintained despite the efforts of the missionaries to impose an exclusively sedentary life and affirms the people's desire to retain autonomy over the order of their lives; a part of a demonstrable resilience and endurance of specific cultural practices.

This is further emphasised when it is remembered that the performance of traditional funeral ceremony business was forbidden at the Roper Mission.[24] Thus, thirdly, the maintenance and endurance of the knowledge of funeral ceremony business through the generations despite nearly 60 years of missionary prohibition is further evidence of extraordinary tenacity and commitment to the maintenance of culture. The decision by the deceased's family and contemporaries, to mark his death in both the traditional way and the Christian way is an honour indicative of his capacity to operate in both spheres and to be acknowledged and respected in the appropriate ceremony for each way.

While there is no doubt that the mission's establishment was motivated by a compassion for the Aboriginal people of the region, without which they may not have survived, the impact of the 'civilising' agenda has left a lasting legacy. The CMS and the majority of its missionaries in Australia were accustomed to believing that there was something particularly Christian about changing people's lifestyle from being nomadic hunters and gatherers to being settled farmers. An article in *The Open Door*, the CMS journal, in 1941 suggested that this was a kind of spiritual healing. 'The healing of the body gives a great opportunity for the healing of the soul. If the Aborigines are to be prepared to take their place in our civilization, they must be brought from a nomadic food-gathering existence to a food-producing village life.'[25] Hunting, fishing and digging yams were not work. Furthermore, building and farming were considered somehow more Christian, whereas hunting and fishing were less Christian. An attitude prevailed where work and the Gospel were intertwined and even indistinguishable. The 'gospel of work' was the attitude and understanding imparted to Aboriginal people when missionaries engaged in training them in the various labouring tasks necessary to create a self supporting, European style community.[26]

One incident reported in a CMS annual illustrates this further:

> One boy requested permission to marry one of the girls, and had now started to build his own house and prepare his garden, with a view to being able to keep himself and family — with the mission behind him to give a hand if he stumbles. We are hoping this couple will be the beginning of our long planned for village settlement, and that others will soon follow in their steps.[27]

Figure 9.4: Mission station at Roper River, no date.

Courtesy of the CMS Hart collection, Darwin.

Figure 9.5: Roper River mission showing gardens, no date.

Courtesy of the CMS Hart collection, Darwin.

Figure 9.6: Mission quarters at Roper River, no date.

(Handcoloured glass slide image, courtesy of the CMS Hart collection, Darwin)

These images are reproduced courtesy of Keith Hart from glass plate positives. Their quality is a result of this source.

As Harris discusses in his history of the CMS presence in the Roper Region, this vision died hard and as recently as the 1960s there were still a few missionaries who dreamed of the self-supporting family unit and spoke of it in sometimes paternalistic terms.[28] For Aboriginal kin groups made up of family extended across generations with extensive group responsibilities and obligations, the Christian order which revised the family dwelling unit to parents and children, required a radical reorientation, with significant consequences for the passing of culture and knowledge between extended kin. Harris concedes that it became evident 'the idealized Christian Aboriginal village, with happy, stable Aboriginal families living in their modest homes and working their little agricultural plots, was never going to happen. CMS was reluctant to let go of the notion of the self-sufficient village altogether. In the 1950s and 1960s the idea of a self-sufficient family gave way to a self-sufficient community'.[29]

During the years when CMS missionaries either believed they were protecting a dying race, or later, when they believed they were preparing Aboriginal people for an English speaking future, they regarded Aboriginal culture as fairly irrelevant. It was only when CMS started appointing linguists that missionaries began to have the opportunity to understand the local culture and society.[30] Since the way in which leadership is exercised in Aboriginal society differs markedly from the way it is exercised in western democratic society, Harris[31] suggests that with the exception of his father, Len Harris, very few, if any, missionaries really knew who the significant people were in community decision-making. Earl Hughes, a reverend appointed to Numbulwar, another CMS mission north of the Roper wrote to Harris about 'the way in which autocratic white mission superintendents ignored tribal leadership, thus contributing hugely to breakdown in community order and discipline'.[32] The ways in which such authority continued to be expressed, despite the ignorance of the missionaries, draws attention to the existence of a concurrent expression of community behaviour, escaping the attention of the missionaries, doubtless continuing to assert its own order over the lives of the residents of the mission settlement. Despite the apparent complicity of the mission population in adopting the missionaries' imposition of structure and order, a traditional cultural order was maintained and the deceased man at the focus of the funeral ceremony described above is one such example of this. He was a 'big boss' for culture. The traditional cultural order with respect to country and ceremony continues still, and is present and publicly expressed in moments such as the negotiation and enactment of a funeral ceremony.

In Minyerri and Ngukurr both Christian orientations to the world and traditional kin-based Aboriginal orientations of relatedness continue to exist concurrently. The contemporary ceremonies enacted to mark the passing of human life have come to embody a significance in which an intersection of orientations to the world and belief structures is continually expressed, negotiated and redefined. Each of these negotiations occurs relative to the deceased individual and the web of relatedness their death draws, particularly from the three contemporary trajectories of authority; Church, State, and Culture. The latter of these three was once the only basis for the allocation of authority and responsibility. While it may be imagined that as a system of authority it was doubtless not innocent of political manoeuvring itself, the contemporary concurrent negotiation of the politics of all three systems of authority reveals an intensely complex and potentially volatile phenomena in marking the death of a kinsmen, as those related to an individual in any of these three spheres may seek to have their relationship to the deceased acknowledged publicly.

For this reason, contemporary funeral ceremonies and the effort that accompanies their negotiation and enactment involve a myriad of political negotiations. My current focus is the manner in which the *spatial arrangement* of such procedures is taken up in expressing relationships between those still living, the expressions of authority they seek to make public through the enactment of the funeral ceremony, and how these negotiations between the living invoke aspects of interpreted significance in their relationship to the deceased in order to re-situate themselves politically. Since communities of Aboriginal people have been living in built environments such as Minyerri and Ngukurr for just less than a century, the ways in which those built environments are taken up by residents in expression of social relationships, casts light upon understanding the impact that settlement life continues to have upon those who live there, how those environments develop through metamorphosing usages, and the impact their usage has on the expression of relatedness between kin and country.

Both historically and in contemporary Minyerri and Ngukurr, particular dwellings or landmarks often stand as a significant marker of country or kin affiliation. In mission times in Ngukurr, the residential camps were spatially separated according to people's affiliation with country, which naturally were also linguistically differentiated. A distinction prevailed in the minds of residents between the 'top camp', 'middle camp' and 'bottom camp'.[33] Each camp embodied its own distinct identity linguistically and socially in relation to the residents it housed and the country from which they originated. Accordingly top camp was Rittharngu camp, middle camp was Nunngubuyu and bottom camp was Ngandi, Wandarang with Mara and Alawa people living nearest the River.[34] This distribution is indicative of these groups' orientation to country; since top camp is the most northern location, where the most northern oriented group, the Rittharngu were camped, and the Nunngubuyu, just south east of them in country, camped south-east of them in the settlement. Ngandi country is in the middle of all these groups, thus they were in middle camp in the settlement. Wandarang are coastal people and their affiliations with Mara and Alawa people, both of whose country lay south of the Roper meant they camped together, and usually Mara and Alawa people were the most southern in the camp, closest to the river and their country on the other side of the river.[35]

While top, middle and bottom camp remain spatially distinct in Ngukurr in contemporary times, generations of intermarriage between the language groups have intensified the associations that any single household may have to several tracts of country, relative to the affiliations of kin who live there. In other Arnhem Land communities, houses have been named after specific country and accordingly will house those with an interest or affiliation with that country.[36] A yard area and communal street area adjacent to a series of houses may have a significance affiliated with certain clans or their country and affiliations. This can occur in an enduring or ongoing sense and/or for a specific temporal period such as during a ceremony. Thus despite the imposition of a grid structure of streets delineating suburban spatial dwelling practices and boundaries, for residents, the spatial order and significance of places within the settlement continues to be structured by residents' relationships to country, kin and thus each other. The structure of living for residents could not be contained by the boundedness of the housing grid. Households are characterised by a constant fluid and evolving process of metamorphosis, in which relationships between individuals and affiliations with webs of kin are constantly negotiated and redefined in relation to disputes, conflict, changes in affiliation and context. Relocations between households are common and a necessary feature in the avoidance of conflict, or temporary resolution of disputes, or claims of sorcery or transgression.

The imposed settlement structure has radically altered the settings for opportunities in which political, ceremonial and cultural negotiation and expression occur and as a result residents constantly renegotiate and redefine the expression of authority on their own terms and thus in their own ways. In the contemporary situation of three systems of authority — Church, State and Culture — the stakes involved in funeral ceremony displays of authority are even more complex. The ways in which the settlement's built environment is adapted to this end, show an acute understanding of the importance of spatial relationships and contexts in situating phenomena. For example, the pink colourbond-clad house from beside which the women emerged, was chosen as an appropriate threshold from which they could embark on their re-entry into public life. The reasons for choosing that house over others was significant, and not an arbitrary choice, but rather one which expressed important aspects of authority, obligation and responsibility between kin and this is expressed in relation to the spatial planning and houses belonging to other kin. Before exploring this in greater depth, it is helpful to contextualise the cultural significance of the events themselves.

Upon the death of a member of the community, the place where they slept is cleared and all their possessions destroyed or removed. This often means that whole families will move house. The house where the deceased person was residing may remain empty for some time until an appropriate cleansing ceremony marks it as able to be inhabited again. It is understood that when an individual is born their spirit has come from a particular place within the earth's features and in order to maintain the enduring life source of that place and keep that country safe, upon an individual's death their spirit must return to it's place of origin. The name of the deceased is not spoken but is replaced by a speech restriction term, lest the speaking of his name should cause his spirit to linger. The immediate relatives of the deceased must move away from their usual living place and conceal themselves, so that if his spirit came looking for them, they would not be recognized. Seeking this concealment, as described at the beginning of this paper, in the women's camp located outside town, they were covering their skin in white body paint to aid in the safe return passage for the spirit of the deceased to his country. In the case of the death at Minyerri, the dwelling of the man was evacuated to ensure that his spirit returned to his country and his relatives hid to ensure that his spirit did not attempt to find them and stay attached to the affiliations of his life. Once the body of the deceased has been buried, his relatives may return to the settlement in a ceremony that marks their absolution from the period requiring concealment. This is followed by a ceremony for the house of the deceased that 'cleanses' it or marks it as safe to inhabit again.[37]

The pink colourbond-clad house from beside which the women at Minyerri emerged during ceremony was chosen because it was located at a sufficient distance; one of the farthest away from the house of the deceased, and also on the perimeter edge of the settlement. Thus it was marked as a threshold of entry back into public settlement life and simultaneously located as far as possible from the deceased's house, which was yet to be 'cleansed'. The relationship between the occupants of that house and the deceased are also of significance. Reciprocal roles of responsibility for country and ceremony are inherited from one's parents (and grandparents) and the significance of these roles depends on the context. In the Roper region the roles carry the names Minggirringi, Junggayi and Darlnyin and each confers different responsibilities in relation to specific sites, land and (by inference) individuals. The terms are sometimes translated into English as 'owner', 'manager' and 'ranger' respectively. An individual is Minggirringi for the sites, ceremonies, ancestral beings and country associated with his or her father and father's father. An individual is Junggayi for sites, ceremonies and historic ancestors associated with his mother's and mother's father's country and father's mother's (brother's) country. Darlnyin are sometimes described as 'half' Minggirringi, 'half' Junggayi, and will be Darlnyin for sites, ceremonies and ancestral beings in his mother's mother's (brother's) country.[38]

The reciprocal relationships, responsibilities and obligations conferred by these roles in relation to country and kin are called forth in different ways relative to context. In the context of the death of a kinsman, the spirit of the deceased must be returned to the country for which he is Minggirringi and the Junggayi of the deceased have an obligation to organise the ceremonies associated with his/her death, since it is their role to ensure that the originating country of the deceased is properly managed, and ensuring the safe return of his spirit to that country is an important part of that management obligation.

The most senior occupant of the pink colourbond-clad house was the most senior Junggayi for the deceased and his country, and thus this Junggayi's house by extension, became the appropriate place, symbolically from which this specific set of ceremonies could be conducted due to the occupant's close reciprocal kin affiliation and responsibility. Thus although this particular country where Minyerri stands has been overlaid with a (rough) grid structure of streets, determined by the imperative of the settlement's 'delivery of services' to individual houses which delineate numerous zones of privacy scaled from the innermost private dwelling practices of 'nuclear' families through to the public life of the street, the residents of Minyerri attribute and distinguish the significance of different places within the settlement using a different structure of order, in fact an order inherent in the Land that existed before the built environment was manifest.

Earlier in the day, I had witnessed the Anglican funeral service (for the same individual) and was struck by the apparent incongruity between the mobile belief structure, that appears to be applicable anywhere, of the Christian doctrines that had found their way to this region, and the particularity of location to which Aboriginal beliefs are anchored. The particularity of location of Aboriginal beliefs in the Roper Region means that the significances of particular places are unique and are unable to be overlaid, imposed upon or transported to other Land (as opposed to the possibility of this in Christian belief structures). The continuation of life requires the nurturance of specific places as the source of life, as the place from whence spirit emerges to give life to human form. Thus it is the particularity of embodiment and a resistance to the mobility offered by the conceptual which allows that continuity and the ontological primacy of Land to be maintained. Unlike the Christian doctrines, applicable in any location just like the conceptually derived Cartesian 'grid' of structures in a settlement, the significance of 'place' for Aboriginal people in the Roper region, as for Aboriginal people in many other areas in Australia, is particular to specific locations and always relationally anchored to webs of other specific places.[39]

So as we witnessed the lowering of the casket and listened to the Aboriginal Anglican minister's sermon promising eternal life in a heavenly city, I wondered, looking at the buildings surrounding us, what exultation these people were supposed to feel might lie in the promise of an afterlife in the 'ethereal' city of heavenly Jerusalem, when their ontological continuum is understood as so connected to the Land, the ground and the particularity of place. Since many people in the region identify as Christian, their capacity to incorporate aspects of the Christian doctrines, while maintaining their adherence to the enduring order of the Land demonstrates their adaptive capacity. The way in which the funeral ceremony was conducted according to customs drawn from both belief structures is indicative of this.

In the Minyerri ceremony the women were led away from the pink colour-bond clad house to an area of ground marked by a group evidently waiting for them. The cleansing procedure continued and the women were absolved from the period requiring concealment; the white paint was washed from their bodies, then each individual was 'smoked', and others of the community, children included, were summonsed to participate in this part of the ceremony if they wished. Branches of leaves were lit, and their burning swiftly smothered, producing smoke that continued for some time. The smoking branches were then waved about the body ensuring the cleansing from the presence of any unwanted spirits. Earth from the ground on which they stood was then placed firmly in the hand of the individuals concerned, and this marked the closure of this part if the ceremony.

It appeared that this last action consolidated their presence and grounded the women in their current location, both temporally and spatially. At that moment it seemed clear that the layout of the surrounding buildings appeared only to represent an order of relatedness that would always be secondary despite colonial attempts continued in contemporary times in structuring Aboriginal lives according to the institutions of behaviour attendant upon settlement life. The order of relatedness for the Aboriginal residents in Minyerri and neighbouring Ngukurr relies primarily on being grounded first and foremost by the Land. While the imposition of built environments in this region remain as structures seeking to re-order the lives of their inhabitants, residents appear to take them up in ways that maintain an adherence to the order of the Land which precedes the built environment. The fixtures of the built environment continue to be taken up with inventive response by residents of the settlement in different contexts with differing political import and are appropriated in the expression and articulation of an order of relatedness between kin and country that has existed and continues to exist beyond the weathering of the corrugated iron cladding.

References

Attwood, Bain 2000, 'Space and time at Ramahyuck, Victoria 1863-85', in Peter Read (ed.), *Settlement: a history of Australian Indigenous housing*, Aboriginal Studies Press, Canberra.

—— 1989, *The making of the Aborigines*, Allen & Unwin, Sydney.

Baker, Brett 2002, '"I'm going to where-is-your-brisket": placenames in the Roper', in Luise Hercus, Flavia Hodges and Jane Simpson, (eds), *The land is a map; Placenames of Indigenous origin in Australia*, Pandanus Books, Canberra: 103-130.

Bauer FH 1964, *Historical geography of white settlement in part of the northern territory, Part 2: The Katherine–Darwin region*, CSIRO Report 64(1), Canberra.

Bern, John 1979, 'Politics in the conduct of a secret male ceremony', *Journal of Anthropological Research* 35(1): 47-60.

Dillon, Jane and Mark Savage 2003, 'House design in Alice Springs town camps', in Paul Memmott (ed.), *TAKE 2 Housing Design in Indigenous Australia*, Royal Australian Institute of Architects.

Edmonds, Angelique 2002, 'Approaching an understanding of the Yuendumu doors', M.Phil thesis, Architecture Department, Cambridge University, U.K.

Edmunds, Angelique 2007, 'Metamorphosis of Relatedness: the Place of Aboriginal Agency, Autonomy and Authority in the Roper River Region of Northern Australia', PhD thesis, The Australian National University.

Elkin, AP 1972, *Two rituals in south and central Arnhem Land*, Oceania Monograph 19, Sydney.

Harris, John 1998, *We wish we'd done more: ninety years of CMS and Aboriginal issues in north Australia*, Open Book Publishers, Adelaide.

—— 1990, *One blood: 200 years of Aboriginal encounter with Christianity — a story of hope*, Albatross, Sydney.

Martin, David 1993, 'Autonomy and relatedness: an ethnography of Wik People of Aurukun, Western Cape York Peninsula', PhD thesis, ANU.

Merlan, Francesca 1978, '"Making people quiet" in the pastoral north: reminiscences of Elsey station', *Aboriginal History* 2(1): 70-106.

Morphy, Howard 1995, 'Landscape and the reproduction of the ancestral past', in E Hirsch and M O'Hanlon (eds), *The anthropology of landscape: perspectives on place and space*, Clarendon Press.

Morphy, Howard and Frances Morphy 1981, 'Yutpundji-Djindiwirritj Land Claim', Northern Land Council.

Myers, Fred 1986, *Pintupi country, Pintupi self: sentiment, place and politics amongst Western Desert Aborigines,* Smithsonian Institute Press, Washington, D.C.

Ogden, Pearl 1992, *From humpy to homestead, the biography of Sabu,* narrated by Peter David Sing, compiled by Pearl Ogden, AIATSIS, Darwin.

Rose, Deborah Bird 1986, *Nourishing terrains, Australian Aboriginal views of landscape and wilderness,* Australian Heritage Commission, Canberra.

Rowse, Tim 1992, *Remote possibilities: the Aboriginal domain and the administrative imagination,* NARU, ANU, Darwin.

Trigger, David 1992, *'Whitefella comin'; Aboriginal responses to colonialism in northern Australia,* Cambridge University Press, Cambridge.

—— 1996, 'Blackfellas and whitefellas: the concepts of domain and social closure in the analysis of race relations', *Mankind* 16(2): 99-117.

ENDNOTES

[1] I attended the ceremony described at the request of adopted family, since I was working with people in the region at the time on a doctoral research project aimed at understanding the impact of sedentary life upon people's relationship to country and their capacity for agency in determining the order of their lives. Although this ceremony occurred early in my stay in the region, my understanding of events from that day grew in retrospect as my experiences as a permanent resident in the region afforded further understanding of the intricacies of the networks of relatedness of kin and country. For further discussion on the importance of Land, see Morphy 1995; Myers 1986; Rose 1996.

[2] Alawa is the predominant language spoken by the residents of Minyerri.

[3] Morphy and Morphy 1981: 4-5.

[4] NTRS and NT Land Title records.

[5] Harris 1990: 696.

[6] Merlan 1978: 87.

[7] Bauer 1964: 157 as cited by Merlan 1978.

[8] Harris 1990: 696-98.

[9] Morphy and Morphy1981: 15.

[10] CMA Instructions from Committee, delivered on Friday July 10th 1908, to Rev. J.F.G. Huthnance, Leader of the party, Mr R. D. Joynt, Mr Charles Sharp CMSF (as cited in Harris 1998: 9).

[11] Harris 1936a: 236 as cited in Harris 1998: 11. John Harris, the author of these texts, was the son of Len and Margery Harris, CMS missionaries who worked in northern Australia. Their relations, Dick and Nell Harris were also contemporary CMS missionaries in the north of Australia. After John Harris' completion of the book *One Blood* in 1990, CMS approached Harris to write *We Wish We'd Done More* since he had significant knowledge and experience of the CMS's presence in the north of Australia and the structure and aims of the Mission stations.

[12] Harris 1998: 326.

[13] Harris 1998: 23.

[14] Harris 1998: 27.

[15] Annual Report of CMA of Victoria 1908: 9 CMSFA (as cited in Harris 1998: 23).

[16] Harris 1998: 330.

[17] Personal communication Gertie Huddlestons, Ngukurr, October 2004.

[18] Gertie Huddleston, 22 October 2004, interview at Old Mission.

[19] See generally Trigger 1992; Martin 1993; Attwood 1989: 1-31, further verified in relation to Roper Mission in interview on 22 October 2004 with Gertie Huddleston, who was born at the old mission in the late 1920s.

[20] Harris 1998: 141.

[21] Mary Crome's diary as cited in Harris 1998: 24.

[22] Trigger 1996: 114-5.

[23] Ogden 1992: 122.

[24] Interview in Ngukurr with Rev. Michael Gumbuli, Helen Rogers, Maureen Thompson, Betty Roberts and Roslyn Munur, 27 October 2004.

[25] *The Open Door* 1941: 11, quoting a National Missionary Council leaflet, cited in Harris 1998: 205.

[26] Harris 1998: 206.

[27] *The Church Missionary Gleaner*, 1 Aug 1926: 20, cited in Harris 1998: 210-211.

[28] Harris 1998: 211.

[29] Harris 1998: 212.

[30] Harris 1998: 156.

[31] Harris 1998: 156.

[32] Harris 1998: 156.

[33] Personal conversations with Ngukurr residents in 2004 including David Daniels, Alan Joshua, John Joshua, Margaret George, Cherry Daniels, Betty Roberts, Freda Roberts, Gertie Huddleston.

[34] Personal conversations with Ngukurr residents in 2004.

[35] Northern Territory Archives Service, Christian Mission Society 873/P1 Box 1, 2 undated maps, read together with Traditional Language Regions map in Baker 2002.

[36] Personal communication Peter Toner, ANU, 11 September 2003.

[37] This was explained to me by my adopted family at the time of the ceremony and in discussion over the following 18 months as I sought to clarify my understanding of the way in which the structures of the built environment had been taken up and incorporated into existing practices ensuring the maintenance of the ontological primacy of the Land.

[38] See Bern 1979; Elkin 1972; Morphy and Morphy 1981.

[39] This understanding was gained through numerous discussions the author has had with Walpiri, Wandarang, Mara, Nunggubuyu, Ritharrngu and Alawa people in the Northern Territory and through sources consulted in the process of my PhD research. For discussion of these issues at greater length see Edmonds 2002 and 2007.

Sinful enough for Jesus: guilt and Christianisation at Mapoon, Queensland

Devin Bowles

The mission at Mapoon is the site of myriad stories. Many have already been lost to time and more will follow as another generation takes its memories to the grave. The narrative related here is not the only one that might be told. It concerns the missionaries who founded Mapoon and, most importantly for this telling, the Aboriginal people who became Christian while these missionaries were there. There were other Aboriginal people who did not become Christian. Some who stayed did not become Christian; others left permanently. They have other stories to be told another time.

This story is a cyclical one. Someone makes a sacrifice for the Christian God and someone else feels guilty because of it. This guilt leads them, in turn, to suffer in spreading God's Word and the cycle is renewed. Europeans repeated it for generations before bringing it to Australia. It is at this juncture, at the point of the spread of the cycle from Europeans to Aboriginal people — in which Aboriginal Christians redefined moral transgression for themselves — that this paper is focused. At Mapoon, the tremendous increase in the guilt felt by Aboriginal people as a result of a new emphasis on sin led to a remarkable degree of Christianisation, which in turn reinforced the new prominence of moral transgression.

The story is an important one for several reasons. It demonstrates some of the ways Aboriginal people creatively adapted Christianity to their own unique needs. It provides an exception to the general rule that Aboriginal Australians have tended not to adopt Christianity without accompanying cultural devastation. In doing so, it points the way to at least part of the role spirituality played in pre-contact Australia. It also suggests why Moravian missionaries have been so effective in populations normally resistant to conversion — because rather than focusing on intellectual persuasion, they relied on Christianity affecting the emotions of potential converts. Moravian practice was marked by a cult-like devotion to Jesus, and at some missions this may have been decisive. At Mapoon, however, the emotional lever with the greatest strength was making people feel indebted and guilty.

Prologue

The arrival and departure of the founding missionaries from Cape York Peninsula in Queensland sets this story in time, from 1891 until 1919. However the beginnings of this story stretch through almost 2000 years of European history to Jesus' death in a Roman-occupied portion of the Middle East, and are planted firmly in pre-contact Australia.

For hundreds of years, Christianity, and the Judaism it grew from, developed in a context in which people were expected to give their allegiance to a ruler. When someone wronged another citizen, vengeance was to come from the king, not the other citizen. People could plead for his mercy, which he could dispense at will, paralleling the situation in Christianity in which all sins were against God and people must seek his mercy to avoid divine retribution.[1] As a result of the sociopolitical context in which Christianity developed, it is notable for its emphasis on rules. For instance, the book of Leviticus is composed almost entirely of God's regulations for His people. God's rules are absolute and incontestable; they separate right from wrong, good from evil, and the sacred from the profane. Out of this conception of immutable boundaries comes the notion of sin: the transgression of God's law. The Christian story is one of humanity's sin and redemption. For this reason, transgression occupies a more central place in Christianity than in most other religions.

Aboriginal society before settlement lacked the top-down social and spiritual control that marked the development of Christianity. People negotiated relationships with each other, ancestral beings, and the land in an interactive way. Relationships were always interdependent and reciprocal. Transgressions resulted in imbalance — social, ecological and spiritual — though the separation of these categories is a European one. Boundaries and their transgressions played an entirely different role in traditional Aboriginal spirituality than in Christianity. Deborah Bird Rose argues that in traditional Yarralin spirituality, evil as Europeans know it does not exist.[2] There are immoral acts, actions which disturb the balance of the world, but not evil. There is no one controlling power; everything is interconnected. There is no punishment from 'on high' for moral transgressions; instead, the result of these acts on the interconnected world is imbalance.

Missionaries' guilt

Understanding why so many Aboriginal people at Mapoon adopted notions of moral transgression similar to those of the missionaries first requires an examination of the missionaries themselves. To have any comprehension of the importance of Jesus and his suffering and resurrection which bridged a degraded humanity and glorious God, to understand the extent of Jesus' love, and to develop one's own love for Him, all fundamental pursuits in Moravian Christianity, one must start with the knowledge that humans are, at base, sinful. Like many European Christians of the day, the missionaries sought to avoid sin in their own lives and save others from sin, in no small part because of what they believed awaited sinners in the afterlife. This emphasis on sin had important consequences for the missionaries.

The word guilt has at least two interrelated meanings. The first definition is what a judge looks for in a criminal trial. It is a violation of a law. This idea took on particular significance for the missionaries who believed that God had created a divine Law. No violation could escape His notice, and all people would be called to account during the Judgement. For the missionaries, guilt was having committed a sin. The second definition is closely related; it is the feeling aroused in a person by the knowledge he or she has done wrong. As a result of the missionaries' belief in an omnipotent Judge watching for transgressions of His absolute moral law, they were acutely aware of any of their own transgressions of this law and felt guilty for what they perceived as their guilt. Rev. Nicholas Hey closely associated the two meanings of guilt when he wrote that the missionaries tried to 'impart a sense of guilt or sin'.[3]

The concept of sin and preoccupation with the feeling of guilt influenced the missionaries' use of this emotion as a lever. For most of the period examined in this article, Nicholas Hey was the senior male missionary and thus had the most influence over the 'official' definition of Christianity. Hey's life was directed by feelings of guilt from a young age. His father, who was unable to fulfil his dream of becoming a missionary, wanted his sons to become missionaries until he died (when Nicholas was 13). His mother had great influence on Nicholas and his siblings.[4]

Arthur Ward's brother, JG, died at Mapoon and Arthur's response was to write a book about the mission. He seems to have obtained much of his information from the missionaries and probably possessed a thorough understanding of their motivations. He writes about Hey's mother, 'She spent hours in prayer for them, and they knew it. She saw that they did not, as was natural, think as she did, and she would have willingly suffered the loss of all things rather than that the soul of one of her children should be lost'.[5] Nicholas rebelled against some of the stricter religious elements of her household, such as not being allowed to dance, and eventually ran away.

> But he found he could enjoy nothing. Pleasure was not pleasant. Go where he would, he felt himself encompassed by his mother's prayers, and at last he gave up the struggle to emancipate himself from her influence, returned home, and quietly settled down to the old strict routine. Not that he was satisfied with it. The Puritan air stifled him, and he began to feel the uncomfortable sensation that there was no chance for him because he was not good enough. He took to reading his Bible systematically, in the hope that some good might come of it.[6]

Guilt was clearly one, if not the, motivating factor in Nicholas Hey's young life. His studies eventually convinced him that the fate of his soul had not been predetermined and that salvation was possible. Yet despite his apparent break with the religion of his mother, 'the best theology he ever learnt was taught him at his mother's feet'.[7] That his parents' lessons made their mark is evidenced by the fact that two of his brothers became preachers while the third became a medical missionary. The effects of Nicholas' upbringing lasted well beyond childhood. Years after the mission had been founded, Arthur Ward could still write, 'The home influences are as strong as ever, though it is years since his mother died'.[8]

Nicholas Hey's 'home influences' were what kept him behaving as he believed a good Christian ought to behave. Even such core elements of his personality as his devotion to Christianity itself and his general way of thinking can be traced back to his early home: 'If one tries to get at the secret of Nicholas Hey's resourcefulness, his earnest piety, and his broad-minded common sense, one is always led back to the days when the boy of 13 left school to become the bread-winner, and to learn from his mother the importance of little things, and the doctrine of stewardship'.[9] As a young man, the missionary path was blocked for Nicholas Hey because he had to care for his sick mother, who was largely confined to bed for the last seven years of her life. By the time she died, he no longer had the same desire to become a missionary but he still felt it was his duty. He wrote to the Moravian Mission Board to put his guilt about the matter to rest, believing that he would be rejected because at 24 he was too old and, further, because he was unworthy of the position. He saw his acceptance by the Board as a sign of God's will which he did not dare transgress.[10]

Guilt was an important part of the other missionaries' lives, too. It is striking that Arthur Ward, while attempting to praise the missionaries and work at Mapoon, portrayed Nicholas Hey as being racked by guilt. This indicates that Nicholas Hey was not exceptional and perhaps even fairly similar to Arthur and JG Ward. In a diary by one of the European females at Mapoon, virtually the only discussion of the author's emotions was written every new year in a prayer to be a better person in the coming year.[11] The missionaries passed along religiously motivated feelings of guilt to Aboriginal people. Many of the Aboriginal people felt as though they sinned against the missionaries when they sinned against God and sinned against God when they sinned against the missionaries.

Passing the guilt

Prior to the mission, the Aboriginal people at Mapoon were largely free of the feelings of intense guilt that marked the missionaries' faith. Upon their arrival, the missionaries made clear that they were suffering in order to bring the Aboriginal people the Christian message. This created an ongoing imbalance that could not be rectified and a situation likely to cause feelings of guilt and indebtedness among Aboriginal people. It would have been difficult for Aboriginal people to accommodate the feelings generated by the new social relations or give these relationships meaning using only their traditional belief systems. The Christianity the missionaries brought with them was, almost by definition, exceptionally well suited to these tasks.

Nicholas Hey writes about the start of the mission: 'Two great difficulties confronted the pioneers at this stage. The first was the language, and the second was the absence of a sense of sin in the native mind'.[12] The missionaries were keen to 'correct' this 'problem' and tried to

> impart a sense of guilt or sin, which is quite foreign to the native mind. They could not see that there was anything wrong in themselves, and even when found out in the very act they said the blame rested with the one who gave them away or discovered their offence. It was a constant battle between darkness and light.[13]

The missionaries endeavoured to pass on their European set of criteria for evaluating behaviour to Aboriginal people.

To the missionaries, Aboriginal 'faults' were not mere differences of belief or custom but absolute moral evils, small but definite victories for the forces of darkness. The missionaries summed up their view of Aboriginal religious beliefs in a report, '"I believe in devils" is the first article of their creed'.[14] Aboriginal people at Mapoon, initially at least, did not divide the world into the forces of good and evil and so could not have thought that they were siding with the forces of darkness in believing and acting as their fathers and mothers had taught them. Convincing Aboriginal people that there were two sides in a great spiritual battle and that they were on the evil and losing side, the side of sin, was a necessary step in what the missionaries viewed as a change of allegiances — conversion. The missionaries sought to teach the Aboriginal people this division intellectually. Aboriginal people were probably more receptive to it because of the new social relationships and the feelings these generated than because of any logical argument offered by the missionaries.

One of the ways missionaries increased Aboriginal feelings of guilt was by assuming a Christ-like role, visibly suffering (much like Hey's mother) for the sake of other people. Like Christ's, their suffering was obviously of a condescending nature. Their message was this: just as God had to lower himself to and endure a human state to redeem humanity, the missionaries had to bear the crosses of leaving 'civilisation' and living amongst savages to bring the Aboriginal people the Gospel. Christ died to give the redeeming Gospel to all of humanity. The missionaries made clear the insalubriousness of the tropical climate. Like many European Australians of the time, the missionaries believed the tropical climate to be inherently unhealthy, a conception no doubt reinforced by JG Ward's death soon after the start of the mission from malaria. Health problems continued to plague the missionaries almost throughout their time at

Mapoon.[15] They were risking, or in JG Ward's case, sacrificing, their lives to save Aboriginal souls, like Christ.

The missionaries' sacrifice was made known to the Aboriginal people at Mapoon, some of whom felt guilty and indebted because of it. Many of the Aboriginal Christians wrote letters to Mrs Ward for her departure. These letters were written on different dates by different people on different types of paper in different places. This and the number of spelling and grammatical errors make it unlikely that any of the missionaries were directly regulating the content, though the writers probably wanted to please Mrs Ward. These letters contain several references to Mrs Ward leaving for her health and having endured bad health for the Aboriginal people. Lena M, for instance, wrote, 'We would like you to stay very much but it would be selfish of us to keep you here when you're always sick and ailing God bless and keep you dear Aunty you were always kind and good to us'.[16] It would not have been necessary for Aboriginal people to believe the Christian message in order for them to experience feelings of deep guilt and indebtedness. They might well remain undecided as to whether or not the Christian story was true but feel indebted to the missionaries for their sacrifices in bringing it to them. Of course, the mere fact that the missionaries were prepared to make these sacrifices may have added weight to their claims. In any event, the feelings of guilt created a situation in which some Aboriginal people found Christian beliefs useful.

In the minds of some of the Aboriginal people, the line between the missionaries and the newfound God was blurry on some levels. The missionaries were like, but not the same as, God or Jesus. Like Jesus, the missionaries were compared to the shepherd going after the one stray sheep. Mackie, one of Mrs Ward's ex-students, wrote, 'We will always have you in our mind and will never forget your teaching us and bringing us back when we went astray'.[17] Theresa wrote to Mrs Ward, 'I am writing to tell you Dear Auntie that I am very very sorry that I grief you and God for all the wrongs that I did. But now I am asking God to forgive me for my sins. And now Dear Auntie I ask you to pray for me'.[18] The new concept of sin was held to be an offence against both God and the missionaries. As though she were a saint, it was believed that Mrs Ward could intercede with God on behalf of the Aboriginal people. It is notable that Theresa wrote that she was asking God for forgiveness as she wrote of repentance in her letter to the missionary. Dolly also believed that Mrs Ward had some special ability to bring Aboriginal people closer to God, 'When I think of Auntie's love I hope it will also bring me nearer Jesus'.[19] Hilda thought Mrs Ward's prayer could bring Aboriginal people closer to God by increasing *their* love for Him, thereby making them less sinful. She wrote, 'Dear Auntie pray for us so that we may come to love our Saviour more and more'.[20]

The parallel between God and the missionaries was important. Aboriginal people developed a relationship with the missionaries that was without precedent in traditional culture. This created a whole new set of emotions. The novel social situation and emotional landscape was difficult to reflect in the Aboriginal people's traditional belief systems. It would have been problematic to accommodate the sustained imbalance of a social debt that could not be repaid in the traditional belief system in which people viewed the universe in terms of interconnection and balance. Traditional Aboriginal beliefs were therefore not well suited to explaining the feelings of guilt that the relationships with the missionaries could generate. However, Aboriginal people had another religious system at their disposal, one they could use to help explain and give meaning to their social environment. In adopting Christian beliefs, they were using a tool that the Europeans brought with them, much as they might have used a metal knife.

Moravian Christianity would have been a very useful tool in this situation, focusing as it did on the suffering of Jesus on the cross. The missionaries would have emphasised this aspect of the Christian story, making Christianity particularly useful to Aboriginal people seeking meaning and explanation in these new circumstances. Gollin describes this Moravian emphasis, 'Since it was essential for the believer to keep the death and suffering of Christ on the Cross before his eyes at all times, the image of Christ became identified almost exclusively with His sufferings, His blood, and His wounds'.[21]

Aboriginal people were receptive to this message. Several of the letters from Aboriginal people to Mrs Ward contain references to the 'cruel cross'. The Christian story made clear that Jesus' suffering, like that of the missionaries, was for them. A letter from Meaffra and Annette is illustrative: 'I don't forget when I was a boy you taught me about the love of Christ and how he died on the cruel cross to save us from going to hell'.[22] Emphasis on the suffering of the Saviour would help explain feelings of guilt. That Aboriginal people chose to emphasise this in their letters buttresses the claim that it was this aspect of Christianity that they were using to help meet their emotional and spiritual needs.

The missionaries brought with them a new set of social relationships and a profound sense of guilt. Many Aboriginal people entered into these new relationships and experienced deep feelings of guilt. To help make sense of the new social structures and feelings, they adopted more or less of the belief system that had coevolved with the social structures and feelings for hundreds of years.

Positive feedback loop of guilt

Aboriginal adoption of Christianity increased their feelings of guilt, thereby increasing the needs that Christianity was meant to be fulfilling. Guilt was critical to a relationship in which the missionaries were viewed as God's messengers to the unknowing and sinful Aboriginal people. This relationship increased Aboriginal acceptance of a moral dichotomy and increased the degree to which Aboriginal people used Christianity as a guide in defining the limits of God's law and what constituted moral behaviour.

Aboriginal acceptance of Christianity increased the imbalance of their relationship with the missionaries. If Aboriginal people felt indebted to the missionaries for their sacrifices when they thought they had come to spread a message of dubious truth value, as well as a new way of life, such feelings would surely have increased when they believed the missionaries brought vitally important spiritual information that saved Aboriginal people from eternal damnation. For their part, the missionaries represented themselves as messengers. As the intermediaries of the Gospel between Jesus and the Aboriginal people at Mapoon, they positioned themselves between God and the Aboriginal people. Aboriginal Christians felt indebted to the missionaries for what they believed to be the salvation of their souls. Such a debt could never be repaid and the missionaries would always be holier than the Aboriginal people. The Christianity guilt produced in turn produced more guilt.

Letters Aboriginal people wrote Mrs Ward are eloquent testimony to the Aboriginal feelings of debt and inferiority. Nearly all of the writers thanked Mrs Ward for coming to teach them about Jesus. One fragmentary letter, whose author is unrecorded, is demonstrative, 'Thank God that he has chosen you to be his messenger and to spread his Gospel to the heathen people at Mapoon and to tell that how our loving Saviour shed his blood on Calvary to save us from going to hell.' The author continues in a vein that is reminiscent of the shepherd analogy, 'And now dear Auntie for many years you have been preaching the Gospel here and have brought many souls to Christ. I also do thank you dear Auntie for bringing me up when I was a girl & telling me about the love of Christ and bringing my poor wandering soul to Christ'.[23]

Aboriginal people were aware of the fact that they had previously been unexposed to Christianity and, according to the missionaries, without Christ's influence. The missionaries' depiction of their presence as a Christ-like sacrifice reinforced this idea. Christ and God were portrayed by the missionaries as being infinitely more moral and powerful than weak and sinful humans. The missionaries' explanation for their presence was to lift up especially weak and especially sinful Aboriginal people to a level closer to, but still below, the European standard. One of the constant themes in the letters to Mrs Ward is the hope that they will meet in heaven. Many of the authors, however, worry that they and other Aboriginal people might not be good enough to enter. Ida wrote, 'We hope if not here on earth to meet you in Heaven, but we know it will be very hard for us as there are many temptations in this world. But through God's help we will overcome them, it is only if we look to Him and ask Him for strength'. She concludes, 'I will try my best to be one of those to meet you in Heaven'.[24] Harry Shadforth echoes this sentiment, 'We hope if not to meet on earth we hope to meet at Jesus' feet that this [sic] if I keep true to the Saviour'.[25] No one expressed any doubt that Mrs Ward would enter heaven when she died.

The Christianity the missionaries brought with them was tied to a particular moral universe and an extensive set of rules for behaviour. In Europe, these ideas evolved in conjunction with one another, and the moral universe was vastly different to the one Aboriginal Australians inhabited before contact. When Aboriginal people at Mapoon made Christianity their own, they also changed the way they viewed morality, even if they did not adopt all or even most of what the missionaries brought with them. Of course their past actions viewed in this new light often failed to measure up. The negotiation of two separate moral universes is exponentially more difficult than the navigation of one. Traditional obligations to relatives for time and resources often conflicted with similar demands by the missionaries. The missionaries were able to increase the weight of their demands because they had some success in portraying themselves as spiritual mediators between Aboriginal people and God.[26] Ironically, mistakes made according to the Aboriginal people's pre-contact ethical code may have led to a Christian-style self-condemnation in a manner foreign to that code.

That Aboriginal Christians did alter their ideas about morality and often judged themselves as committing ethical breaches is evidenced in their letters to Mrs Ward. Bella Busch writes,

> When I was naughty and in bad temper how you tell me that's not right for me to do, then you tell me about Jesus love, you taught me just like your own girl ... But your kindness never ceased from me when I go a stray and do things that's not right in our Saviour side. You always teach me what is right. Your talking always touch my heart and your saying a great feeling to me when you tell me of Jesus and his love ... How you bring my wandering soul back to the Shepherds fold. So I thank God that you are a servant of God ... Also I will remember all what you have taught me how to live a better life.[27]

Perhaps the clearest statement about how radical the shift in morality was comes 'out of the mouths of babes', from Annie, 'I hope to be a good girl and don't give any trouble and to obey every little thing even when I at school or at play'.[28] Annie gets to the heart of the matter in equating the good side of the newly introduced good-bad dichotomy with adoption of missionary values.

The dichotomised worldview the missionaries put forward undermined Aboriginal self-confidence and self-justification. Not only were the Aboriginal people taught that all people were sinners, but that Aboriginal people had fallen farther than the rest of humanity. In many of their letters to Mrs Ward, Aboriginal people wrote about being good with God's help or the missionaries' prayers. Many accepted their need for moral improvement; some even doubted their ability to do this without the help of God or the missionaries. They became so fixated on God's power that they rested their own futures on it rather than themselves. In his letter to Mrs Ward, Alexander asks her to keep in touch so they know how she is 'But I'll leave it all to Jesus he knows what is best for you and I'.[29] The adoption of Christianity to assuage feelings of guilt created more guilt, which of course increased the usefulness of Christianity to alleviate these feelings.

The cycle begins again

It is not surprising that Aboriginal Christians sought to alleviate the feelings of guilt and inadequacy they felt. The social conditions at the mission and particularities about Moravian Christianity meant that many did so by spreading Christianity to others and beginning the cycle again.

The social conditions that saw those spreading the Word in a superior position to those to whom it was being spread was an inducement to join the ranks of the former. Many missionaries, including the pioneer missionaries at Mapoon, often saw their work as never finished because they believed the faith of the newly converted was still fragile and needed protection from someone with stronger faith, the missionary. It takes little imagination to envision at least some of the ways in which ideas of racial and cultural superiority complemented this view. The perspective from the other side of the missionary experience at Mapoon — that of the newly converted — was very different. The people who accepted more or less of the Christian story were aware that those who brought them the Gospel did not feel most of them had developed or were responsible enough to be left alone with it, furthering the already strong feelings of guilt and inadequacy discussed above. From the European Christian perspective at Mapoon, missionaries were always the powerful, knowledgeable, generous ones giving of themselves and spreading the Word while Aboriginal people were, initially at least, not seen by the missionaries as having anything of spiritual value to share. With time, Aboriginal people sought and found ways to become givers and share the Word themselves. The hierarchy of savers and saved the missionaries brought also meant that by becoming givers in this relationship, they were simultaneously moving up the moral ladder. Spreading their faith both alleviated the guilt and increased the social status of Aboriginal Christians at Mapoon.

This degree to which sharing the Gospel was a liberating and empowering activity was especially true at Moravian missions. One of the Moravian Church's distinguishing features is its emphasis on missionary work.[30] Missionary work was a task always before devout Moravians whether or not they were venturing into the mission fields themselves. Even marriage was viewed as an opportunity to help a member of the opposite sex improve their relationship with God. One consequence of the importance placed on missionary work was the high social and spiritual status accorded to missionaries among Moravians.[31]

Aboriginal Christians at Mapoon realised the liberating effects that spreading, rather than just receiving, Christianity could have. It was not long after a Christian community had formed among Aboriginal people at Mapoon that Aboriginal Christians began to work to assist in other Christian pursuits. Older Aboriginal people built a church and helped support a Christian teacher for Aboriginal people. Younger Christians made crafts in an effort to contribute to other missions and the Red Cross.[32]

Some Aboriginal people at Mapoon went to help convert other Aboriginal people elsewhere in Australia. In a 1918 report, Nicholas Hey wrote,

> The great event of the year was the marriage of 5 couples on June 19, two of whom left the following day to join the staff of the Wesleyan Aboriginal Mission at Goulburn Island Northern Territory. A third couple is prepared to go to Mornington Island if required & a fourth couple will be married shortly & proceed to Weipa to assist Mr. & Mrs Hall. We felt sorry to lose such promising workers, yet we rejoice also that we had the honour to send forth missionaries from our midst.[33]

Through these activities, Aboriginal people helped shape other people's religious views as the European missionaries had helped shape their own. Working for Christian causes allowed Aboriginal people to become active participants in part of a worldwide network labouring for God. This investment of time and money would have helped cement people's faith. Further, those who contributed time or money to the greater Christian cause would be repaid in additional pride, a resource that was often scarce at settler institutions for Aboriginal people. Such activities also would have probably been the most effective way for Aboriginal people to palliate their new burdens of guilt.

Conclusions

The passing of guilt along with Christian faith began well before the first missionaries came to Cape York Peninsula and continued after their departure. The period of time examined in this article, however, is uniquely important because it gives particular emphasis to the question of power in the process of spiritual change and because it sheds light on several important areas of the history of missions. The story sheds light on some hitherto understudied ways in which Aboriginal people made Christianity their own. It provides an exception to the general rule that Aboriginal people do not convert to Christianity or take up a European-Christian worldview if there is any semblance of the traditional social structure remaining. This, in turn, points to the psychological function of spirituality for Aboriginal Australians at the time of contact. Finally, it helps explain the remarkable success Moravian missionaries have had in their missions.

The field of Aboriginal studies currently gives great weight to the previously neglected task of identifying how Aboriginal people shaped the frontier. In this context, the question 'Were Aboriginal people creative actors in becoming Christian?' must be asked, because despite the earlier comparison, an Aboriginal person using Christianity to meet psychological needs is not exactly the same as using a metal knife to skin a kangaroo. For at least two reasons, the answer has to be 'yes'.

Much ink has been used by social scientists trying to discover the determinants of religious change and conversion. While little agreement exists, most hypotheses suggest that religion meets (usually unconscious) psychological needs and that spiritual change is an attempt to satisfy these needs.[34] Even among theorists who emphasise social factors as important in religious changes, these alterations in beliefs and practices are seen as meeting individual needs or arising from individual agency,[35] though some have noted conversion is socially defined[36] and that the change in religious designation does not come from the convert.[37] Seen in this light, conversion is at base an individual act, even if it not one over which people have conscious control. So using Christianity to assuage feelings of guilt differs from using a metal knife to skin a kangaroo in that it is not consciously employed, but both are employed by individuals to meet those individuals' needs.

The adoption of Christian beliefs differs from the use of a metal knife also in that it is far more creative because it requires much more modification of and integration with other beliefs and practices. The amount of integration required in everyday life would have made it impossible for Aboriginal individuals not to be creative in their understanding and expression of these beliefs. The comparison between the use of Christianity and a metal knife is useful in its emphasis that when Aboriginal people adopted Christian beliefs at Mapoon, they were not merely imitating Europeans. They were using all of the spiritual material at their disposal to make emotional sense of their world.

There is a second reason that Aboriginal Christians must be seen as actively shaping their own faith: the Christian perspective the missionaries brought and Aboriginal Christians more or less adopted emphasised that conversion and religious change were primarily individual acts. While no one would deny that the missionaries were a necessary condition for Aboriginal people becoming Christian, people at Mapoon probably would have argued that their presence was not a sufficient condition. This Protestant Christian viewpoint emphasises nothing if not a one-on-one relationship with God, even if it allows one to ask for others' prayers for strengthening one's faith. The importance of individual responsibility was the heart of the realisation Nicholas Hey made in Europe when he decided to read 'his Bible systematically, in the hope that some good might come of it'.[38] This Christianity sees conversion as the quintessential creative act. People are reborn: Saul became Paul. Aboriginal Christians at Mapoon may have felt terribly indebted to the missionaries for bringing them Christianity, but certainly thought that their own beliefs were largely their own responsibility, even if God's help was required.

The story of Christianity and guilt at Mapoon is especially interesting because it provides an exception to the general rule that Aboriginal people adopt Christianity only when their traditional social structures have been decimated.[39] Resistance to becoming Christian is seen even when Aboriginal people have incorporated Christian stories and personages, such as Noah and Jesus, into their spiritual landscapes.[40] Aram A. Yengoyan argues that Aboriginal people adopted Christian beliefs and practices in a significant way only in conditions of 'economic need or social deprivation or both. In such examples, the tribal ethic or structure has been destroyed with much of the Aboriginal population'.[41] According to Yengoyan, it is impossible to change directly from traditional spirituality to Christianity because of the 'prior text' in traditional spirituality, which does not allow people to make the switch.

The mission at Mapoon under the co-leadership of the Hey and Ward families, however, is remarkable for the number of people who adopted Christian beliefs. In 1891, when the Moravian missionaries first arrived at what would become Mapoon mission on the western coast of Cape York, most of the Aboriginal people were totally unexposed to the Christian notion of sin. Less than 30 years later, sin occupied a prominent place in the intellectual and emotional life of the Aboriginal people at Mapoon. Yengoyan's criteria for Aboriginal adoption of Christianity do not seem to have been met at Mapoon. It is difficult to determine how much of the 'tribal ethic or structure' had 'been destroyed' prior to the missionaries' arrival, given the lack of recordings of European contact with Aboriginal people there. Nevertheless, with the possible exception of some Aboriginal people who came to the mission from other places, it does not seem to have been the sort of massive devastation Yengoyan has in mind.[42] After the missionaries arrived, devastation does not seem to have occurred at Mapoon on anywhere near the scale as in many other missions which were less successful at promulgating Christianity.[43]

It would not do to give the impression that every Aboriginal person at Mapoon adopted Christianity, nor would it be appropriate to deny that factors other than guilt might have influenced Aboriginal people's changes toward Christianity. Some Aboriginal people at Mapoon, mostly older ones, did not accept Christianity. This was true for a number of reasons, not least because they were emotionally and socially invested in traditional spirituality. Additionally, they had less contact with missionaries, who actively divided the Aboriginal population into Christians and pagans. After a certain point, the missionaries were reluctant to expend their resources attempting to convert these older Aboriginal people and concentrated their efforts on younger Aboriginal people. It is also reasonable to assume that some younger Aboriginal people simply left the area. Beyond these non-converts, the Aboriginal people who were regarded by themselves and by the missionaries as Christians did not fully accept every aspect of the Christianity the missionaries brought. They modified Christianity and made it their own; all converted populations do. What is remarkable is how much of the missionaries' Christianity they accepted with so little modification in so short a time.

Other factors guided the population toward Christianity. The dormitory system probably impeded Aboriginal cultural transmission. Immigration of Aboriginal people from other groups may have increased spiritual tensions and threats while the immigrants themselves were probably spiritually homesick, both problems that Christianity may have been able to help alleviate.[44] While each of these factors was important, there were a number of missions in Australia where they were replicated and Aboriginal people have still been much more reluctant to accept the Christian ideas. Since these factors are not unique to Mapoon, they cannot be used to explain why so many people at this Moravian mission adopted Christianity and the Christian view of moral transgression when so few Aboriginal people at many other missions did. In this paper I have argued that the notable degree and rapid pace of the adoption of Christianity was due largely to importance the missionaries placed on the emotion of guilt and the way in which Christianity's notion of transgression helped make sense of and give meaning to this emotion.

The time period at Mapoon examined in this article also helps explain why the Moravian Church has had such success in its missionary work. The Moravian Church has long placed an emphasis on missionary work. It has devoted a very high proportion of its resources to setting up a number of missions far exceeding that which would be expected of so small a denomination.[45] What is most remarkable, however, is the success these missions have had in Christianising people who have been resistant to spiritual change.[46] One might hypothesise that Yengoyan's thesis that the 'prior text' of a group's spirituality can inhibit Christianisation if its values and view of the universe are very different from Christianity holds true for groups outside Australia as well, and that Moravian missionaries often find some way to get around this.

As discussed above, guilt played a major role in the emotional and spiritual lives of most Moravians.[47] It is notable that while there is no single blueprint for how Moravian missions should be run, missionaries were instructed not to talk too much about God or the trinity but instead focus on Christ's suffering and forgiveness.[48] These emphases imply an understanding of, and preoccupation with, sin. Perhaps the Moravians' success as missionaries is explained by, and therefore supports, the hypothesis that the creation of guilt in a population can dramatically increase its probability of adopting Christian beliefs and practices. This is especially true where the 'prior text' of the population's spirituality makes it resistant to other methods of spreading Christianity by focusing on balance rather than hierarchy, on interrelations and reciprocity rather than debt and guilt.

As an exception to Yengoyan's rule, Mapoon's population points to a primary cause of spiritual change during colonisation and, beyond that, to a fundamental role of spirituality in Aboriginal life during colonisation. The population at Mapoon underwent massive changes to its material way of life, but so did many other Aboriginal populations that did not undergo a shift in spirituality toward Christianity. Aboriginal spirituality must not have been a mere reflection of material life or just an intellectual tool used to cope with the major social and ecological changes taking place.

Spirituality gave meaning to and made sense of the emotional landscape of individual Aboriginal people. The violence and dispossession of colonisation mostly did not require Christianisation because traditional spirituality could usually meet the demands this made on Aboriginal people without drastic modifications. Colonisation was a massive disruption to equilibrium, and therefore within the purview of traditional spirituality. The guilt experienced by many Aboriginal people at Mapoon, however, was not. Guilt implies both a degree of hierarchy and a dichotomy between good and evil not found in traditional Aboriginal spirituality. Many Aboriginal people at Mapoon, therefore, adopted much of the missionaries' Christianity and its understanding of and emphasis on transgression in an effort to locate and give meaning to new feelings of guilt.

References

Primary sources

Records of Mapoon and Weipa 1893-1967, MF 305, Presbyterian Church of Australia, Board of Ecumenical Mission and Relations, Australian Institute of Aboriginal and Torres Strait Islander Studies.

Secondary sources

Combs-Bowles, Devin 2004, 'Southern Crossroads to Damascus: Christianities at three Australian Missions', MA thesis, The Australian National University.

Ferry, John 1979, 'The Failure of New South Wales Missions to the Aborigines Before 1845', *Aboriginal History* 3(1): 25-36.

Geertz, Richard 1966, 'Religion as a Cultural System', in M Banton (ed.), *Anthropological Approaches to the Study of Religion*, Tavistock Publications, London.

Gollin, Gillian Lindt 1967, *Moravians in Two Worlds: a study of changing communities*, Columbia University Press, New York.

Gunson, Niel (ed.) 1974, *Australian reminiscences and papers of LE Threlkeld, missionary to the Aborigines, 1824-1859* (2 vols), Australian Institute of Aboriginal Studies, Canberra.

Hefner, Robert W 1993, 'On Faith and Commitment: Christian conversion in Muslim Java', in Robert W Hefner (ed.), *Conversion to Christianity: historical and anthropological perspectives on a great transformation*, University of California Press, Berkeley.

Hey, Rev. JN 1931a, *A Brief History of the Presbyterian Church's Mission Enterprise among the Australian Aborigines*, New Press, Sydney.

—— 1931b, *The Moravian Church: (Unitas Fratrum), or the Unity of Brethren*, J.N. Hey, Sydney.

Horton, Robin 1971, 'African Conversion', *Africa* 41(3): 85-108.

—— 1975a, 'On the Rationality of Conversion', part 1, *Africa* 45(3): 219-235.

—— 1975b, 'On the Rationality of Conversion', part 2, *Africa* 45(4): 373-399.

Lampe, Armando 2001, *Mission or Submission? Moravian and Catholic Missionaries in the Dutch Caribbean during the 19th century*, Vandenhoeck & Ruprecht, Göttingen.

Lewis, AJ 1962, *Zinzendorf the Ecumenical Pioneer A Study in the Moravian Contribution of Christian Mission and Unity*, SCM Press Ltd, London.

Lofland, John and Rodney Stark 1965, 'Becoming a World-Saver: a theory of conversion to a deviant perspective', *American Sociological Review* 30(6): 862-75.

MacIntyre, Ronald G 1931, 'Foreword', in JN Hey (author), *The Moravian Church: (Unitas Fratrum), or the Unity of Brethren*, J.N. Hey, Sydney.

McDonald, Heather 2001, *Blood, Bones, and Spirit: Aboriginal Christianity in an East Kimberley town*, Melbourne University Press, Carlton South.

Merrill, William L 1993, 'Conversion and Colonialism in Northern Mexico: the Tarahumara response to the Jesuit mission program, 1601-1767', in Robert W Hefner (ed.), *Conversion to Christianity: historical and anthro-*

pological perspectives on a great transformation. University of California Press, Berkeley.

Murphy, William P 1981, 'The Rhetorical Management of Dangerous Knowledge in Kpelle Brokerage', *American Ethnologist* 8(4): 667-685.

Ng, Kwai Hang 2002, 'Seeking the Christian Tutelage: agency and culture in Chinese immigrants' conversion to Christianity', *Sociology of Religion* 63(2): 195-214.

Pollock, Donald K 1993, 'Conversion and "Community" in Amazonia', in Robert W Hefner (ed.), *Conversion to Christianity: historical and anthropological perspectives on a great transformation*, University of California Press, Berkeley.

Rose, Deborah Bird 1988, 'Jesus and the Dingo', in T Swain and D Rose (eds), *Aboriginal Australians and Christian Missions,* Australian Association for the Study of Religion, Bedford Park: 361-375.

—— 1992, *Dingo Makes Us Human: life and land in an Australian Aboriginal culture,* Cambridge University Press, Cambridge.

—— 1994, 'Ned Kelly Died for our Sins', *Oceania* 65: 175-186.

Sharp, Nonie 1992, *Footprints Along the Cape York Sandbeaches*, Aboriginal Studies Press: Canberra.

Ward, Arthur 1908, *The Miracle of Mapoon, or, From Native Camp to Christian Village*, S. W. Partridge & Co, London.

Yang, Fenggang 1998, 'Chinese Conversion to Evangelical Christianity: the importance of social and cultural contexts', *Sociology of Religion* 59(3): 237-257.

Yengoyan, Aram, A 1993, 'Religion, Morality, and Prophetic Traditions: conversion among the Pitjantjatjara of central Australia', in Robert W Hefner (ed.), *Conversion to Christianity: historical and anthropological perspectives on a great transformation*, University of California Press, Berkeley.

ENDNOTES

[1] See generally McDonald 2001.

[2] See generally Rose 1992 especially chapter 11.

[3] Hey 1931a: 10.

[4] Ward 1908: 35-42.

[5] Ward 1908: 36-7.

[6] Ward 1908: 37.

[7] Ward 1908: 37-8.

[8] Ward 1908: 41.

[9] Ward 1908: 41-2.

[10] See generally Ward 1908.

11 See generally Records of Mapoon and Weipa: 1893-1967 Reel 2. The author of the diary may be Mrs Ward, but it is not certain.

12 Hey 1931a: 10.

13 Hey 1931a: 10-11.

14 Records of Mapoon and Weipa Reel 2: 50.

15 Records of Mapoon and Weipa Reel 2: 50.

16 Records of Mapoon and Weipa Reel 2: 554.

17 Records of Mapoon and Weipa Reel 2: 564.

18 Records of Mapoon and Weipa Reel 2: 561.

19 Records of Mapoon and Weipa Reel 2: 600.

20 Records of Mapoon and Weipa Reel 2: 557.

21 Gollin 1967: 11.

22 Records of Mapoon and Weipa Reel 2: 571.

23 Records of Mapoon and Weipa Reel 2: 571-2.

24 Records of Mapoon and Weipa Reel 2: 588.

25 Records of Mapoon and WeipaReel 2: 558.

26 See Murphy 1981 for a discussion of brokers as mediating between people and the supernatural.

27 Records of Mapoon and Weipa Reel 2: 596-7.

28 Records of Mapoon and Weipa Reel 2: 580.

29 Records of Mapoon and Weipa Reel 2: 576.

30 See generally Gollin 1967; MacIntyre 1931.

31 Gollin 1967: 97, 101, 200.

32 See generally Records of Mapoon and Weipa Reel 2.

33 Records of Mapoon and Weipa Reel 2: 84.

34 See generally Geertz 1966; Horton 1971, 1975a, 1975b; Lofland and Stark 1965.

35 See generally Ng 2002; Yang 1998.

36 See generally Pollock 1993.

37 Merrill 1993: 153-4.

38 Ward 1908: 37.

39 See generally Ferry 1979; Yengoyan 1993.

40 See generally Rose 1988, 1992, 1994.

41 Yengoyan 1993: 234.

42 See generally Records of Mapoon and Weipa; Sharp 1992.

43 See generally Combs-Bowles 2004; Ferry 1979; Gunson 1974; Yengoyan 1993.

44 Combs-Bowles 2004 chapter 4.

45 See generally Gollin 1967.

46 Lewis 1962 chapter 5; see generally Hey 1931b.

47 See generally Gollin 1967.

48 Lampe 2001: 37.

Corrupt desires and the wages of sin: Indigenous people, missionaries and male sexuality, 1830-1850

Jessie Mitchell

In 1841, Reverend Francis Tuckfield of the Buntingdale mission near Geelong, Victoria, recorded a conversation he had recently had with a group of Aboriginal men. The men were impressed by a new hut being built on the mission and announced to Tuckfield that they wanted huts of their own, but these would have to be spacious, to accommodate their three wives each. Tuckfield told them sternly that if they wanted the material benefits of European housing they should also adopt the moral benefits of European monogamy. The men were more puzzled than offended by Tuckfield's lecture on the sin of polygamy, and asked with surprise why God would be interested in such an ordinary matter and why He would deny the privilege of multiple wives even to the missionaries who talked so much about Him. They rejected Tuckfield's suggestion that they abandon two wives each, explaining, much to his outrage, that they needed lots of women to do their hard work. Tuckfield felt his worst fears had been confirmed: the men, he believed, had no respect for women or monogamy, not so much because of lust, but because of laziness, greed and amorality — these, the missionary assumed, were typical qualities of savages.[1]

Tuckfield, like his fellow missionaries, was attempting to impart Christian sexual morality to Aboriginal people, a task that provoked reactions ranging from curiosity and confusion to determined opposition. Such encounters formed an important part of daily life on missions and protectorate stations in New South Wales and Port Phillip during the early nineteenth century. The 1830s and 1840s — an era when violence, dispossession and Indigenous depopulation occurred alongside enthusiastic humanitarian endeavour — saw interesting developments in Aboriginal–missionary relations. Aboriginal people, while impoverished and traumatised by invasion, were not yet under strong government control, and retained many elements of pre-colonial life. The roles of evangelical Protestant missionaries and government-appointed protectors were also at a unique stage. Although missionaries' power as colonising agents would increase greatly in the twentieth century, during these early decades they still lacked economic power, strong government support or social acceptance in the Australian colonies. The first protectors — most of whom had strong religious backgrounds and saw their job largely in missionary terms — had government backing but inadequate physical power or social support.[2] They trod an uneasy balance between enticing

Aborigines to their stations and trying to discipline them when they arrived. The relationships they formed arguably relied as much on negotiation and exchange as they did on coercion. The limited power of these early humanitarians has led many historians to focus largely on the reasons for their failure,[3] an approach which is unfortunate, as it does not consider the complex encounters and relationships that developed between Aboriginal people and the first protectors and missionaries. Missionaries' lack of strong authority made these encounters all the more intricate, marked by a mixture of arrogant paternalism, cultural bewilderment and reluctant accommodation.

One particular area generally neglected by historians is the attitude of these early missionaries and protectors towards Aboriginal men's sexuality. This is a topic worth exploring both because of the immediate impact of missionary activities on Aboriginal people's lives and also because missionary and protectorate writings helped to shape British and colonial attitudes — mostly amongst religious humanitarian communities — towards Aboriginal humanity and future potential. This brief study considers missionaries' and protectors' concerns about Aboriginal men's sexual behaviour — real and imaginary — including desires for black and white women and other men and involvement in prostitution. These views, in turn, must be situated within general European ideas of 'black' or 'native' men as sexually deviant, ideas that took a particular shape in the early Australian colonies. Some forms of sexual 'deviance' attracted more missionary attention than others, arguably because of their perceived relevance to broader questions about Aboriginal men's economic and social roles. Aboriginal responses to missionary civilising agendas at this time were largely pragmatic but nonetheless varied, and their reactions to these particular campaigns of sexual civilisation encompassed tolerance, opportunism, angry opposition and bored rejection.

Recently there has been growing interest in how white Australia has represented and exploited Aboriginal women's sexuality, a topic explored by historians including Patricia Grimshaw, Susan Hunt, Mary Anne Jebb, Anna Haebich, Ann McGrath and Patty O'Brien.[4] There has not really been any equivalent body of work produced on European portrayals of the sexuality of Aboriginal men, however, particularly during this early colonial period. Some historians claim that Indigenous men have been commonly depicted as brutally lustful savages, hyper-masculine in their sexual aggression but lacking masculine self-control (identified as a European quality). Patty O'Brien, Jan Pettman, Anna Haebich and Raymond Evans point out that these stereotypes were used to rationalise European men's economic and political dominance and acquisition of Aboriginal women and land. These historians stress the particular importance to colonial agendas of stories about Aboriginal men posing a sexual threat to white women.[5] These historians consider the issue only briefly, however, focusing largely on popular colonial stereotypes from the late nineteenth and early twentieth centuries. An examination of sexual politics on the first missions and protectorate stations reveals rather different sexual ideas, emerging from a different intellectual and social climate.

Belief in the sexual savagery of non-European men predated the colonisation of Australia. By the sixteenth century, ancient European folk myths of wild men of the woods — described as animalistic, filthy, violent and promiscuous — were being reshaped and racialised by the medieval custom of depicting devils as black men and the circulation of European travellers' stories of Africa as a place of wild, unregulated sex.[6] However, the expansion of the slave trade and European imperialism, combined with growing European interest in natural history and human biology, must be seen as essential in encouraging these initially vague and unsystematic ideas of black male sexual savagery to become much more common, vicious and biologically determinist, keeping pace with intellectual trends and rationalising developing colonial power structures.[7]

Given missionaries' and protectors' ambiguous place within the power structure of colonial Australia — as aggressive cultural colonisers and self-avowed Christian philanthropists — their sexual agendas become particularly interesting. Unlike settlers, the first missionaries and protectors had little desire to dehumanise Aborigines or portray them as a doomed, impotent race. Nor did they wish to justify sexual relationships between European men and Aboriginal women. Rather, as evangelical Christian colonisers, they were particularly concerned about sexual immorality and keen to implement systems of bodily and mental surveillance and control. They sometimes portrayed Aboriginal societies as promiscuous, probably referring to both traditional practices of polygamy and bestowing women, and colonial prostitution. Protector James Dredge, working in Taungurong country along the Goulbourn River in the 1840s, described 'sins of the most obscene and revolting description, alike destructive to the body and to the soul'.[8] Rev William Watson of the Wellington Valley mission in Wiradjuri country in the 1830s deplored Aborigines' 'corrupt desires' and 'lowest and most obscene' practices, and Rev James Günther's wife, Lydia, was disgusted by their 'vile wretched habits and moral degradation'.[9] In most of these cases, the immoral desires seem to have been implicitly attributed to men; while missionaries often considered Aboriginal women degraded and corrupt, they rarely credited them with enough free will to determine their own sexual behaviour.

When the first missionaries and protectors discussed Aboriginal men's lusts, they usually referred to desire for Aboriginal women. The possibility of sexual relationships between Aboriginal men was a topic missionaries and protectors mentioned only occasionally. Given this scarcity, it is difficult to say exactly how such behaviour (real or imagined) was viewed, but some suggestions can be made. Living in an era before firm medical, legal or social definitions of homosexuality in Europe, missionaries generally did not imply that such sexual behaviour made certain Aboriginal men inherently strange and marginalised, or that these men necessarily lacked masculinity. Rather, the 'awful crime of "Sodomy"',[10] as missionaries characterised it, was depicted as a degenerate heathen act rather than a permanent identity. When travelling around Wellington Valley, missionary JCS Handt was surprised and disturbed when a party of young Wiradjuri men and boys refused to follow him to the mission, despite his talking to them about God and giving them pipes and tobacco. He concluded (with an intriguing leap of logic) that the men must have wished to keep the boys to 'commit with them the horrid sin of Sodom'.[11] Protector Edward Stone Parker of the Loddon River district in Port Phillip also suspected that 'unnatural offences are not uncommon among these degraded people ... most of the single men are guilty of this horrible crime ... the young boys are brutally forced to become their victims'.[12] As with the prostitution of Aboriginal women, missionaries and protectors varied between blaming original heathen sin and corrupt European influences. Handt blamed such behaviour on Aboriginal customs, saying of male initiation at Moreton Bay 'such filthy acts attend the whole of the ceremony as are best buried in silence'.[13] Chief Protector GA Robinson, in contrast, was more inclined to blame settlers. When travelling in the Goulbourn River district, he saw boys being offered to white stockmen 'for the purpose of committing unnatural offence' and was told 'plenty of white fellows on the Goulbourn always did that'.[14] Parker, similarly, blamed the European removal of Aboriginal women, since, he said, this 'crime' was only committed by single men, who stopped once they were married.[15]

Whether these stories were true or not, they indicate a particular European view of male sexuality. The emphasis on sodomy as a sinful act rather than an intrinsic identity squares with what Robert Aldrich, Craig Johnston and Robert Johnston have identified as general concerns about convicts' sexual behaviour in early colonial Australia. Sex between men was depicted as a degrading criminal act to be eradicated through physical punishment, not necessarily a symptom of any radically different sexual or gender identity.[16] These missionary accounts are also suggestive of broader European ideas about masculinity. While the younger, passive sexual partners are 'made victims' and thus feminised, there is no suggestion that the sexual aggressors have lost their masculine dominance. Missionaries apparently made no attempt to discover whether Aboriginal people viewed sexual roles in this way or not. Furthermore, there is no evidence of the men allegedly involved in sodomy being singled out by missionaries as a separate problematic group. Rather, their behaviour was considered simply more evidence of the general Aboriginal need for Christian conversion. Thus, the proposed solution was religion and respectable marriage, to be guaranteed through missionary or protectorate supervision. The suggestion by a government doctor that young men could be straightened out through military service was dismissed by Robinson, on the grounds that a military environment would only encourage 'the disgusting practice'. Protector Parker added testily that he believed the word of God was stronger than 'the drill sergeant's cane'.[17] Overall, however, there is little evidence of concrete steps being taken to police relationships between men. This indicates not only the limitations of missionary power, at a time when pre-colonial forms of authority and ceremonial life remained powerful and when Aboriginal people were not being physically forced onto missions, but also the fact that same-sex encounters, while considered savage and sinful, were not the greatest sexual issue to attract missionary concern.

Another issue, which attracted only a small amount of missionary concern, was the idea that Aboriginal men posed a sexual threat to white women. Stories of sex between white women and black men are notorious for exciting horror and violence in European colonies, as well as providing a pretext for curtailing colonised people's rights. However, in Australia during the early nineteenth century, the issue arises in missionary accounts only a handful of times. In a letter to his missionary society colleagues in 1832, JCS Handt of the Wellington Valley mission related two such stories. There was a tale circulating in the colony, he said, of a white woman shipwrecked near Moreton Bay and held prisoner by Aborigines; the woman, Handt believed, had several 'Mulatto' children.[18] This rumour reminded him of his own recent experience in Sydney, when an apparently white woman with a child on her arm had approached him during the annual Parramatta native feast and asked him for bread. Handt was astonished to hear that she 'belonged to the blacks'. The first women he depicted as a suffering victim, the second, he assumed, must have 'abandoned herself to such a wretched life and company'.[19] This seemed credible to Handt, who considered most colonial white women immoral.[20]

Meanwhile, Rev Lancelot Threlkeld of the Lake Macquarie mission near Newcastle described an Aboriginal man educated at the Male Orphan School in Sydney, who eloped with a settler's daughter. The story could have been used to invoke the supposed sexual threat of Aboriginal men and the dangers of trying to integrate 'savages' into European society, but this was not how Threlkeld portrayed it. Rather, he stated that the man was intelligent and very handsome and that the couple eventually settled as respectable farmers.[21] Elsewhere, Threlkeld expressed concern that the Native Police might attack white and black women, but merely concluded that they needed to be taught military self-discipline.[22] These examples are too isolated to be conclusive, but they do not convey a strong, general sense of racial or sexual paranoia, and variables like the behaviour, class and level of 'civilisation' of the men and women involved seem to have strongly influenced missionaries' final conclusions. This is suggestive of a climate where racial and sexual views were in something of a state of flux, and where local variations could be significant. Perhaps the very isolation of these accounts is the most important element here; the issue of sex between Aboriginal men and European women simply does not seem to have concerned missionaries or protectors very much at all.

It might be assumed that they avoided the topic for fear of inciting racial violence, but such sexual stories do not seem to have featured prominently in many government or settler accounts either. There were, of course, exceptions to this, perhaps most notably the story of Eliza Fraser's shipwreck in south-eastern Queensland, which emerged in the late 1830s, and the frontier legends about the 'White Woman of Gippsland', which were first told in the 1840s. The Fraser captivity narratives — whose racial, sexual and class politics have been discussed by Kay Schaffer — did not feature in missionary or protectorate accounts at this time. Indeed, Schaffer's work suggests that during the 1830s the story attracted more interest in Britain and the United States than in Australia, being linked to British class and political turmoil and America's negotiation of its own frontier history through stories of white people captured by 'natives'.[23] During this period, the White Woman of Gippsland stories seem to have had greater local resonance. These stories told of a woman stranded by a shipwreck, held prisoner by the Kurnai and forced to marry an elder, Bungelene. These rumours, not coincidentally, circulated at the same time as the violent dispossession of the Kurnai people. Missionaries, incidentally, did not discuss this story, and protectors dismissed it as unlikely and an excuse for colonial violence.[24]

This is one of the few stories involving sex between Aboriginal men and white women during this era to have received much attention from historians, but even here, gaps in the historiography of Australian racism are evident. It is only recently that Julie Carr has discussed in depth how this legend reflected changes in colonial society and politics. (Interestingly, Carr also notes that stories about sex between European women and Indigenous men were, overall, rare in Australia, particularly compared to North America.)[25] Apart from Carr's work, other historians who have narrated the story, like Michael Cannon, have tended not to examine its sexual and racial significance in depth. Even Kate Darian-Smith, who discusses the importance of the figure of the frontier white woman to Australian national identity, still tends to link events from the 1840s unproblematically with racism from later decades.[26] Meanwhile, Schaffer's work on Eliza Fraser arguably focuses more on situating the 1830s versions of Fraser's story within British imperial literature than within Australian representations of Aboriginality.[27] Thus, greater discussion is still needed on how sexualised racism has evolved in colonial Australia.

It is interesting to speculate on why colonists appeared to pay a relative lack of attention to sex between Aboriginal men and European women in the early nineteenth century. The small number of European women in rural districts at this time was no doubt relevant. However, the fact that sexualised nationalist ideology had not yet strongly emerged in the Australian colonies was also significant. The image of the white woman as a force of purity and morality on the frontier and a symbol of racial and sexual vulnerability for white men to protect would become vital during the late nineteenth and early twentieth centuries, feeding into a number of developments like the rise of Australian nationalism, concerns about the white birth rate, and the emergence of disciplines of racial and sexual science.[28] However, during the 1830s and 1840s, it seems to have been less of a general concern.

Another reason for this may well have been a general colonial downplaying of Aboriginal men's sexual vitality. Some portrayals of Aboriginal men disregarding chastity and monogamy and brutally seizing as many wives as they wanted were put forward by explorers, including David Collins and Edward John Eyre, and settlers and journalists like George Arden, Edward M Curr and George Hamilton.[29] While these accounts may have referred to real events, the way these were portrayed was almost certainly shaped by the pre-existing idea that sexual brutality was normal behaviour for 'savages', and by the continuing desire to rationalise Aboriginal dispossession.

However, what is more surprising is that in the early nineteenth century such descriptions of Aboriginal men as brutally lustful seem to have been, overall, quite rare. Few settlers or explorers portrayed lust as Aboriginal people's defining quality — instead, they emphasised traits like laziness, cruelty or treachery. (Some examples of this attitude are evident in the works of David Collins, Charles Sturt, John Henderson, Francis Barrallier, RJ Massie and James Malcolm.)[30] Furthermore, even sexualised colonial accounts still tended to place greater stress on stories of men beating their wives or lazily depending on women's work. For example, Eyre, Arden and Peter Cunningham, whose descriptions of Aborigines were quite sexual in some ways, still explained Aboriginal polygamy in economic terms, describing Aboriginal women as servants (rather than concubines), valued mainly for their hard labour.[31] Pre-existing European ideas of black men as virile and sexually deviant, while popular in other parts of the world, appear to have generally been secondary in Australian colonial accounts, when mentioned at all.

The fact that few early colonial accounts defined Aboriginal men in terms of savage lust is, I would suggest, no accident. During this period, the new sciences of anatomy, biology, physiology and palaeontology were becoming sophisticated, popular and entangled in world politics, and human development was being increasingly viewed as naturally hierarchical and progressive. The extermination of so-called weaker races was often depicted as a natural, positive part of this process. For Europeans unsettled by rapid industrialisation and social change and seeking to rationalise their own growing imperial dominance, such ideas could be strongly appealing.[32] While many colonial sources attributed indigenous depopulation to changeable material causes, the notion that this demise was inevitable and necessary was growing in North America, New Zealand and, increasingly, Australia.[33] Herman Merivale, lecturing at Oxford in the 1840s, noted the increasing popularity of the claim that Aboriginal improvement was hopeless — 'the feebler race must yield to the stronger; the white is destined to extirpate the savage … the mere contact of Europeans is fatal to him [the Aborigine] in some unknown manner'.[34] Perhaps the fullest scientific expression of these ideas in an Australian context came from naturalist PE de Strzelecki, who in 1845 asserted that indigenous demise occurred worldwide as the result of a mysterious process by which indigenous women, through sex with white men, became unable to have children by indigenous men.[35]

Colonists were not necessarily being self-conscious and cynical when they constructed or embraced stereotypes of Aborigines as sterile and doomed; such ideas were in keeping with international trends in Western thought. However, there is no doubt that such stereotypes could be appealing and useful in the Australian colonies. The figure of the virile, promiscuous black man whose sexuality must be regulated by a white master — important to the rationalisation of American slavery — was less attractive in Australia, where colonialism did not rely on the breeding and exploitation of Indigenous people so much as on their supposedly inevitable deaths. In a colonial setting where the legal, physical and cultural *absence* of Aboriginal people from the land became crucial to national development and white Australian identity, and where Aborigines were repeatedly described as a dying race, a portrayal of Aboriginal men as oversexed, lustful and reproductive would not necessarily have appealed to colonists. Nor would it have fit in with growing international beliefs in indigenous peoples in settler colonies as 'doomed races'. (As an interesting comparison, Robert Wokler points out that some eighteenth-century commentators, including Thomas Malthus, attributed the decline in the indigenous American population to lack of male virility.)[36]

Protectors and missionaries during the early nineteenth century rarely depicted Aborigines as inevitably doomed and sterile, although the question of how they may have been privately or subconsciously influenced by such arguments would make an interesting topic for further discussion. However, like other colonists, they seemed less interested in Aboriginal men's lusts than in some of their other activities, particularly the lending or prostitution of Aboriginal women to European men. The bestowing of women began as a traditional method of forging family and economic alliances between different Aboriginal groups. In a colonial context, it was sometimes an initial response to European presence, an attempt to incorporate Europeans into Indigenous social systems.[37] Later, however, as Aboriginal poverty worsened, sex became more directly related to immediate needs for food and supplies. This 'prostitution', as missionaries defined it, troubled humanitarians for several reasons. Not only was prostitution considered sinful in principle, but its connection to the spread of venereal disease, the dangerously low Aboriginal birth rate and violent clashes between European and Aboriginal men led many missionaries to cite prostitution as a major cause of imminent Aboriginal 'extinction'.[38]

I would also argue that missionaries linked Aboriginal men's involvement in prostitution to broader concerns about hard work and property ownership. As Elizabeth Fee has explored, imperial discourse frequently linked the supposed sexual looseness of 'savages' with lack of property sense. Many nineteenth-century historians, anthropologists and philosophers asserted that in 'savage' societies women and children belonged to the horde and that the emergence of patrilineal descent systems, monogamous marriage and the nuclear family were key signs of progress. The development of bourgeois forms of male authority over women and children was linked to the growth of private property and liberalism and the reduction of women's public labour.[39] Thus, accusations of indigenous promiscuity could serve not only to depict colonised peoples as primitive, but also to reinforce claims that they lacked property sense, which in turn helped to rationalise the theft of their land and resources.[40]

While missionaries did not necessarily wish to justify this theft, they did wish to transform Aboriginal people's ideas about labour and property, and some of these concerns were sexualised. Unlike some colonists, though, missionaries did not equate alleged Aboriginal promiscuity with total indifference to property. They often claimed that Aboriginal men treated their wives as servants, insisting on women's economic and sexual work to support their families. Missionary William Watson of Wellington Valley, for example, saw Aboriginal women as slaves, coerced into manual and sexual labour. He claimed that every European in the neighbourhood had at least one woman living with him — some, Watson said, kept several girls as young as eight — with the cooperation of their male relatives, who were being bribed.[41] Meanwhile, Methodist Joseph Orton claimed the men treated their wives like horses and bullocks, and protector James Dredge claimed that Aboriginal women were forced into prostitution — 'were they to refuse to yield to the directions of their savage lords ... they would ensure an unmerciful beating, if not be killed on the spot'.[42] Thus, to missionaries, prostitution did not demonstrate that Aboriginal men lacked a sense of their wives as sexual property. Rather, missionaries implied, by renting their wives to other men instead of controlling them monogamously, Aboriginal husbands showed a lack of Christian chastity, but also assumed an economic role that seemed parasitical, receiving what Rev James Günther of Wellington Valley called 'the wages of sin'.[43] The claim that Aboriginal men refused to earn their keep honestly was in keeping with missionaries' and protectors' frequent general complaints about Aboriginal 'vagrant habits', 'remarkable aversion to labour', 'indolence', 'fecklessness' and 'erratic', 'fickle' behaviour.[44] Thus, Handt, when lecturing Aboriginal men on the sin of prostitution, emphasised that their 'idleness' was the main cause behind this, and one report from the Wellington Valley mission claimed that prostituted Aboriginal women were 'the unwilling victims of their husbands' indolence'.[45]

The project of reshaping Aboriginal men's sexuality would, missionaries hoped, involve conveying a different version of masculine control. This European masculine ideal entailed firm control over one's own sexual urges and strict but benevolent control over one's legal monogamous sexual partners. In the mission context, however, this was problematic, as Aboriginal men, often described as lazy and undisciplined (and thus, in some respects, childlike), could not necessarily be trusted with such control. Through dependence on and obedience to the missionaries, Aboriginal men would supposedly learn correct masculine behaviour, but at the same time this dependence and obedience reinforced their low status. For example, Watson claimed proudly that men who read the Bible became possessive of their wives and left them on the mission away from predatory Europeans.[46] Here, Aboriginal men were demonstrating the monogamy and possessiveness missionaries had hoped to impart. But they were expected to do this by submitting themselves and their wives to missionary sexual supervision. Presumably, missionaries envisaged Aboriginal men eventually moving beyond this immature sexual stage, but this future prospect was rarely discussed.

Attempts to alter and control Aboriginal sexuality involved different types of physical restriction and emotional manipulation. These often varied according to gender. The physical power of missionaries and protectors at this time was not great; Aboriginal people in many districts were still able to survive off missions, and missionaries' and protectors' relationships to government and police were often troubled and uncooperative.[47] However, force was sometimes used to restrain the sex lives of women and girls. This included locking girls in the mission overnight, using police to remove women from 'debauched' living arrangements with European men, and, occasionally at Wellington Valley, beating young girls for sexual behaviour.[48] Attempts to change Aboriginal men's sexual behaviour, in contrast, hardly ever involved direct physical force.

Missionaries' main tactic for teaching their sexual values to Aboriginal men was through conversation and lecturing, through which they hoped to induce feelings of morality and shame. The way missionaries saw their role was not unlike that of strict Protestant parents of the period, trying to impart self-control to their children. Through frequent lecturing and daily Christian routine, the child — or, in this case, the native — would internalise a sense of guilt and of being watched at all times by a stern God.[49] Thus, when reproving Aboriginal men for sexual sin, missionaries reminded them that monogamous marriage had been set down by God, that God was always watching and judging them, and that illicit sex was proof that they did not yet have a 'new heart' and would not be saved.[50]

Missionaries and protectors also tried to cultivate an image of themselves as powerful moral observers hurt by evidence of sin. For instance, one night at Wellington Valley the missionaries were woken by whispering in the girls' bedroom, and rushed in in time to see two young men vanishing up the chimney. Upon catching one of the guilty youths, Goongeen, Mr and Mrs Watson reproved him — 'you know Goongeen that it is very wrong, you have been told so very many times, and your conduct makes us very sorry, it makes us that we cannot eat or drink or sleep'. Goongeen, who had a close, if vexed, relationship with the missionaries, knew enough to at least give the impression of repentance.[51] Thus, emotional connections and observation by God were used to try to cultivate a guilty conscience.

Aboriginal men's responses to these moral campaigns varied but tended to demonstrate the limitations of missionary power. Attempts to incorporate missionaries into sexual relationships for money or supplies were very rare, presumably owing to their obvious disgust at such relationships and their general willingness to provide supplies in return for church attendance and farm work. I have found only one example of an Aboriginal man trying to forge a serious marital link with a missionary or protector. When protector Charles Sievwright was travelling around Keilambete, he visited the camp of Burguidenang, a man from the Terang region, whom he had helped to release from prison. Burguidenang embraced Sievwright closely, welcomed him as an honoured guest, and, accompanied by the elders, offered his infant daughter in betrothal to Sievwright's 11-year-old son. Sievwright delicately refused but was touched by the gesture.[52] This story seems to have been unique, however, prompted by an unusually strong bond between the two men.

On other occasions, Aboriginal men used protectors to help remove their wives from sexual relationships with other men. Protector Sievwright, for example, was asked in 1839 by a group of Barrabool (Wathaurung) men to help retrieve three women being forcibly held in a convict servant's hut. The men threatened that if Sievwright was unsuccessful they would set fire to the hut and spear the white men. Sievwright removed the women and had the guilty servants flogged.[53] In the same year, at protector William Thomas's camp near Melbourne, an Aboriginal man confidently demanded Thomas's help in looking for his missing wife, insisting that Thomas search the house of a neighbouring European and the miams of visiting Aborigines, and threatening to report Thomas to the police if he did not cooperate.[54] These men may have been taking advantage of the protectors' opposition to illegitimate sex, but the confidence with which they acted indicates that they also believed they had the right to expect help, as they had been told the protectors were there to represent their interests.

However, many Aboriginal men's responses to missionary sexual agendas were less cooperative. Many continued to have relationships with girls and women on the missions and tolerate or encourage their wives' prostitution, and others ignored, mocked or challenged missionaries' lectures on sexual propriety. Some men questioned missionaries' opposition to prostitution, wanting to know why other Europeans found it acceptable and why missionaries did not lecture them. At Wellington Valley in 1833, Watson lectured a man called Woowah on the Christian necessity of having one wife only and not lending her to others. Woowah responded 'white fellow all about make a light God, Black fellow all about very stupid. What for white fellow always say you lend me yeener [woman] belonging to you … then I give you bread, I give you milk, shirt etc?'[55] The missionary could not adequately respond to this. When one man at Wellington Valley responded to James Günther's lectures against promiscuity by asking 'Why don't you talk that way to White fellas?' Günther acknowledged 'It is melancholy but the Black has some sight and must be in some respect justified for passing a remark like that'.[56] Handt reproved another man for prostituting his wife, and the man replied 'that white men should know that it was wrong, and not have asked her of him as they know about God'. To this, Handt responded 'A just reply indeed.'[57]

More serious disputes arose when Aboriginal men saw missionaries as exercising too much control over the women. Protector Thomas, for example, caused considerable turmoil by interfering in the betrothal of a Kulin woman, Kitty, whose uncle had removed her from her husband to marry her to someone else. Thomas was far more concerned about the sanctity of marriage than about Kitty's wishes; he dragged her forcibly away from her female relatives and threatened her with prison if she left her husband again. Thomas's actions disturbed Kitty's husband, Benbow, who begged him not to interfere, and angered her uncle, Ningollobin, who protested 'before white man came Black fellows did as they like with Lubras what for now sulky no good that'.[58] It should be noted, though, that the most direct coercion Thomas used was against the woman herself, and that the issue was only resolved through compromise with traditional practices; Benbow took Kitty back but had to give one of his female relatives to Ningollobin. Thus, the protector's authority was evident but also limited.[59]

Disputes with Aboriginal men over women were particularly evident at Wellington Valley, where the local police magistrate claimed that Aboriginal men had asked him to forcibly remove the women from missionary custody.[60] One Wiradjuri man, Frederick, was furious when missionaries refused to let him marry a mission girl despite his attempts to negotiate by promising to build a house at the mission and leave his wife there most of the time. Upon being rejected, Frederick threatened to borrow muskets from local Europeans and remove all the girls by force. To this, Watson could only respond with warnings of spiritual, rather than physical, punishment, saying 'Well Frederick … you have not yet got a new heart, you are not a Christian.'[61] Other men accused the missionaries of keeping the women for sex. One man, Kabbarin, told Watson 'you like yinars [women] too much … what do you want with Black yinars? … Why don't you go to Sydney? plenty white yinars sit down there. Yes yes you get plenty of children by and by.' Watson was furious, especially when the other people listening laughed at him.[62] These accusations and threats may not have been sincere, but the men's resentment at missionary interference in betrothals was strongly felt, and was one of the many reasons why the first missions were unsuccessful.

Attempts by the first missionaries and protectors to reshape Aboriginal sexuality by arranging respectable Christian marriages is a topic where much research has yet to be done. At present, it seems that perhaps the most significant point here is the general *absence* of such marital plans in the south-east in the early nineteenth century. The poverty, prostitution and violence of the frontier and the general lack of committed Aboriginal Christians may have made missionaries and protectors too pessimistic to plan marriages. Some also noted that few Europeans would consider marrying Aborigines, and few Aborigines were considered sufficiently Christianised to marry decently amongst themselves.[63] Some missionary attempts to plan marriages also met with considerable Aboriginal resistance when they interfered with pre-existing betrothals or linked young people forbidden to each other under traditional law.[64] This would make a significant topic for further investigation.

The first protectors and missions operated at a time when colonial understandings of Aboriginal sexuality were influenced by stereotypes of savages as lazy, uncontrolled and amoral, as well as by a particular feature of settler colonialism: the attraction of portraying Indigenous people as doomed and sterile, rather than as lustful, uncontrolled breeders. This intellectual climate seems to have influenced to some extent missionary attitudes towards Aboriginal men's sexuality. However, their attitudes were also shaped by particular concerns about the relationships between sex and heathen sin, imported vices, hard labour and property ownership. A study of missionaries' and protectors' attempts to instil self-discipline and shame in Aboriginal men, and the men's varied responses to this — including cooperation, opportunism and aggressive resistance — helps to illuminate a mission both sympathetic and chauvinistic in its intentions and limited in its power.

References

Primary sources

Aboriginal Affairs Records, (AAR), VPRS4467, Victorian Public Records Office.

Dredge, James, *Diaries, Notebooks and Letterbook: ?1817-1845*, (JDD), MS11625, State Library of Victoria.

Thomas, William, *Journal and Papers, 1834-1844*, (WTP), MF323, Australian Institute of Aboriginal and Torres Strait Islander Studies.

Tuckfield, Francis, *Journal: 1837-1842*, MS11341, Box 655, State Library of Victoria.

Wellington Valley Project, (WVP): Letters and Journals relating to the Church Missionary Society Mission to Wellington Valley, New South Wales, 1830-45, a critical electronic edition, Hilary M Carey and David A Roberts (eds), University of Newcastle, <http://www.new-castle.edu.au/centre/wvp/>

Wesleyan Methodist Missionary Society Archive, Australasia 1812-1889, (WMMS), Boxes 1 and 2, Mp2107, National Library of Australia.

Secondary sources

Adams, David Wallace 1995, *Education for Extinction: American Indians and the Boarding School Experience, 1875-1928*, University of Kansas Press, Lawrence.

Aldrich, Robert 2003, *Colonialism and Homosexuality*, Routledge, London and New York.

Arden, George 1843, 'Civilization of the Aborigines', in *Arden's Sydney Magazine of Politics and General Literature*, vol. 1, no. 1, September: 65-82.

Arkley, Lindsey 2000, *The Hated Protector: The Story of Charles Wighton Sievwright, Protector of Aborigines, 1839-42*, Orbit Press, Mentone.

Barrallier, Francis 1975, *Journal of the Expedition into the Interior of New South Wales, 1802*, Marsh Walsh, Melbourne.

Barthelemy, Anthony Gerard 1987, *Black Face, Maligned Race: The Representation of Blacks in English Drama, from Shakespeare to Southerne*, Louisiana State University Press, Baton Rouge and London.

Bowler, Peter J 1984, *Evolution: The History of an Idea*, University of California Press, Berkeley.

—— 1989, *The Invention of Progress: The Victorians and the Past*, Basil Blackwell, Oxford.

Brantlinger, Patrick 2003, *Dark Vanishings: Discourse on the Extinction of Primitive Races, 1800-1930*, Cornell University Press, Ithaca and London.

Bridges, Barry John 1970, 'James Dredge in Australia', *Descent* 5(1): 1-16.

—— 1978, 'The Church of England and the Aborigines of New South Wales, 1788-1855', PhD thesis in History, University of New South Wales, Sydney.

Campbell, Alastair H 1987, *John Batman and the Aborigines*, Kibble Books, Malmsbury.

Cannon, Michael (ed.) 1982, *Historical Records of Victoria: The Aborigines of Port Phillip, 1835-1839*, vol. 2A, Victorian Government Printing Office, Melbourne.

—— 1983, *Historical Records of Victoria: Aborigines and Protectors, 1838-1839*, vol. 2B, Victorian Government Printing Office, Melbourne.

—— 1990, *Who Killed the Koories?* William Heinemann, Port Melbourne.

Carr, Julie E 2001a, '"Cabin'd, Cribb'd and Confin'd": the White Woman of Gipps Land and Bungalene', in Barbara Creed and Jeanette Hoorn (eds), *Body Trade: Captivity, Cannibalism and Colonialism in the Pacific*, Routledge, New York: 167-179.

—— 2001b, *The Captive White Woman of Gipps Land: In Pursuit of a Legend*, Melbourne University Press, Carlton South.

Christie, Michael 1979, *Aborigines in Colonial Victoria, 1835-86*, University of Sydney Press, Sydney.

Cohen, William B 1980, *The French Encounter with Africans: White Responses to Blacks, 1530-1880*, Indiana University Press, Bloomington and London.

Collins, David 1798, *An Account of the English Colony in New South Wales, With Remarks on the Dispositions, Customs, Manners, etc, of the Native Inhabitants of that Country*, vol. 1, Reed/Royal Australian Historical Society, Sydney.

Corris, Peter 1968, *Aborigines and Europeans in Western Victoria*, Australian Institute of Aboriginal Studies, Canberra.

Critchett, Jan 1990, *A 'Distant Field of Murder': Western District Frontiers 1834-1848*, Melbourne University Press, Burwood.

Cunningham, Peter 1827, *Two Years in New South Wales*, vol. 2, Henry Colburn, London.

Cunningham, Hugh 1995, *Children and Childhood in Western Society Since 1500*, Longman, London.

Curr, Edward M 1883, *Recollections of Squatting in Victoria, then called the Port Phillip District (from 1841-1851)*, Melbourne University Press, Carlton.

Darian-Smith, Kate 2001, 'Material Culture and the "Signs" of Captive White Women', in Barbara Creed and Jeanette Hoorn (eds), *Body Trade: Captivity, Cannibalism and Colonialism in the Pacific*, Routledge, New York: 180-192.

Dredge, James 1845, *Brief Notes on the Aborigines of New South Wales*, James Harrison, Geelong.

—— 1983, 'Journal', in Michael Cannon (ed.), *Historical Records of Victoria: Aborigines and Protectors, 1838-1839*, vol. 2B, Victorian Government Printing Press, Melbourne.

Evans, Raymond 1999, *Fighting Words: Writing About Race*, University of Queensland Press, St Lucia.

Eyre, Edward John 1845, *Journals of Expedition of Discovery into Central Australia and Overland from Adelaide to King George's Sound in the years 1840-1*, vol. 2, T and W Boone, London.

Fee, Elizabeth 1974, 'The Sexual Politics of Victorian Social Anthropology', in Mary S Hartman and Lois Banner (eds), *Clio's Consciousness Raised: New Perspectives on the History of Women*, Harper Torchbooks, New York: 86-103.

Fels, Marie Hansen 1988, *Good Men and True: The Aboriginal Police of the Port Phillip District, 1837-1853*, Melbourne University Press, Burwood.

Frauenfelder, Peter (ed.) 1997, *Aboriginal Communities: the Colonial Experience, Port Phillip District*, Education Centre of the State Library of Victoria, Melbourne.

Gilman, Sander L 1985, *Difference and Pathology: Stereotypes of Sexuality, Race, and Madness*, Cornell University Press, Ithaca.

Gipps, Sir George, to Lord John Russell, 7 May 1840, in *Historical Records of Australia*, series 1, vol. XX, February 1839 – September 1840, Library Committee of the Commonwealth Parliament, Sydney, 1924: 607-647.

Goodall, Heather 1996, *Invasion to Embassy: Land in Aboriginal Politics in New South Wales, 1770-1972*, Allen & Unwin, St Leonards.

Greven, Phillip 1977, *The Protestant Temperament: Patterns of Child-Rearing, Religious Experience and the Self in Early America*, Alfred A. Knopf, New York.

Grimshaw, Patricia 1994, *Colonialism, Gender and Representations of Race: Issues in writing women's history in Australia and the Pacific*, University of Melbourne History Department, Parkville.

Haebich, Anna 2000, *Broken Circles: Fragmenting Indigenous Families, 1800-2000*, Fremantle Arts Centre Press, Fremantle.

Hamilton, George 1879, *Experiences of a Colonist Forty Years Ago, and a Journey from Port Phillip to South Australia in 1839*, Frearson & Brother, Adelaide.

Henderson, John 1832, *Observations on the Colonies of New South Wales and Van Diemen's Land*, Baptist Mission Press, Calcutta.

Henningham, Nikki 2000, '"Hats off, Gentlemen, to our Australian Mothers!": Representations of White Femininity in North Queensland in the Early Twentieth Century', in Martin Crotty, John Germov and Grant Rodwell (eds), *'A Race for a Place': Eugenics, Darwinism and Social Thought and Practice in Australia*, University of Newcastle, Callaghan: 156-166.

Huhndorf, Shari H 2001, *Going Native: Indians in the American Cultural Imagination*, Cornell University Press, Ithaca and London.

Hunt, Susan 1986, *Spinifex and Hessian: Women in North-West Australia, 1860-1900*, University of Western Australia Press, Perth.

Jebb, Mary Anne and Haebich, Anna 1992, 'Across the Great Divide: Gender Relations on Australian Frontiers', in Kay Saunders and Raymond Evans (eds), *Gender Relations in Australia: Domination and Negotiation*, Harcourt Brace Jovanovich, Sydney: 20-41.

Johnston, Colin and Johnston, Robert 1988, 'The Making of Homosexual Men', in Verity Burgmann and Jenny Lee (eds), *Staining the Wattle: A People's History of Australia since 1788*, Penguin, Ringwood: 87-99.

Langhorne, George, to Colonial Secretary, 31 December 1837, in Michael Cannon (ed.), *Historical Records of Victoria: The Aborigines of Port Phillip, 1835-1839*, vol. 2A, Victorian Government Printing Press, Melbourne, 1982: 208-209.

—— to CJ LaTrobe, 15 October 1839, in Michael Cannon (ed.), *Historical Records of Victoria: Aborigines and Protectors, 1838-1839*, vol. 2B, Victorian Government Printing Press, Melbourne, 1983: 507-510.

de Lepervanche, Marie 1989, 'Breeders for Australia: A National Identity for Women', *Australian Journal of Social Issues* 24(3), August: 163-180.

Malcolm, James 1997, Evidence, 'Report from the Select Committee on the Condition of the Aborigines, 1845', in Peter Frauenfelder (ed.), *Aboriginal Communities: the Colonial Experience, Port Phillip District*, Education Centre of the State Library of Victoria, Melbourne: 55-63.

Malthus, Thomas 1986, 'An Essay on the Principle of Population', in EA Wrigley and David Souden (eds), *The works of Thomas Robert Malthus*, vol. 1, William Pickering, London.

Markus, Andrew 1990, *Governing Savages*, Allen & Unwin, Sydney.

Massie, RJ, to Colonial Secretary, 31 December 1847, in *Historical Records of Australia*, series 1, vol. XXVI, October 1847 – October 1848, Library Committee of the Commonwealth Parliament, Sydney: 393-394.

McGrath, Ann 1990, 'The White Man's Looking-Glass: Aboriginal-Colonial Gender Relations at Port Jackson', *Australian Historical Studies* 24(95), October: 186-206.

McGregor, Russell 1997, *Imagined Destinies: Aboriginal Australians and the Doomed Race Theory, 1880-1939*, Melbourne University Press, Carlton South.

Merivale, Herman 1861, *Lectures on Colonization and Colonies*, first delivered 1839-1841, London, Oxford University Press.

Miner, Earl 1972, 'The Wild Man Through the Looking Glass', in Edward Dudley and Maximillian E. Novak (eds), *The Wild Man Within: An Image in Western Thought from the Renaissance to Romanticism*, University of Pittsburgh Press, London: 87-114.

O'Brien, Patty 1998, 'The Gaze of the "Ghosts": Images of Aboriginal Women in New South Wales and Port Phillip (1800-1850)', in Jan Kociumbas (ed.), *Maps, Dreams, History: Race and Representation in Australia*, Department of History, University of Sydney, Sydney: 313-400.

Pettman, Jan 1992, *Living in the Margins: Racism, Sexism and Feminism in Australia*, Allen and Unwin, North Sydney.

Rae-Ellis, Vivienne 1988, *Black Robinson, Protector of the Aborigines*, Melbourne University Press, Collingwood.

Reece, Robert 1974, *Aborigines and Colonists: Aborigines and Colonial Society in New South Wales in the 1830s and 1840s*, Sydney University Press, Sydney.

Robertson, Priscilla 1988, 'Home As A Nest: Middle Class Childhood in Nineteenth Century England', in Lloyd deMause (ed.), *The History of Childhood: The Untold Story of Child Abuse*, Peter Bedrick Books, New York: 407-431.

Robinson, George Augustus 1998a, *Journals: Port Phillip Aboriginal Protectorate*, Ian D Clark (ed.), vol. 1, 1 January 1839 – 30 September 1840, Heritage Matters, Melbourne.

—— 1998b, *Journals: Port Phillip Aboriginal Protectorate*, Ian D Clark (ed.), vol. 4, 1 January 1844 – 24 October 1845, Heritage Matters, Melbourne.

—— 1997, Evidence, 'Report from the Select Committee on the Condition of the Aborigines, 1845', in Peter Frauenfelder (ed.), *Aboriginal Communities:*

the Colonial Experience, Port Phillip District, Education Centre of the State Library of Victoria, Melbourne: 51-54.

—— 2001, '1848 Annual Report', in Ian D Clark (ed.), The Papers of George Augustus Robinson, Chief Protector, Port Phillip Aboriginal Protectorate, vol. 4, Clarendon, Heritage Matters: 139-156.

Russell, Penny 1994, A Wish of Distinction: Colonial Gentility and Femininity, Melbourne University Press, Carlton.

Russett, Cynthia Eagle 1989, Sexual Science: The Victorian Construction of Womanhood, Harvard University Press, Cambridge, Massachusetts.

Schaffer, Kay 1995, In the Wake of First Contact: The Eliza Fraser Stories, Cambridge University Press, Cambridge.

Schiebinger, Londa 1993, Nature's Body: Gender in the Making of Modern Science, Beacon Press, London.

Sievwright, Charles 1994, 'Report: September 1839 – May 1840', in Mira Lakic and Rosemary Wrench (eds), Through Their Eyes: An Historical Record of Aboriginal People in Victoria as Documented by the Officials of the Port Phillip Protectorate, 1839-1841, Museum of Victoria, Melbourne: 115-127.

Sommerville, C John 1982, The Rise and Fall of Childhood, Sage Publications, Beverly Hills.

Stepan, Nancy 1982, The Idea of Race in Science: Great Britain, 1800-1960, MacMillan Press, London.

Strzelecki, PE de 1845, Physical Descriptions of New South Wales and Van Diemen's Land, Longman, London.

Sturt, Charles 1833, Two Expeditions into the Interior of Southern Australia, Smith, Elder & Co., London.

—— 1861, First Report of the Central Board Appointed to Watch over the Interests of the Aborigines in the Colony of Victoria, Melbourne, Government Printer, GMF105, Box 2, State Library of Victoria.

Threlkeld, LE 1974, 'Correspondence and Early Reports relating to the Aboriginal Mission, 1825-1841', in Niel Gunson (ed.), Australian Reminiscences and Papers of L. E. Threlkeld, Missionary to the Aborigines, 1824-1859, vol. 2, Australian Institute of Aboriginal Studies, Canberra: 177-306.

Tyrell, Alex, 1993, A Sphere of Benevolence: The Life of Joseph Orton, Wesleyan Methodist Missionary (1795-1842), State Library of Victoria, Melbourne.

Walker, David, 1999, Anxious Nation: Australia and the Rise of Asia, 1850-1939, University of Queensland Press, St Lucia.

White, Richard 1981, *Inventing Australia: Images and Identity, 1688-1980*, Allen and Unwin, Sydney.

Wokler, Robert 1995, 'Anthropology and Conjectural History in the Enlightenment', in Christopher Fox, Roy Porter and Robert Wokler (eds), *Inventing Human Science: Eighteenth Century Domains*, University of California Press, Berkeley: 31-52.

ENDNOTES

[1] Francis Tuckfield, *Journal: 1837-1842*, 11 May 1841, MS11341, Box 655, State Library of Victoria; Francis Tuckfield to General Secretaries, 30 October 1841, Wesleyan Methodist Missionary Society Archive, Australasia 1812-1889 (WMMS), Box 2, 'Correspondence, Australia, 1840-1852', Mp2107, National Library of Australia.

[2] For example, Cannon 1983: 366; Cannon 1990: 132; Christie 1979: 90-94, 101-05; Corris 1968: 73-79, 93-94; Haebich 2000: 348-51; O'Brien 1998: 383-85, 395.

[3] For example, Bridges 1970, 1978; Cannon 1990; Christie 1979; Corris 1968; Rae-Ellis 1988; Reece 1974.

[4] Grimshaw 1994; Hunt 1986; Jebb and Haebich 1992; McGrath 1990; O'Brien 1998.

[5] Evans 1999: 136-37, 156-58; Jebb and Haebich 1992: 34; O'Brien 1998: 321-23; Pettman 1992: 26-28.

[6] Barthelemy 1987: 5; Cohen 1980: 20; Miner 1972: 89, 95.

[7] Barthelemy 1987: 6-12, 120; Cohen 1980: 13-19.

[8] Dredge 1845: 11.

[9] Lydia Günther to William Jowett, 12 January 1839: 2-3, Wellington Valley Project (WVP); William Watson, *Journal*, 8 May 1835: 6, WVP.

[10] Cannon 1990: 135.

[11] JCS Handt, *Journal*, 17 February 1835: 10, WVP.

[12] Edward Stone Parker, 14 July, 'Quarterly Journal', 1 June – 31 August 1842, Aboriginal Affairs Records (AAR), VPRS4467, Reel 2, Victorian Public Records Office.

[13] Bridges 1978: 810.

[14] Robinson 1998a: 285.

[15] Cannon 1990: 135-36.

[16] Aldrich 2003: 219-224; Johnston and Johnston 1988: 87.

[17] Cannon 1990: 136.

[18] JCS Handt to T Woodrooffe and Dandeson Coates, 23 April 1832: 1, WVP.

[19] JCS Handt to T Woodrooffe and Dandeson Coates, 23 April 1832: 1, WVP.

[20] Bridges 1978: 307-08.

[21] Threlkeld 1974, vol. 2: 300.

[22] Threlkeld 1974, vol. 2: 264.

[23] Schaffer 1995: 29-96.

[24] Robinson 2001: 143; Thomas, *Journal and Papers, 1834-1844* (WTP), 7 October 1846, 29 January 1847, 21 and 23 February 1847, MF323, Reel 3, AIATSIS; Thomas 1861: 9.

[25] Carr 2001b: 93.

[26] Carr 2001a: 167-79; Cannon 1990: 205-217; Darian-Smith 2001: 180-92.

[27] Schaffer 1995: 29-125.

[28] Significant works in these areas include Fee 1974; Gilman 1985; Henningham 2000; Lepervanche 1989; Markus 1990; McGregor 1997; Russell 1994; Russett 1989; Stepan 1982; Walker 1999; White 1981.

[29] Arden 1843: 67; Collins [1798] 1975, vol.1: 463; Curr 1883: 114-15, 120; Eyre 1845, vol.2: 319-22; Hamilton 1879: 31-32.

[30] Barrallier 1975: 22-23; Collins [1798] 1975, vol.1: 463, 485-89, 498-99; Henderson 1832: 149, 153; Malcolm 1997: 59; Massie 1847; Sturt 1833: 55.

[31] Arden 1843: 67; Cunningham 1827, vol.2: 19; Eyre 1845: 319-22.

[32] Bowler 1984: 90-92; Bowler 1989: 1-13; Schiebinger 1993: 84-100.

[33] Adams 1995: 24-25; Brantlinger 2003: 157-60; Huhndorf 2001: 14-15, 20-22, 27-31, 56-58.

[34] Merivale 1861 [1839-41]: 540.

[35] Strzelecki 1845: 344-55.

[36] Malthus [1798] 1986 vol.1: 18; Wokler 1995: 41.

[37] Goodall 1996: 27; McGrath 1990: 193-94.

[38] For example, JCS Handt, *Journal*, 13 August 1835: 12, WVP; Benjamin Hurst to CJ LaTrobe, 22 December 1841, AAR, VPRS4467, Reel 1; Benjamin Hurst to J McKenny, 8 March 1842, WMMS, Box 2, Mp2107; Threlkeld 1974, vol. 2: 227.

[39] Fee 1974: 86-101.

[40] Fee 1974: 92-93.

[41] William Watson, *Report 1: 1832*: 3, WVP; William Watson to William Jowett, 17 January 1837: 1, WVP.

[42] James Dredge, 'Journal' in Cannon (ed) 1983, vol. 2B: 712; Tyrell 1993: 152.

[43] James Günther to Dandeson Coates, 30 November 1838: 2, WVP.

[44] For example, Edward Stone Parker to GA Robinson, 1 April 1840 (Cannon (ed) 1983, vol.2B: 695); William Porter to Dandeson Coates, 22 February 1841: 4, WVP; Thomas, WTP, 31 October 1844, MF323, Reel 3; William Thomas to G. A Robinson, 1 March 1841, AAR, Reel 2; William Thomas to GA Robinson, 1 June 1846, AAR, VPRS4467, Reel 2; William Watson to Dandeson Coates, 31 December 1832: 2, WVP.

[45] JCS Handt, *Journal*, 13 August 1835: 12, WVP; William Watson and JCS Handt 'Report on the Mission to the Aborigines of New Holland, 14 December 1833', WMMS, Box 2, Mp2107.

[46] Bridges 1978: 778.

[47] For discussion of protectors' and missionaries' relationships with police, see particularly Arkley 2000: 21-22, 326-29; Bridges 1978: 594-95, 642, 674; Campbell 1987: 206-7; Christie 1979: 83-84; Fels 1988: 95, 141-50.

[48] For example, James Günther, *Journal*, 26 January 1838: 8, 11 April 1838: 3, 22 April 1838: 5-6, WVP; Robinson 1998b, vol. 4: 282; Charles Sievwright to GA Robinson, 1 June 1840 (Lakic and Wrench (eds), 1994: 131); Watson, *Journal*, 1 March 1834: 17, 29 December 1835: 11, WVP.

[49] Cunningham, 1995: 48; Greven, 1977: 33-52; Robertson, 1988: 415; Sommerville, 1982: 125.

[50] For example, Watson, *Journal*, 26 April 1833: 4-5, 16 March 1837: 17, WVP.

[51] Watson, *Journal*, 6 November 1834: 7, WVP.

[52] Arkley 2000: 141-42; Critchett 1990: 27-28.

[53] Arkley 2000: 19.

[54] Thomas, WTP, 15 November 1839, MF323, Reel 1.

[55] Watson, *Journal*, 26 April 1833: 5, WVP.

[56] Günther, *Journal*, 14 March 1838: 19-20, WVP.

[57] Handt, *Journal*, 28 April 1833: 3, WVP.

[58] Thomas, WTP, 24 August 1844, MF323, Reel 3.

[59] Thomas, WTP, 24 and 25 August 1844, MF323, Reel 3.

[60] Henry Fysche Gisbourne, quote in Gipps 1840 (1924): 618.

[61] Watson, *Journal*, 16 February 1837: 15-17, WVP.

[62] Watson, *Journal*, 29 December 1835: 11-12 , WVP.

[63] GM Langhorne to CJ LaTrobe, 15 October 1839 (Cannon (ed) 1983, vol. 2B: 508); GA Robinson, 1845 in Frauenfelder (ed) 1997: 53.

[64] Bridges, 1978: 709; George Langhorne to Colonial Secretary, 31 December 1837 in Cannon (ed), 1982, vol.2A: 208; Günther, *Journal*, 23 April 1838: 7, WVP.